W Farwell '98

The Consuming Passion

Christianity &
the Consumer Culture

Edited by Rodney Clapp

InterVarsity Press
Downers Grove, Illinois

InterVarsity Press
P.O. Box 1400, Downers Grove, IL 60515
World Wide Web: www.ivpress.com
E-mail: mail@ivpress.com

InterVarsity Press® is the book-publishing division of InterVarsity Christian Fellowship/USA®, a student movement active on campus at hundreds of universities, colleges and schools of nursing in the United States of America, and a member movement of the International Fellowship of Evangelical Students. For information about local and regional activities, write Public Relations Dept., InterVarsity Christian Fellowship/USA, 6400 Schroeder Rd., P.O. Box 7895, Madison, WI 53707-7895.

Cover photograph: Michael Goss

ISBN 0-8308-1897-9

Printed in the United States of America ⊜

Library of Congress Cataloging-in-Publication Data

The consuming passion : Christianity and the culture of consumption /
   Rodney Clapp, editor.
     p. cm.
   Includes bibliographical references.
   ISBN 0-8308-1897-9 (alk. paper)
     1. Consumption (Economics)—Religious aspects—Christianity.
   2. Christianity and culture. I. Clapp, Rodney.
   BR115.C67C66 1997
   241'.68—dc21   *97-44349*
                                                     CIP

20	19	18	17	16	15	14	13	12	11	10	9	8	7	6	5	4	3	2	1
15	14	13	12	11	10	09	08	07	06	05	04	03	02	01	00	99	98		

Introduction
Consumption & the Modern Ethos *RODNEY CLAPP*

1 1856H

STATE   MARKET

POLITICS   ECONOMICS

Introduction

Consumption &
the Modern Ethos
Rodney Clapp

Modernity is that period in history that has allowed for only two public institutions: the state and the market. If Aristotle's Greece saw friendship as a public and political concern, and Christendom understood the church as a public and societal body (one of Augustine's two "cities"), modernity privatized "personal relationships" and religion.[1] For people of faith, this relegation to the private has meant that any access of religion to the public sphere has necessarily been through the state or the market. Partly on behalf of privatized, and thus marginalized, religious voices, Margaret Thatcher and Ronald Reagan popularized worries about the sprawling and overweening state, with its governmental tentacles intruding into everything. But significantly, when Thatcher and Reagan sought leverage for their assault on big government, they turned to the other public institution of modernity, the market.

While concerns about an all-permeating state should not be forgotten, perhaps it is time for people of faith to focus some attention on the powers and effects of the other leviathan of modernity. After all, one of the indisputable concerns of religions—at least of Christianity and Judaism—is with ethos: the fundamental character, dispositions and pursued goods of a people. Consumerism names that ethos of the modern market that is at least as inescapable as the state. Thus, modern persons are increasingly defined in all our relationships or endeavors as consumers. We are no longer "students" but "educational consumers," no longer "worshipers" but "church shoppers," no longer "patients" but "health consumers," and so on. Some may brush aside such labels as "mere language," but language is crucial to any ethos. Language makes all the difference in how we perceive and define the issues of everyday life, and so how we respond to them. For instance, regarding consumption, is the shopper who walks away from a bargain exercising the Christian virtue of self-control or exhibiting the marketer's "sales resistance"? At work are two different rationalities, two different construals, and so two different plans for proceeding.[2]

Reading as Consumption

Such an example, of course, points up tensions between the ethos of Christianity and the ethos of consumption. Christians, however, have not always been quick to recognize such tensions and have in some ways been avid architects of consumerism. The historian R. Laurence Moore reminds us that religious reading itself was earlier the very vanguard of modern practices of consumption. With their emphasis on the importance of the Bible, Protestant Christians promoted literacy and reading. As literacy spread and the technology of printing developed, "the most typical commodity that the print market offered for sale was some form of devotional material."[3] Even into the seventeenth and eighteenth centuries, religious works were the most widely circulated books in library collections. In the nineteenth century, stereotype printing and steam-powered presses made print materials available on a revolutionary scale, at unprecedented quantities and affordable prices. There quickly developed a growing market for newspapers and other nonreligious reading.[4]

In the United States, of course, there was no established, state-supported church, and ministerial influence began to wane precipitously in the eighteenth century. In 1740, for instance, clergy made up 70 percent of all professionals in Massachusetts. By 1800 that figure had declined to 45 percent. Perhaps inevitably, American ministers decided to fight fire with fire. With no state support to fall back on, the American church entered the marketplace of reading. Pastors became authors. Denominations established publishing houses and produced increasingly entertaining material. In so doing, Moore notes, "Protestants solidified a new base for religious authority . . . that depended heavily on market strategies."[5]

In the early nineteenth century, the religious publisher would certainly not describe its books as "entertainment." Ministers never uttered the word approvingly without putting "useful" or "instructive" in front of it. Even the Harper brothers, who ran the largest printing establishment in the country, behaved along these lines. All four of the brothers were staunch Methodists who lived frugally and honestly and emphasized character over capital in their business. As late as 1830 they advertised that they would publish no books "but such as are interesting, instructive, and moral."[6] So it was significant when, in 1834, the American Tract Society began to portray its material as "short," "interesting" and, yes, unqualifiedly "entertaining." Yet even then the Tract Society refused to publish fiction, since it departed from "truth" and gave pleasure by encouraging readers in the free play of their imaginations.[7] These and most other objections to "virtuous fiction" gave way by the end of the nineteenth century, however. This happened, as these things usually do, in stages.

First, ministers endorsed "true narratives" or "truthful tales," exciting accounts of real-life conversions and religious heroism. These evolved into real-life narratives that, ostensibly in order to more effectively make their moral point, included lurid details about immoral and destructive behaviors. A reading of the titles by one of the most popular authors in the genre, an Episcopal minister named Mason Locke Weems, provides a sense of this approach: *God's Revenge Against Adultery* and *God's Revenge Against Gambling.* Moore summarizes another of Weems's books, *The Drunkard's Looking Glass,* by describing it as the

> tale of a man, who, after falling before Satan's temptation to get drunk, violates his sister, kills his father, and hangs himself. Calamity follows calamity, all bloody, all violent. Drunkards die in their vomit. One inebriated young man falls from his horse, and the brutal

impact leaves "no sign of a nose remaining on his face . . . completely scalping the right side of his face and head. . . . One of his eyes was cleanly knocked out of its socket; and, held only by a thin string of skin, there it lay naked on his bloody cheek."[8]

So we soon enough arrive at what Moore calls "moral pornography," with its display of seduction, rape, torture, enforced prostitution, sadomasochism, incest and necrophilia condoned so long as these practices suffered, in the same text, explicit moral condemnation.

Thanks to this growing appetite for sensationalism and milder amusement, Moore notes, nineteenth-century Protestants played an important hand in a "revolution in reading that had a major impact on the development of consumer culture." The commodification of religion produced a much greater number of books and "involved a basic shift in psychology, one that fed a habit of addictive buying." People learned not to linger over or reread a book, to savor again and again particular passages. Now they read quickly and moved on to the next book. What the scholars call "intensive" reading was transformed into "extensive" reading.[9] As Moore asks in ominous retrospect:

> Once the Bible was offered as an item for display and sale, as a proof of the affluence of capitalism and its ability to invent endlessly in service to the pleasures of consumerism, what restraints remained on thinking about religion not merely as an influence on the taste of buyers but also as something that itself had to satisfy the reigning taste?[10]

A Few Who Resisted

Such is but one example of how closely Christianity and consumption have interacted throughout modernity. It would be a gross mistake, however, to suggest that no modern Christians were concerned about the ethos of consumerism and how it might affect the ethos of Christianity. Though they rapidly became minority and overwhelmed voices, a number of significant Christian figures recognized the dangers of consumer culture and spoke out against it. Four will be briefly mentioned here.

G. K. Chesterton visited Broadway and Times Square in 1922. The Catholic pundit was somewhat taken with skyscrapers and electric signs. But he objected that all the "colours and fire" were attached to commodities. Powerful sacred meanings had once been linked to the spectacle of light and fire, yet today the "new illumination has made people weary of proclaiming great things, by perpetually using it to proclaim small things." More profoundly, Chesterton believed the burgeoning business corporations of consumer capitalism were inherently antidemocratic. The problem with this culture, he averred, "is not that it is vulgar, but that it is not popular." No one saw the glory of God in consumeristic displays, and no one voted for them to appear on roadways and buildings. "These modern and mercantile legends are imposed upon us by a mercantile minority and we are merely passive to the suggestion. The hypnotist of high finance or big business writes his commands in heaven with a finger of fire. We are only the victims of his pyrotechnic violence; and it is he who hits us in the eye."[11]

Baptist social gospeler Walter Rauschenbusch worried in 1907 that "competitive commerce spreads things before us and beseeches and persuades us to buy what we do not want." Speaking very much in the language of character formation, Rauschenbusch worried that proponents of consumerism "try to break down the foresight and self-restraint which were the slow product of moral education, and reduce us to the moral habits of savages who gorge today and fast tomorrow."[12]

Catholic Monsignor John Ryan (1869-1945) was a lifelong critic of consumer capitalism, insisting in echo of the church fathers that all "superfluous wealth" should be shared with the poor. He asserted that there was an "unbridgeable gulf between Catholic and capitalistic conceptions of life" and upheld "frugal comfort," fulfilling work and charity in opposition to consumerism's "diversified satisfaction of the senses."[13]

Lastly, evangelical statesman William Jennings Bryan championed farmers, wage earners and local merchants displaced by growing consumer capitalism throughout his career. In 1896 he argued against overweening corporations, protesting, "The man who is employed for wages is as much a business man as his employer; the attorney in a small town as much a business man as the corporation counsel in a great metropolis. . . . The miners who go down a thousand feet in the earth . . . and bring forth . . . the precious metals to be poured into the channels of trade are as much business men as the financial magnates who . . . corner the money of the world."[14]

The Wisdom of *Centesimus Annus*

These brief samplings of history should make it adequately clear that the consumptive ethos is exceedingly complex—one often, but by no means always, supported by Christians. All its elements are not simply good or bad. It is pervasive in both grossly obvious and infinitely subtle ways. It is profoundly rooted in faith, culture and society as we now know them. To the degree it is toxic, it is an ivy in a garden with its tendrils wrapped around and through our most beautiful flowers and our most essential vegetables. It could not be violently or wholly extirpated without destroying much that we rightly prize and protect. But like just such a vining plant, it has grown too abundant and thick, so that it is now choking the life out of precious flowers and indispensable vegetables. Christians and other people of faith are among those who must gird themselves for a long, intricate and difficult pruning.

The times appear to call for a critique and response similar to what many Christians and other citizens, as we have noted, are already calling for in the area of government. Such manifestations of big government as the welfare state have shown themselves to have limitations and drawbacks. Still, hardly anyone is calling for the elimination of government or denying that government has an important role to play in a salutary way of life. What we are sure about is that government has become too pervasive and needs to be curtailed, put back in its place. Likewise, it might be argued that the market has become too pervasive and needs to be put back in its place. It plays an important— indeed, an unexcelled—role in the efficient exchange and distribution of material goods. But it should not arbitrate and define our faith, family life, friendships and so much else. Consumption makes a fine slave but a tyrannous master; it provides an abundantly stocked pantry but a lousy way of life.

Such a judicious yet radically Christian response is well articulated in Pope John Paul II's encyclical *Centesimus Annus.* In this document the Pope warns against the dangers of pervasive government and readily affirms the free market as "the most efficient instrument for utilizing resources and effectively responding to needs."[15] When the free market is eliminated, "self-interest is violently suppressed [and] replaced by a burdensome system of bureaucratic control which dries up the wellsprings of initiative and creativity."[16] But John Paul II also insists that we should "try to avoid making market mechanisms the only point of reference for social life."[17] The efficiency of the market is appropriate only for needs and resources that are genuinely marketable. We should strive for a society that is "not directed against the market, but demands that the market be appropriately controlled by the forces of society and the State, so as to guarantee that the basic needs of the whole of society are satisfied." This entails, for example, that "profitability is not the only indicator of a firm's condition. . . . In fact, the purpose of the business firm is not simply to make a profit, but is to be found in its very existence as a *community of persons* who in various ways are endeavouring to satisfy their basic needs, and who form a particular group at the service of the whole of society."[18]

Echoing the ancient Christian tradition, the pope advises that we cannot hold up negative freedom, a merely formal freedom of choice, as the highest good. (Consumerism, of course, posits just such freedom of choice as its highest good.) Such freedom is freedom separate from truth, and it fosters "self-love carried to the point of contempt for God and neighbour, a self-love which leads to an unbridled affirmation of self-interest and which refuses to be limited by any demand of justice."[19] In fact, in Christian perspective such "freedom" is not freedom at all:

> A person who is concerned solely or primarily with possessing and enjoying, who is no longer able to control his instincts and passions, or to subordinate them to obedience to the truth, cannot be free: *obedience to the truth* about God and man is the first condition of freedom, making it possible for a person to order his needs and desires to choose the means of satisfying them according to a scale of values, so that the ownership of things may become an occasion of growth for him.[20]

From this deeply Pauline and Augustinian base, John Paul II launches an incisive critique of consumerism, worth quoting at length:

> The manner in which new needs arise and are defined is always marked by a more or less appropriate concept of man and his true good. A given culture reveals its overall understanding of life through the choices it makes in production and consumption. It is here that *the phenomenon of consumerism* arises. In singling out new needs and new means to meet them, one must be guided by a comprehensive picture of man which respects all the dimensions of

his being and which subordinates his material and instinctive dimensions to his interior and spiritual ones. If, on the contrary, a direct appeal is made to his instincts—while ignoring in various ways the reality of the person as intelligent and free—then *consumer attitudes and life-styles* can be created which are objectively improper and often damaging to his physical and spiritual health. Of itself, an economic system does not possess criteria for correctly distinguishing new and higher forms of satisfying human needs from artificial new needs which hinder the formation of a mature personality. *Thus a great deal of educational and cultural work* is urgently needed, including the education of consumers in the responsible use of their power of choice, the formation of a strong sense of responsibility among producers and among people in the mass media in particular, as well as the necessary intervention by public authorities.[21]

The Essays in This Book

In terms of ethos and character formation, *Centesimus Annus* is especially helpful in its recognition that consumer attitudes and ways of life are created, so that if such formation is to be corrected it must be answered by alternative "cultural work." Though none of the contributors to *The Consuming Passion* would be so bold as to put his essay on par with a papal encyclical, the chapters that follow have a similar aim. They seek to clarify what consumption is, what its ethos entails and how faith traditions might best respond.[22]

Craig Gay bolsters and deepens the thesis of this introduction, asserting that consumerism reveals the highest ideals of modernity. He boldly argues that a determinedly Christian response to consumerism will entail criticizing and even rejecting key aspects of the modern ethos. John Tropman gets both of the twin leviathans of modernity—the state and the market—in his sights. He suggests that Catholic (or communalistic, and friendlier to the state) and Protestant (or individualistic, and friendlier to the market) ethics should be held in a complementary tension to best serve the public good. Both essays help us better understand the nature of the beast we call consumption.

Bill McKibben and David Myers, in their separate essays, examine respectively the effects of modern consumption on the earth's ecology and on the actual happiness of human beings. McKibben vividly represents the grave damage creation has suffered in modernity and urgently calls people of faith to an ethos or way of life that will alleviate and repair the damage. Myers examines social scientific studies that provide some empirical information for answering the question, Does consuming more make people happier?

The next five essays look at consumption from the vantage point of particular theological traditions. Tsvi Blanchard, drawing on rabbinic sources, models an initially affirmative, but not uncritical, approach to the habits of consumption. Economist John Mason, though a Protestant Christian, also relies heavily on the Jewish tradition, examining what the Jewish and Christian practice of the sabbath can still teach us about the stewardship of time, which seems to be increasingly scarce in consumer society. Kenneth Paul Wesche, writing as an Orthodox Christian theologian, crystallizes stewardship as it was understood by the church fathers. His profoundly theological essay demonstrates how Christians might address consumerism from the heart of Christian metaphysics, namely Christology and the Incarnation. John Schneider relies on his own Protestant Reformed tradition to present another view of Christian stewardship, one that, like Rabbi Blanchard's, is careful to recognize what may be good about the (consumeristic) "good life." Pastor Clifford Jones, on the other hand, writes from the perspective of African-American Christians who have not shared so widely in this good life. He is suspicious of consumerism's advertising and other wiles, and includes many examples from his own pastoral experience of how the church can help people economically in a more realistic way than consumption-oriented institutions and practices.

The book closes with my essay, which resumes key themes of this introduction and tries to explore the ethos of consumption in light of Christian theological convictions and practices. The essay is an expanded version of an article that originally appeared in *Christianity Today*.[23] All the essays in *The Consuming Passion* were, in fact, initially presented at a March 1996 conference sponsored by *Christianity Today* and the Pew Global Stewardship Initiative. The magazine's editors and I are eager to express our appreciation for Pew's gracious funding and encouragement, without which the conference and this book would never have come to pass.

Part 1

••••••••••••••••••••••••••••••••••••••

Consumption & Its Effects

1
Sensualists Without Heart

Contemporary Consumerism in Light of the Modern Project

Craig M. Gay

We have entered on a new phase of culture—we may call it the Age of the Cinema—in which the most amazing perfection of scientific technique is being devoted to purely ephemeral objects, without any consideration of their ultimate justification. It seems as though a new society was arising which will acknowledge no hierarchy of values, no intellectual authority, and no social or religious tradition, but which will live for the moment in a chaos of pure sensation.—CHRISTOPHER DAWSON (1931)[1]

*M*y *thesis in the following essay is that contemporary consumer behavior,* often pejoratively labeled "consumerism," far from representing abnormal or aberrant behavior within modern society and culture, actually discloses modernity's highest ideals. The modern project, it seems, was launched with the deliberate decision to forswear philosophical and theological judgment—or what we might term a genuinely religious view of life—for the sake of the comfort and convenience that were to be made possible by scientific and technological development. Contemporary consumer behavior ultimately stems from this decision. It is precisely toward modern consumerism that modern thought, supported by a variety of modern institutions, has been striving for the last several hundred years.

Beyond the importance of this thesis for analysis, the most important implication of this suggestion that contemporary consumer behavior represents the highest ideals of modernity is that, if we are not happy with this behavior—if we think it narrow, wasteful, irresponsible, per-

haps even immoral—then we will need to subject the root propositions
of modernity to criticism. Put somewhat differently, we cannot seriously
redress the problem of contemporary consumerism unless and until
we are willing to address the problem of modernity itself.

To suggest that consumerism discloses modernity's highest ideals is
not to say that the authors of the modern project would necessarily
have been pleased with contemporary consumer behavior, for they
likely would not be pleased with it. Theory, after all, frequently becomes tarnished in practice. Rather, the point is simply to encourage
us to see two things: first, that our culture invites us to locate the sum
total of human happiness here and now and in the consumption of the
fruits of the technological economy; and second, that we have not been
tricked into this, but that we actually chose this path several hundred
years ago and continue to choose it on a more-or-less daily basis.

In defending the thesis that modern consumerism discloses modernity's highest ideals, I plan to work back from several recent
sociological interpretations of contemporary consumer behavior to
a number of observations that were made about similar behavior
over a century ago, and in some cases even earlier. Something very
much like contemporary consumerism, it seems, has actually characterized our culture for some time. In this connection, I would like
to suggest that the essence of contemporary consumerism consists
in two closely related commitments. The first is the commitment to
self-creation and autonomous self-definition. We are told today that
we are, or at least ought to be, entirely free to make whatever we
would of ourselves; and so long as our projects of self-construction
do not obviously interfere with anyone else's, we must not be
hindered by tradition, custom, law or outmoded notions of "human
nature" as we fashion our own identities. This commitment amounts
finally to a repudiation of the belief in moral order. The second
commitment entails shrinking the range of possible human aspirations to those circumscribed by secular existence. We may construct
ourselves entirely as we see fit, so we are also told today, as long as
we remain within the confines of this world and within the limits of
the here and now. These twin commitments go some distance
toward describing the quality of contemporary consumerism. They
also define the essence of the modern project.

Consumerism: Definitions and Interpretations

"Consumerism" is occasionally used to denote the "consumer movement" and advocacy on behalf of consumers vis-à-vis the producers of consumer products. The term is also infrequently used to refer to the economic theory that suggests that the growth of consumption is always good for an economy. Normally, however, "consumerism" is lamented as a significant behavioral blemish in modern industrial society. It suggests an inordinate concern—some might even say an addiction—with the acquisition, possession and consumption of material goods and services. Even more seriously, consumerism suggests a preoccupation with the immediate gratification of desire. It implies foolishness, superficiality and triviality, and the destruction of personal and social relationships by means of selfishness, individualism, possessiveness and covetousness. The prevalence of consumerism in contemporary society, then, suggests a general contraction of the compass of modern culture.

Contemporary consumer behavior is occasionally interpreted as a natural and instinctive behavior. People will naturally adopt a "consumer mentality," so this sort of argument runs, with respect to whatever goods and services become available. And there is clearly some truth in this. The tendency toward hedonism does appear to be something of a human constant, and this behavior has, in fact, accompanied the spread of consumer capitalism around the world during this last century.

Yet it is important to stress that there are a number of aspects of modern consumer behavior that appear to distinguish it from traditional hedonism as such. In his provocative study entitled *The Theory of the Leisure Class* (1899), Thorstein Veblen argued that consumerism is the uniquely modern expression of the age-old desire for status and prestige. The motive that lies behind ownership, Veblen argued, is "emulation," or the desire to be esteemed in the eyes of one's peers on the basis of what one is able to possess and consume. Traditionally, this motive gives rise to predatory activity in which the strong simply take what they desire from the weak. Yet as civilization has advanced, Veblen opined, the lawful accumulation of property has replaced "trophies of predatory exploit as the conventional exponent of prepotence and success."[2] Modern consumerism subsequently emerges as the owners of property compete with each other for status and prestige by means of further accumulation. Veblen termed this competitive behavior "pecuniary emulation" and suggested that it gives rise to both "conspicuous leisure" and "conspicuous consumption."

Veblen was not the first to observe that modern society makes good use of certain apparently "natural" instincts, in this case transforming the desire for prestige into "pecuniary emulation." Adam Smith had already said as much—though in a slightly different way—a century earlier in his celebrated contention that the "invisible hand" of the market economy actually transforms the selfishness of individuals into the larger social benefit. Several generations after Smith, French political philosopher Alexis de Tocqueville also made a number of penetrating observations about the natural penchant for selfishness and how it had been incorporated into the American social fabric. "In the first place," Tocqueville noted in his remarkable study *Democracy in America,*

> I see an innumerable multitude of men, alike and equal, constantly circling around in pursuit of the petty and banal pleasures with which they glut their souls. Each one of them, withdrawn into himself, is almost unaware of the fate of the rest. Mankind, for him, consists in his children and his personal friends. As for the rest of his fellow citizens, they are near enough, but he does not notice them. He touches them but feels nothing. He exists in and for himself, and though he may still have a family, once can at least say that he has not got a fatherland.[3]

One of Tocqueville's concerns in *Democracy in America* was to indicate that the petty and individualistic quality of American culture might actually be a kind of unintended byproduct of democracy. Because the democratic institutionalization of liberty and equality had liberated the Americans from all traditional sources of authority, Tocqueville reasoned, it left the matters of goodness and justice up to each one of them to decide for him or herself. Democracy had declared all individuals to be equal, in other words, but in the process it had disconnected them from divine revelation and from one another, and it had left them alone and self-determining. Along this line, Tocqueville suggested that the Americans were actually, albeit unwittingly, the world's most faithful disciples of Descartes. They were individualistic, skeptical, largely secular in outlook, materialistic, pragmatic and activistic.

Tocqueville went on to suggest that the democratic habit of relying only on oneself had created a character that was extremely practical but also profoundly restless and ultimately quite narrow. "Most of the people in these [democratic] nations," Tocqueville wrote,

> are extremely eager in the pursuit of immediate material pleasures and are always discontented with the position they occupy and always free to leave it. They think about nothing but ways of changing their lot and bettering it. For people in this frame of mind every new way of getting wealth more quickly, every machine which lessens work, every means of diminishing the costs of production, every invention which makes pleasures easier or greater, seems the most magnificent accomplishment of the human mind.[4]

As Tocqueville noted, however, the Americans' success in the realm of practical achievements had the effect of encouraging them to imagine that everything in the world must somehow be explicable in largely technical-rational terms. "Hence," Tocqueville observed, "they have little faith in anything extraordinary and an almost invincible distaste for the supernatural."[5]

Tocqueville also noticed that the institutionalization of equality had had an apparently unintended impact on the principle of stratification within democratic society, making the possession of money far more important than it had been previously in the feudal or aristocratic context. "One usually finds," he noted, "that love of money is either the chief or a secondary motive at the bottom of everything the Americans do. This gives a family likeness to all their passions and soon makes them wearisome to contemplate."[6]

Tocqueville's greatest fear for us Americans, then, was that the "pursuit of immediate material pleasures" and the love of money might eventually extinguish our spirit. "The prospect really does frighten me," Tocqueville lamented, "that they may finally become so engrossed in a cowardly love of immediate pleasures that their interest in their own future and in that of their descendants may vanish, and that they will prefer tamely to follow the course of their destiny rather than make a sudden energetic effort necessary to set things right."[7]

A number of Tocqueville's concerns were restated earlier in this century by Spanish philosopher José Ortega y Gasset in a study provocatively entitled *The Revolt of the Masses* (1932). As the title suggests, Ortega y Gasset's concern focused on the emergence of "mass" society and culture which, he argued, is the product of "hyperdemocracy" in conjunction with the fabulous expansion of modern consumer goods by means of industrial technology. Within this nascent mass society, Ortega y Gasset lamented, cultural and political aspirations had, in effect, been surrendered to the lowest common denominators of comfort, convenience and safety. "We live at a time," Ortega y Gasset opined,

> when man believes himself fabulously capable of creation, but he does not know what to create. Lord of all things, he is not lord of himself. He feels lost amid his own abundance. With more means at its disposal, more knowledge, more technique than ever, it turns out that the world today goes the same way as the worst of worlds that have been; it simply drifts.[8]

Of course, in addition to linking modern consumer behavior to mass democracy, consumerism has also been interpreted as a reflection of a particular kind of economy and society. Marxists and neo-Marxists, for example, commonly assume that modern consumerism is simply the necessary counterpart on the side of consumption of modern capitalism's dramatic expansion of commodity production. Consumerism, from this perspective, is engineered by the producers of commodities and is the result of the artificial stimulation, principally by means of manipulative advertising, of ever-increasing "needs" for mass-produced consumer products. The emphasis in this interpretation is thus upon the triumph of commodity logic and instrumental rationality, a process in which culture is transformed from a meaningful order into a commodity whose "meaning"—if it can even be called that—is tied only to its exchange value. As one author recently summarized the position of the Frankfurt School theorists, for example: "Once the dominance of exchange-value has managed to obliterate the memory of the original use-value of goods, the commodity becomes free to take up a secondary or ersatz use-value. . . . Advertising in particular is able to exploit this and attach images of romance, exotica, desire, beauty, fulfillment, communality, scientific progress and the good life to mundane consumer goods such as soap, washing machines, motor cars and alcoholic drinks."[9]

German social theorist Georg Simmel also interpreted the quality of modern consumer culture in terms of the peculiar features of the modern industrial economy. In his essay "The Metropolis and Mental Life" (c. 1900), Simmel suggested that the superficiality so frequently associated with contemporary consumer behavior is really only the subjective reflection of the pervasive use of money in the modern industrial context.[10] The sheer complexity of modern urban existence, Simmel reasoned, would be psychologically intolerable were it not for the fact that money enables us to render the flood of objects and relations that we encounter comparable in terms of price. Money quickly and conveniently reduces all concrete and qualitative relationships to comparability, making rational choice possible. As money rationalizes our experience of the world by making everything arithmetically comparable, however, so we actually begin to experience the world as a place devoid of qualities. "By being the equivalent to all the manifold things in one and the same way," Simmel observed,

> money becomes the most frightful leveler. For money expresses all qualitative differences of things in terms of "how much?" Money, with all its colorlessness and indifference, becomes the common denominator of all values; irreparably it hollows out the core of things, their individuality, their specific value, and their incomparability. All things float with equal specific gravity in the constantly moving stream of money. All things lie on the same level and differ from one another only in the size of the area which they cover.[11]

Simmel used the term *blasé* to describe the peculiar modern outlook in which qualities have been reduced to calculations of quantity. "The essence of the blasé attitude," he wrote, "consists in the blunting of discrimination . . . [and all things] appear to the blasé person in an evenly flat and grey tone; no one object deserves preference over any other."[12] Søren Kierkegaard lamented in a similar fashion:

> In the end, money will be the one thing people will desire, which is moreover only representative, an abstraction. Nowadays a young man hardly envies anyone his gifts, his art, the love of a beautiful girl, or his fame; he only envies him his money. Give me money, he will say, and I am saved. . . . He would die with nothing to reproach himself with, and under the impression that if only he had had the money he might really have lived and might even have achieved something great.[13]

The net effect of the pervasive use of money in modern industrial context, then, is the creation of a culture in which, as the old saying goes, individuals "know the price of everything but the value of nothing."

The narrowly individualistic quality of contemporary consumer behavior has also been interpreted as a reflection of the "privatization" of individual biography. Along this line, sociologist Thomas Luckmann has observed that, although traditional religious understanding has become unbelievable for many people in modern societies, the contemporary situation has seen the rise to a kind of "proto-religious" mentality that is characterized by a subjectivistic consumer orientation. The same people who are largely indifferent to traditional religious doctrine and discipline, in other words, are nevertheless attracted by astrology, the occult, modern forms of gnosticism and so forth. The reason for this, Luckmann argues, is that as the larger "public" sphere of modern society has become increasingly rationalized and impersonal, individuals have, in effect, been left to themselves to provide themselves with meanings and purposes. "To an immeasurably higher degree than in a traditional social order," Luckmann observes,

> the individual is left to his own devices in choosing goods and services, friends, marriage partners, neighbors, hobbies and ... even "ultimate" meanings in a relatively autonomous fashion. In a manner of speaking, he is free to construct his own personal identity. The consumer orientation, in short, is not limited to economic products but characterizes the relation of the individual to the entire culture.[14]

Indeed, we might go as far as to say that the consumer orientation characterizes the relation of the individual to the entire cosmos.

This division of individual biography into "public" and "private" aspects, then, helps to interpret the contemporary preoccupation with therapy and "lifestyle," as well as the phenomenon of modern individualism. It also helps to explain the odd coincidence of individualism and mass conformity in contemporary culture, for the consumer orientation ensures that the possibilities of self-construction will be limited by the range of "identity products" developed for mass consumption.

Contemporary consumerism thus appears to be far more than simply a kind of abnormal behavior within modern industrial culture. Indeed, it appears to be a more-or-less direct reflection of the increasingly rationalized quality of modern social life. As more and more aspects of modern social life are subjected to a purely technical-rational calculus, individuals have increasingly been cut loose from the discipline of community, and they have been left almost entirely alone to construct satisfying meanings and purposes for themselves. Yet this has left them highly vulnerable to fashion, and to the seductive claims of various mass-marketed products and techniques that have been developed in recent years to facilitate private self-construction. It is not terribly surprising, then, that the meanings and purposes that individuals choose for themselves in the contemporary context are often irrational and ephemeral, for not only are individual identities constructed in the absence of social and/or institutional support, but individuals do not expect to have to submit their identity-constructs to any kind of reasoned discipline. Here we might recall Max Weber's ominous comments at the conclusion of his celebrated book *The Protestant Ethic and the Spirit of Capitalism* (1904-1905). Weber had just described modern rationalized existence as kind of "iron cage" from which there is very little hope of escape. He continued:

> In the field of [modernity's] highest development, in the United States, the pursuit of wealth, stripped of its religious and ethical meaning, tends to become associated with purely mundane passions, which often actually give it the character of sport. . . . For the last stage of this cultural development, it might well be truly said: "Specialists without spirit, sensualists without heart; this nullity imagines that it has attained a level of civilization never before achieved."[15]

What better way to capture the peculiar quality of contemporary consumer behavior than with the theme "sensualists without heart"?

Identifying the "Spirit" of Modern Consumerism
At first blush it appears that many of the peculiar features of modern consumer culture—the preoccupation with "petty and banal pleasures," as Tocqueville commented—emerged within North American society and culture at least as early as the beginning of the nineteenth century, apparently simultaneously with the revolution in modern production techniques. Yet recent historians have noted that many of the features of modern consumer culture—including the individualistic preoccupation with consumption, manipulative advertising, the

deliberate stimulation of desire, and so forth—had already begun to emerge in the eighteenth century and so actually antedate the modern revolution in production by a considerable margin. British social historian Colin Campbell, for example, has recently suggested that the peculiar spirit of modern consumerism actually appears to have emerged independently of the modern revolution in production.[16] The key to modern consumer behavior, Campbell contends, is the "want to want."[17] The modern consumer does not simply want to consume but actually enjoys the process of desiring, wanting, musing over products and shopping for them. This, Campbell argues, is what distinguishes modern hedonism from its traditional counterpart. Campbell then goes on to suggest that this curiously insatiable spirit, this "wanting to want under all circumstances," first developed out of Romanticism's commitment to creative individuality and out of the Romantic quest for self-liberation by means of the consumption of experiences. Indeed, the Romantics appear to have believed that the commitment to self-liberation by means of the consumption of novel experiences was actually a kind of obligation one owed oneself. Describing the novelty of the eighteenth-century Romantic ethic, Campbell notes:

> The "self" becomes, in effect, a very personal god or spirit to whom one owes obedience. Hence "experiencing," with all its connotations of gratificatory and stimulative feelings becomes an ethical activity, an aspect of duty. This is a radically different doctrine of the person, who is no longer conceived of as a "character" constructed painfully out of the unpromising raw material of original sin, but as a "self" liberated through experiences and strong feelings from the inhibiting constraints of social convention.[18]

It was this Romantic ethic, Campbell reasons, that gave rise to the revolution in consumption habits in modern society, and that eventually precipitated a revolution in modern techniques of production.

Interestingly, Campbell traces the development of the Romantic ethic back to evangelical Protestant sources. In a manner similar to Weber's original Protestant ethic thesis, Campbell argues that Romantic sensibilities originated in Calvinism. While Weber had focused, among other things, on the seventeenth-century Reformed doctrine

INNER LIFE
WORLD OF WORK — ONE'S PERFORMANCE

of double predestination, however, Campbell examines a later Calvin-ism tempered by the Arminian preclusion of double predestination. The "other Protestant ethic," as Campbell calls it, that developed out of this later Calvinism also revolved around concern to find signs of one's election in one's performance, but rather than seeking for these signs in the world of work, it stressed examining one's inner life for indications of the action of God's grace. Sorrow for sin, empathy for the plight of one's neighbor, and a generally melancholic disposition were held to be sure indications of one's election to grace. However, Campbell observes that this originally Christian piety devolved eventu-ally into a kind of spurious religiosity within which strong sentiments were sought for their own sake. "One way of looking at this change," Campbell suggests, "is to regard the Puritans as having developed a 'taste' for the strong meat of powerful religious emotion, and when their convictions waned, seeking alternative fare with which to satisfy their appetite."[19]

Sentimentalism, in turn, contributed to the Romantic emphasis on the cultivation of feeling by means of the consumption of immediate experi-ences, from which the peculiar spirit of modern consumerism appears to have emerged. "It is now possible to conclude," Campbell writes,

> that there were two, and not one, powerful cultural traditions of thought and associated "ethics" which developed out of English Puritanism in the eighteenth century. The first, which corresponds to that identified by Weber and is consequently commonly referred to as "the Protestant ethic," stressed rationality, instrumentality, industry and achievement, and is more suspicious of pleasure than of comfort. . . . The second, traceable from the Arminian revolt against predestination . . . and incorporating an "optimistic," "emo-tionalist" version of the Calvinist doctrine of signs, develops first into the cults of benevolence and melancholy, and then into a fully fledged Sentimentalism. For both, the culture-carriers are the mid-dle classes, and each, in its own way, has a vital contribution to make to the accomplishment of the Industrial Revolution and the legiti-mation of an essentially "bourgeois" way of life.[20]

Taking the Analysis Several Steps Further
Although Campbell's Romantic ethic thesis appears to interpret the

peculiar style of modern consumerism, it does not really explain why modern consumer behavior is so narrowly confined to the consumption of *material* products and services and why these products and services are so largely "harmless," to use the contemporary expression. After all, the Romantic ethic might just as well have prescribed self-construction by means of the heroic pursuit of pain and self-abnegation, or in wars of conquest, or in exposure to dangerous risk. Yet we find that modern consumer behavior, while admittedly hedonistic in just the ways that Campbell suggests, is actually highly risk averse and geared largely toward relatively mundane and antiheroic creature comforts. An additional problem with Campbell's Romantic ethic thesis, as he himself notes, is that Romantic sensibilities appear to have emerged out of an increasingly *secularized* Protestantism, a Protestantism in which, for whatever reasons, the object of Christian belief had been eclipsed by interest in the subjective act of believing. It would appear to be just as important, therefore, and perhaps even more important, to identify the reasons for this secularization of Protestantism as to trace the "spirit" of modern consumerism back to the Romantic ethic. We apparently need to extend the analysis back even further than the eighteenth century.

In this connection, we may recall that Tocqueville interpreted the American distaste for the supernatural in terms of a kind of unconscious Cartesianism. I believe Tocqueville was right, and that the key to the secular and relatively mundane quality of modern consumer behavior owes a great deal to the impact of the scientific method on the modern imagination, care of the likes of Spinoza, Descartes and Bacon. C. S. Lewis, among others, was very insistent on this point. In his essay *The Abolition of Man* (1943), Lewis argued that the mastery of nature, including human nature, by means of science and technology must result finally in the surrender of the human spirit to mere impulse. The reason for this, Lewis reasoned, is that the scientistic suggestion that the traditional belief in moral order is really nothing but a reflection of the emotional states of particular peoples at particular times and places inevitably becomes a kind of self-fulfilling prophecy within modern culture. It simply gives contemporary men and women license to surrender themselves to their own supposedly "natural" appetites and impulses. "Such is the tragi-comedy of our age," Lewis laments, "we continue to clamour for those very qualities we are rendering impossible. . . . We make men without chests [i.e., people who no longer believe in goodness and moral order] and expect of them virtue and enterprise. . . . We castrate and bid the geldings be fruitful."[21] Lewis's brilliant analysis helps to explain not simply the impulsive quality of modern consumer behavior but also its secularity and superficiality. In effect, we have become mere consumers because there is really nothing else left for us to become. Modern consumerism does not result in "the abolition of man" so much as it is an expression of the fact that genuinely human moral agency has already been abolished within modern scientific understanding.

A slightly different reading of the relation between consumerism and modern science was provided recently by Lesek Kolakowski in a book of essays entitled *Modernity on Endless Trial* (1990). In one of these essays, "The Illusion of Demythologization," Kolakowski suggests that it is not the logic of science as such that has abolished genuinely religious striving from contemporary culture so much as it has been our decision to submit ourselves to the logic of science for the sake of trying to achieve more effective control over our circumstances. The conflict between science and religion, Kolakowski observes, "is cultural, and it is about our hierarchy of preferences: our *libido dominandi* [our needs for comfort and safety] against our need to find meaning in the universe and in our lives."[22] The former, Kolakowski feels, has taken precedence over the latter. Indeed, the shallow quality of contemporary consumer behavior does suggest that our need to find meaning in the universe has, by and large, been eclipsed by our desire for creature comforts. We have, in effect, abandoned the religious quest for truth and meaning for the sake of comfort and convenience. It is this tradeoff that interprets the pervasiveness of consumptive romanticism and the utter absence of any kind of ascetic impulse in modern culture.

A concise analysis of this portentous modern decision to trade meaning for comfort was given a number of years ago by political philosopher Leo Strauss under the heading "the crisis of modernity." This crisis, Strauss wrote,

> reveals itself in the fact . . . that modern western man no longer knows what he wants—that he no longer believes that he can know

what is good and bad, what is right and wrong. Until a few generations ago, it was generally taken for granted that man can know what
is right and wrong, what is the just or the good or the best order of
society. . . . In our time this faith has lost its power."[23]
Strauss went on to argue that although the secularity and superficiality
of modern consumer culture is most commonly interpreted sociologi-
cally, that is, as a reflection of presumably more basic social forces, the
crisis of modernity must ultimately be traced back to a number of
deliberate philosophical decisions made by the intellectual architects
of the modern project. What united the likes of Machiavelli, Descartes,
Bacon, Hobbes, Locke and Rousseau, Strauss observed, was their
repudiation of the classical philosophical—and biblical—understanding of natural, created and eschatological limits to human freedom.

Representatives of the classical philosophical tradition, for example,
had stressed that nature was a "Good" wholly independent of human
willing, for which one must be willing to patiently seek and to which
one must acquiesce if one is to find happiness. Representatives of the
biblical tradition, furthermore, had stressed that the kingdom of God
is something for which one must be willing to sacrifice earthly happiness and for which one must be willing to wait. In sharp contrast to
both of these traditions, modern (and now "postmodern") philoso-
phers have insisted that human happiness is something human beings
must construct for themselves and by themselves *now.* Put somewhat
differently, modernity began in the decision to abandon the philosophical and theological attempt to penetrate behind immediate experience to the transcendent meaning of things. "Meaning," modern
thinkers have replied in effect, "is in the eye of the beholder. It lies only
in what we choose to make meaningful."

For Strauss, Machiavelli provides the archetype for this repudiation
of the classical and biblical conception of moral order. Machiavelli,
Strauss observed,

rejects the whole philosophic and theological tradition. . . . One
must start from how men do live; one must lower one's sights. The
immediate corollary is the reinterpretation of virtue: virtue must not
be understood as that for the sake of which the commonwealth
exists, but virtue exists exclusively for the sake of the commonwealth.

... This is a guarantee for the solution of the political problem [i.e., the realization of the good society] because a) the goal is lower, i.e., in harmony with what most men actually do desire; and b) chance [nature] can be conquered. The political problem becomes a technical problem.[24]

Of course, for our purposes the critical assertion in the above passage is that we must "lower our sights." We cannot realize the best society of which we are presently capable, so the modern argument runs, if we insist upon wasting our time dreaming about utopian futures and arguing about such things as the "will of God." All such theological disputation must be dispensed with, Machiavelli reasoned, if we are to be free to make the best of our circumstances here and now. "Criticism of religion," Marx was to put this same point several centuries later, "is the premise of all criticism."[25] Or, as Freud contended in his famous essay on religion "The Future of an Illusion" (1927):

Men cannot remain children forever. . . . Need I confess to you that the sole purpose of my book is to point out the necessity for this forward step? . . . By withdrawing their expectations from the other world and concentrating all their liberated energies into their life on earth, they will probably succeed in achieving a state of things in which life will become tolerable for everyone and civilization no longer oppressive to anyone.[26]

And so we have, since the seventeenth century and repeatedly thereafter, been encouraged to lower our sights philosophically and religiously for the sake of peace, prosperity, comfort and convenience.

The problem to which the superficiality and triviality of modern consumerism attests, however, is that the human goal did not simply have to be lowered a little bit; it had to be lowered a lot. Indeed, by the middle of the nineteenth century the human goal had been lowered to the point that Nietzsche condemned modern urban humanity as a kind of mindless herd possessing no transcendent ideals or aspirations. Thus, according to Nietzsche, spoke Zarathustra:

"Alas, the time is coming when man will no longer give birth to a star [i.e., conceive heroic aspirations]. Alas, the time of the most despicable man is coming, he that is no longer able to despise himself. Behold, I show you the last man. . . .

"The earth has become so small, and on it the last man, who

makes everything small. His race is as ineradicable as the flea-beetle; the last man lives longest.

" 'We have invented happiness,' say the last men, and they blink. They have left the regions where it was hard to live, for one needs warmth. . . .

"Becoming sick and harbouring suspicion are sinful to them: one proceeds carefully. . . . A little poison now and then: that makes for agreeable dreams. And much poison in the end, for an agreeable death.

"One still works, for work is a form of entertainment. But one is careful lest the entertainment be too harrowing. One no longer becomes poor or rich: both require too much exertion. Who still wants to rule? Who obey? Both require too much exertion.

"No shepherd and one herd! Everybody wants the same, everybody is the same: whoever feels different goes voluntarily into a madhouse. . . .

" 'We have invented happiness,' say the last men, and they blink."

And here ended Zarathustra's first speech . . . for at this point he was interrupted by the clamor and delight of the crowd. "Give us this last man, O Zarathustra," they shouted. "Turn us into these last men!"[27]

Nietzsche captured the essence of the modern project in his assertion that the last men believe that they have "invented happiness" and in his indictment of their pitiful avoidance of "exertion." For at the heart of this project lies the deliberate decision to surrender aspirations to transcendence for the sake of peace and prosperity. It is precisely this decision that is still so tellingly evident in modern consumer behavior.

Briefly reviewing our argument thus far, it is important to stress that although we often interpret modern consumerism as a kind of spiritual sloth—that is, as though it stemmed simply from a lack of resolve to pursue higher ideals—the deliberate decision not to pursue higher ideals actually precedes the emergence of modern consumer behavior by several centuries. Indeed, this decision discloses half of the Faustian bargain with which modernity began. The other half lay in the hope that by redirecting our energies toward the practical projects of peace and prosperity, we might be better able to take control of our circumstances here and now. This bargain has by now become very deeply embedded in the institutional fabric of modern society and culture.

The surrender of aspirations to transcendence is evident in the typically modern assumption that political life is not really grounded in any kind of "natural" or created order as much as it simply reflects a kind of standard deviation of human desires at any given time and place. The modern repudiation of a religious view of life is also evident in science's objectification of the natural world and in our technological utilization of "resources" and the "environment," both of which we now deem meaningful only to the extent that they are useful to us. In the economic realm, furthermore, the modern rejection of a religious view of life is evident in the so-called subjective theory of value and in our reliance on the market mechanism to determine "values" solely by means of price signals. And in the realm of culture, the modern repudiation of metaphysics discloses itself in what Philip Rieff so aptly termed "the triumph of the therapeutic." "Religious man," Rieff lamented, "was born to be saved, [modern] psychological man is born to be pleased."[28]

Of course, the thinkers who launched the modern project recognized that this lowering of our sights, as it were, was somewhat regrettable, but they hoped that the material payoff would more than adequately compensate us for our sacrifice of idealism and spiritual heroism. In effect, these thinkers replied to Jesus' assertion that man does not live by bread alone with the retort: "On the contrary, man lives quite well by bread alone so long as he can be distracted—by means of entertainment and therapy—from asking imponderable religious questions." Modernity's ultimate product is thus the individual who has been liberated to construct him or herself, but only within the confines of the here and now, and only by means of consuming the fruits of technological production, and only in the privacy of his or her own home, and only in such a way as not to disturb the peace by impinging materially upon his or her neighbor's equally autonomous self-construction—the modern consumer. While Nietzsche called this kind of individual "the last man," I think we might call him a Prometheus with a very small *p*.

A Christian Diagnosis of Modern Consumerism
Understood as a preoccupation with the consumption of material

goods and services, modern consumerism has little to commend it from a Christian point of view. In the first instance, it suggests a kind of mindlessness on the part of modern consumers. As essayist Wendell Berry recently observed in a provocative piece entitled "The Joy of Sales Resistance," the contemporary preoccupation with marketing, salesmanship and consumption could arise only in a society whose members are expected "to think and do and provide very little for themselves."[29]

Modern consumer behavior also discloses a remarkable lack of wisdom, particularly with respect to the relentless logic of desire. One of the Desert Fathers, St. Neilos the Ascetic (d. 430), is said to have advised his disciples to remain within the limits imposed by our basic needs and to strive with all their power not to exceed them. "For once we are carried a little beyond these limits in our desires for the pleasures of this life," Neilos warned, "there is no criterion by which to check our onward movement, since no bounds can be set to that which exceeds the necessary."[30] Neilos went on to outline the sorts of absurdities that inevitably result from attempting to satisfy material desires beyond the reasonable limits of need, and in so doing he described something very much like late-twentieth-century consumer culture. And it is certainly the case that a good deal of the dissatisfaction and disappointment that so pervades modern life owes to the insatiable logic of "need" in consumer culture. The "more is better" attitude of modern consumer culture makes it difficult, if not impossible, to say when enough is enough.

Yet the most serious indictment we must level at contemporary consumer behavior is that it is "spiritless." It betrays a decision to sacrifice all noble and truly human aspirations at the altars of comfort, convenience and safety. In this connection, Søren Kierkegaard was one of the most perceptive Christian critics of modern consumer behavior. The inventive term Kierkegaard used to describe this behavior is "philistine-bourgeois mentality," a mentality so mired in this-worldly matters that it cannot even bring itself to imagine the possibility of a human destiny that transcends this world. The philistine-bourgeois mentality, Kierkegaard observed,

> lacks every qualification of spirit and is completely wrapped up in probability, within which possibility finds its small corner; therefore it lacks the possibility of becoming aware of God. Bereft of imagination,

as the philistine-bourgeois always is, whether alehouse keeper or prime minister, he lives within a certain trivial compendium of experiences as to how things go, what is possible, what usually happens. In this way, the philistine-bourgeois has lost his self and God. In order for a person to become aware of his self and of God, imagination must raise him higher than the miasma of probability, it must tear him out of this and teach him to hope and to fear—or to fear and to hope—by rendering possible that which surpasses the *quantum satis* [sufficient standard] of any experience. But the philistine-bourgeois mentality does not have imagination, does not want to have it, abhors it. So there is no help to be had here. And if at times existence provides frightful experiences that go beyond the parrot-wisdom of routine experience, then the philistine-bourgeois mentality despairs, then it becomes apparent that it was despair; it lacks faith's possibility of being able under God to save a self from certain downfall.[31]

To be "completely wrapped up in probability," as Kierkegaard put it, is simply to be committed to the typically modern assumption, following the likes of David Hume, that we must limit "reasonable" discourse to the realm of the probable, and that we must never allow either reason or hope to extend beyond this-worldly experience. Although this sort of assumption is practically useful and undergirds modern scientific and technological praxis, it is profoundly stultifying in the realm of the spirit because it rules out the possibility that something really new might actually happen—say, a revelation from God or the resurrection of Jesus Christ from the dead. This is why Kierkegaard argued that the philistine-bourgeois personality discloses a fundamental sickness of the soul.

Of course, Kierkegaard's philistine-bourgeois mentality is simply a gloss on Jesus' simple yet penetrating questions: "What good will it be for a man if he gains the whole world, yet forfeits his soul? Or what can a man give in exchange for his soul?" (Mt 16:26). To imagine that we can create or sustain ourselves by means of our possessions or consumption habits, Jesus suggests, is tragically mistaken. It is also stupid. For such things have no lasting future. If we stake our identities—our selves—to these things, then we will pass away with them.

Responding Christianly to Modern Consumerism

In forming a Christian response to contemporary consumerism it may help to recall that the original meaning of *consume* is to burn, to exhaust and to destroy completely. The object of our response to consumerism, then, is to try, with the Lord's gracious help, to avoid destroying ourselves in this behavior and to try to prevent our neighbor from being destroyed by such behavior as well. Our first duty, then, as Wendell Berry insists, is to "resist the language, the ideas, and the categories of this ubiquitous sales talk, no matter from whose mouth it issues."[32] We must also encourage our neighbor to look beyond the mundane horizons of material existence for truly human meanings and purposes. "When someone faints," Kierkegaard wrote, "we call for water, eau de Cologne, smelling salts; but when someone wants to despair [i.e., when they become mired in this-worldly probability] then the word is: Get possibility, get possibility, possibility is the only salvation."[33]

Yet in suggesting that we must encourage our neighbor to look beyond consumerism to truly human meanings and purposes, we must recognize that we face something of a fork in the road at present with respect to this matter, with the followers of Nietzsche pointing in one direction and with Jesus Christ pointing in quite a different direction. The postmodern followers of Nietzsche would have us transcend the narrow confines of modern bourgeois-philistinism by sheer acts of will. From this point of view, it is precisely the autonomous will-to-self-definition, the will-to-power, that is authentically human, and it is believed that it will be through the exertion of our will-to-power that we will somehow "transcend" present circumstances. Needless to say, the potential for brutality and death in this Nietzschean "spirituality" is very great. In sharp contrast to this postmodern Nietzscheanism, Jesus Christ exhorts us to heroic self-transcendence by means of love understood in terms of servanthood. "The kings of the Gentiles lord it over them," Jesus reminded his disciples, "and those who exercise authority over them call themselves Benefactors. But you are not to be like that. Instead, the greatest among you should be like the youngest, and the one who rules like the one who serves" (Lk 22:25-26). From a Christian point of view, then, the path of genuine self-transcendence, of authentic heroism, of possibility, lies in giving one's self away for the sake of one's neighbor. It is the way of the cross.

Conclusion

It may also help to juxtapose the modern obsession with acquisition, grasping and possessing with the Christian virtues of gratitude, generosity and hope. Far from encouraging us to accumulate and/or consume as much as we possibly can, the Scriptures exhort us to view our lives as a gracious gift from God for which we are to be grateful. We are further exhorted to express our gratitude by giving ourselves generously away in the love of God and in the love of our neighbor (see 1 Tim 6:18). Finally, because the plausibility of consumerism depends entirely upon the apparent permanence of life in this world, we must continually remind each other and ourselves that this world and its lusts are indeed passing away (1 Cor 7:30-31). "Sell your possessions and give to the poor," Jesus says to us. "Provide purses for yourselves that will not wear out, a treasure in heaven that will not be exhausted, where no thief comes near and no moth destroys" (Lk 12:33). Jesus also exhorts us to "use worldly wealth to gain friends for yourselves, so that when it is gone, you will be welcomed into eternal dwellings. . . . If you have not been trustworthy in handling worldly wealth, who will trust you with true riches?" (Lk 16:9, 11).

2
Returning God to the Center

•••

Consumerism & the Environmental Threat

Bill McKibben

Christmas has become, for most in the affluent West, the high holy day of consumerism. It used to be so for our family. But now, come November and December, we look forward to Christmas, with no dread of busyness and no fear of drowning in commercialism.

I know what Christmas Eve will be like: We'll cut the tree in the afternoon and bring it in and decorate it. We'll go to church, where I will sweat with my Sunday-school class as they try to remember their lines for the pageant, and then I'll relax in the knowledge that it is the small mistakes (the drooping halo, the three-year-old shepherd using his crook as a hockey stick) that really stick most fondly in people's minds. We'll come home, read the Christmas story once more, put up our stockings and go to bed. In the morning we'll open the stockings and find the candies and pencils and tiny jokes inside; we'll exchange one or two homemade presents—photo albums, raspberry jam made in the summer's heat—and then we'll go outside to play in the snow, or into the kitchen to prepare a great dinner. It will be a completely normal Christmas—minus the mounds of presents.

The story of how my family arrived at this quiet and beloved Christmas (which means, of course, a much quieter December than most of our friends experience, without a single trip to the mall, and a January without credit card debt) has many parts: carbon dioxide levels in the atmosphere, worries about what a consumer culture meant for our daughter, and the conviction, nurtured by our church, that there was more real joy to be had from Christmas if only we could unplug it. For us this has meant more real connections with that glad day than in the past.

To understand what I mean, let us begin by looking hard at what we have done to this planet. One can guess with some accuracy a human being's behavior by looking at his physical and social surroundings. If a parent is self-absorbed, lazy or forced by economic pressure to be absent, then a family often falls apart. On a slightly larger scale, when a community's institutions—schools, parks, churches—begin to wither, we know its people have succumbed to a kind of privatized selfishness.

If we look at the largest measures of environmental health, we can make similar judgments: the ever-increasing levels of carbon dioxide, the steadily rising rates of ultraviolet radiation, the fast-growing list of extinctions. These testify not so much to technological failure as to human failure. We need to confront that failure in the hopes of building something new and joyful in its place.

We need to begin with a few basics. I find as I travel that there is a tendency, even among those who care about such issues, to underestimate the pressures on the natural world. We tend to list "the environment" as one issue alongside a hundred others, such as drugs and the deficit. But it is much more than that; it is less an issue than a context, the basic context in which we all must live our lives. And it is coming unraveled.

In the next fifty years we will probably see Earth's population hit its maximum. Toxic pollution, fossil fuel use, ozone depletion, soil erosion and a dozen other phenomena that environmentalists have been warning us about will put enormous pressure on this planet.

In the area I study most closely, global climate change, the world's scientists have now reached a broad consensus that we have begun to warm the planet. This warming is in its very early stages. 1995 was the warmest year to date, but it reflects only about a fifth of the warming scientists say we will see by midcentury. Still, already we can begin to see results of this gradual increase in temperature. Over seven hundred died in a short Chicago heat wave—you can't "prove" that this resulted from global warming, only that it coincides neatly with what the computer models tell us to expect from the early years of the greenhouse era. New data shows that severe storms have increased 20 percent across the North American continent during the twentieth century, another match with the predictions, another portent of things to come.

We do not yet realize the danger. The most recent presidential campaign, with its call from both sides for cutting gas taxes, is proof of that. One reason we do not is because of the casual way we discuss environmental problems. By grouping together everything from global warming to river pollution, we obscure crucial differences and delude ourselves about the progress we have made.

What Goes In . . .

Although we have made major strides in addressing some ecological problems, such as urban air pollution, lake contamination, and lead poisoning, it does not follow that we have the same capacity to solve other environmental problems, because other problems are fundamentally different.

Consider what comes out of the tailpipe of a car. One byproduct of burning gas is carbon monoxide, the chief ingredient in the brown, dirty and dangerous-to-breathe substance known as smog. Smog has now largely been eliminated by the installation of catalytic converters, which is why Los Angeles is noticeably cleaner than it used to be.

However, carbon dioxide still comes pouring out that exhaust pipe. When you burn a gallon of gasoline, which weighs about eight pounds, you release five and a half pounds of carbon dioxide. The average car releases its own weight in carbon dioxide annually. It is invisible and does nothing to us directly. But it is the chief heat-trapping gas now altering the most basic terrestrial forces on the planet. Its molecular structure traps heat that would otherwise radiate back out to space. And here is the real catch: there is no catalytic converter, no technology, that can do anything about it. All that can be done is to drive smaller cars, and drive them less; but few, of course, are doing either, and so the carbon dioxide continues to build up in the atmosphere.

There is a difference between environmental problems such as smog, rivers that catch on fire and radiation leaks from atomic plants on the one hand, and global warming, habitat destruction and over-fishing on the other hand. The first type of problem is caused by some mistake, something that has gone wrong. It can therefore be fixed with relative ease. The second is caused by things operating as they should, at simply much too high a level. These more serious and deeper problems concern me most. We are in the fast-moving water above the rapids, and there is no way to paddle backwards. It will take all the skill and cohesion we can muster to get through intact.

Think of it this way: we have vastly increased the speed of change in our societies and economies in the twentieth century, and seen people and communities strain, and in some cases crack, as they try to keep up. Now as the twenty-first century dawns, we are taking the physical systems that have always been stable before and forcing them to speed up just as quickly. But there is no good reason to suppose they will adapt.

Job Talks Back

For people of faith, however, the problem is even deeper than the practical one I have described. People have always polluted, always needed to alter and manipulate the land around the places they lived or farmed. But that did not raise the deepest theological questions. Now, in the short period of ten or twenty years, we have so quantitatively increased the scope of our alterations that they have become qualitatively different. We are altering the most basic forces of the planet's surface—the content of the sunlight, the temperature and aridity—and that raises powerful questions about who is in charge.

If you wanted to give a name to this theological problem, I think you could say that we are engaged in decreation. God, before getting around to humans, created birds and sea creatures and beasts and creeping things, and he pronounced them all good. Later he saved a breeding pair of each aboard the ark. Now, metaphorically, we toss them off the ark.

In the book of Job, God speaks from the whirlwind, taunting Job's powerlessness. Where were you, he asks, when I set the boundary of the oceans? Can you summon forth the rain clouds and crack them open? Job chose to sit down and shut up, but increasingly we brazenly talk right back to God. We can spit in his face, the old geezer. Our habits and behaviors, by raising the earth's temperature, now threaten to determine how high the seas rise, and where it will rain and where it will not.

Our Behaviors, Not Our Technologies

Let us look again at global warming. Carbon dioxide is an inevitable byproduct of burning fossil fuel. If you buy an electric car and hook it up to a power plant that burns fossil fuel, then you have simply moved the problem upstream: now the carbon dioxide pours out of the power plant's smokestack.

What if you double the efficiency of your car's engine so it burns only half as much gasoline? That is possible; in fact, it has been done over the last decade. But in the United States we have simultaneously doubled the total number of miles driven, and therefore wiped out the whole gain. A massive, much-heralded EPA project to reduce energy use by half at the American Express Corporation was wiped out by only seven hundred people switching from cars to sport utility vehicles or four-wheel-drive pickup trucks. With constant pushing by the electric utilities, the average American household added a compact fluorescent bulb during the 1980s—and seven incandescent bulbs as well, one reason that per capita electric consumption increased an average of 11 percent. If you double fuel efficiency while simultaneously doubling the size of the economy, you get nowhere.

We need technical change, but more than that we need behavioral change. Much more than electric cars, we need buses and bicycles and shifts in our ideas of what is desirable that would lead us to use them. The American way of life, insofar as it revolves around consumption, drives our environmental problems.

Consumption is an issue uniquely suited for faith communities. Among the institutions of our society, only the communities of faith can still posit some reason for human existence other than the constant accumulation of stuff. Our businesses thrive on constant growth; our politicians avoid hard choices by flogging the economy to grow more quickly (in the immortal words of Bill Clinton, "It's the economy, stupid"); even our educational institutions have designed themselves to fit easily into this happy picture. We have made important decisions in recent decades as individuals and as a nation by answering the question, Is it good for the economy?

Religious institutions that grew up before this trend inherited a different set of concerns (in many ways, a contradictory set of concerns), and the resulting contradictions, among other things, have weakened the power of religion in the economic era. We profess to believe that we cannot worship both God and mammon. We profess to worship someone who told us to give away, not accumulate. We profess to follow a tradition that in its earliest and purest forms demanded communal sharing of goods and money. But we have by and large bracketed off those central portions of the message. We are not alone in this. Virtually every religious and philosophic tradition has similar figures and similar teachings, in a line that runs from Buddha through Jesus and St. Francis to Thoreau and Gandhi. Martin Luther King Jr. said at the end of his life that it was not racism or imperialism or militarism that represented our root problem—it was materialism. But for all our pious lip service, we have regarded those people as unrealistic cranks.

This is a powerful moment for rehabilitating Christ the crank. What are the atmospheric chemists telling us? What are the climatologists saying? In many ways, the same things we have heard from Christ and his disciples: Simplicity. Community. Not because it is good for our souls or for our right relation with God, but because without simpler lives, the chances of stabilizing the planet's basic workings are slim. Without community, the chances for buses and trains and other necessary efficiencies are nil. This confluence of the hardheaded and the softhearted may make for a powerful moment, an unpredictable time when the world could turn quickly in new directions.

The $100 Christmas

If we in religious communities are going to do anything about it, we have to recognize just how strong the consumerist ethos is. It has taken root in all of us, basically unchallenged. Fertilized by a million commercials, it has grown like a wolf tree, a tree whose canopy spreads so

wide that it blots out the sun. In the same way, the consumerist ethos
blots out the quiet word of God. Churches, obviously, do not have the
power to compete head-on, and few of us junkies are ready to go cold
turkey. But increasingly there are signs that people are asking, "Isn't
there something more than this?" Churches can help build this momentum in important ways, beginning with those things it has the most
psychological control over.

Chief on this list is the celebration of Christmas. Not only the most
beloved of church holidays, Christmas is also the most powerful celebration of consumerism—so powerful, in fact, that it has become a
major gift-giving holiday in Japan, despite the conspicuous lack of
Christians there.

Christmas is a school for consumerism. In it we learn to equate
delight with materialism. We celebrate the birth of One who told us to
give everything to the poor by giving each other motorized tie racks.

With a couple of friends a few years ago, I launched a campaign in
the conference of the United Methodist Church to which we belong
for "Hundred Dollar Holidays," recommending that families try to
spend no more than a hundred dollars on Christmas. When we began
we were long-faced, talking about the environmental damage that
Christmas caused (all those batteries!), the money that could instead
go to social justice work and so on. But we found that this did not do
the trick, either for us or for our fellow congregants.

What did the trick, we discovered, was focusing on happier holidays.
Though we continued to stress the $100 figure as an anchor for families
pushed and pulled by the tidal forces of advertising and social expectation, we talked about making Christmas more fun. The poster we
used suggests many alternatives to a store-bought Christmas, things
that involve people doing things for each other and for creation.

We were amazed at how well this worked, even on the limited scale
in which we were trying it. Many people thanked us for "giving them
permission" to celebrate Christmas "the way I always wanted to celebrate it." This taught me some useful lessons: that the effect of
consumerism on the planet is mirrored precisely in its effect on the
soul, that finding true joy means passing up momentary pleasure, and
that joy, deep bubbling joy, is the only really subversive force left in
our society. The only way to make people doubt, even for a minute,

the inevitability of their course in life is to show them they are being cheated of the truest happiness. Christmas is a good school for this education, because it can be such a wonderfully giddy party for the birth of a baby.

It also turns out to be a pretty radical idea. The retail economy is massively geared toward the fourth quarter, banking annually on the fact that people will rush into stores to buy things they do not need. To question the wisdom and the pleasure of that consumption is to question an awful lot about our consumer society. Several newspaper columnists attacked our campaign on the grounds that while we might be right, we would also undermine the sacred economy. This gave us a good opportunity to reply that surely American consumer capitalism, defended always as the most rational of all systems, does not demand the corrupted celebration of Christ's birth in order to make ends meet.

Great American TV Turnoff

Another practical idea involves a feature of our lives even more entrenched than Christmas—television. Television has become the essential anchor of the growth culture and our endless moral tutor. American children spend more time staring at it than they spend in school; when asked if they wanted to spend more time with the tube or with their father, more than half chose the TV. New research indicates that watching television makes us fatter and less physically healthy and, more profoundly, changes the shape of our minds. Are you worried about a decline in family values, in community spirit? Then you are worried about television.

The debates over things like violence on television miss the point, I think. I wrote a book once that involved watching everything that came across the largest cable system then in existence on a single day. I had 2,400 hours of videotape by day's end, and I spent a year looking at them, asking myself, *What would the world look like if this was your main source of information?* If you distilled all those thousands of game shows and talk shows and sitcoms and commercials down into a single notion, it would be this: "You are the most important thing on the face of the earth. Your immediate desires are all that count. Do It Your Way. This Bud's for You." We are led daily, hourly, into temptation.

There is something else: television and its attendant technologies create a constant buzz around us, an unrelenting torrent of image and sound that make it difficult for us to think for ourselves anymore, to rise to occasions. That is one reason I am a board member of a group called TV Free America, which every year sponsors a turnoff week in schools around the nation. Last year three million kids took part. Increasingly the idea is spreading to churches. Not only are the turnoffs endorsed by the American Medical Association, the Children's Defense Fund and the Natural Resources Defense Council, but also by the Congress of National Black Churches, the National Religious Partnership for the Environment and the Family Research Council. Last winter the pope called for TV-free Lent, a campaign we are just beginning here.

Again, the emphasis will not be on renunciation; it will be on the great pleasure that comes when you turn off the television and rejoin the living world, and on the opportunity to reflect, to think, in the stillness of the unplugged world. Solitude and silence and darkness have always been key parts of the religious life, but they have been banished by television. We need to reclaim them, and in so doing to break the materialist enchantment that now holds us in its thrall, to shrug off some of the witchcraft that makes us long constantly for things that will not satisfy us.

The Center of Our Lives

Questions about consumption, like the questions about the new environmental damage, get near the deepest theological questions. If we were built, then what were we built for? We know what hawks were built for; it is announced in every fiber of their bodies. But what about us? Why do we have this amazing collection of sinews, senses and sensibilities? Were we really designed to recline on the couch, extending our wrists perpendicular to the floor so we can flick through the television's offerings? Were we really designed in order to shop some more so the economy can grow some more? Or were we designed to experience the great epiphanies that come from contact with each other and with the natural world? Were we designed to witness the goodness all around us and to protect and nourish it? Just as "the environment" is a context, not an issue, so is "consumption." It defines at the moment who we are, and who we are not.

This is a profound moment for religious people. On the one hand, our species asserts itself as never before. We have grown large enough to alter creation, by the single great explosion of a nuclear weapon or the billion muffled explosions of pistons inside engines spewing out carbon dioxide. As Oppenheimer said on that afternoon testing of the atomic bomb, we have become as gods: not just the nuclear engineers, but anyone with a car, anyone with a credit card.

Yet at the same moment we have acquired the intelligence to see what we are doing: not only the scientific understanding of things like the greenhouse effect, but also the dawning ecological understanding of the way that everything is linked to everything else, that creation is a fabric far richer than any of our predecessors could have understood (though, of course, they may have sensed it more deeply than we do). The age-old struggle between God and mammon, always before a personal and never-ending battle, now has a time limit and a bottom line.

The issue is who or what we put at the center of our lives. In the environmental debates there has been a lot of discussion about anthropocentrism versus biocentrism versus theocentrism. Most of this debate seems empty to me, assuming as it does that most of us put any of these things at the center. If we followed any of them in a sincere fashion, we would be well on the way to solving our environmental and social problems. Anthropocentrism, if we lived as though we really believed it, would lead inevitably to the kind of sharing necessary to heal the environmentally destructive gaps between rich and poor. Were we truly anthropocentric, we would feel grave shame at our own overconsumption. But of course we are not. We are me-centric. We are I-dolatrous. That is what consumer society has schooled us to be.

The question now is, How can we break out of it? Some have criticized secular environmentalists as "pagans" because they profess a biocentrism, a view of the world that puts all living things at its center. But they are far closer to orthodoxy than most of the rest of us who still place ourselves there. We need to put God in the center. Then we need to realize that this involves more than the smug announcement that we have done so.

Having God at the center imposes certain limits on our behavior. If we are not to wreck God's creation, then there are certain things we simply must not do; we simply must not continue consuming as we now are. And there are certain things we must do; we must share our bounty with those in need in the rest of the world, finding somewhere a middle ground so they do not follow our path to consumer development. These things are in one way extraordinarily difficult. But we know the deep and certain joy they can bring, and so we can say with some confidence that at least they are possible. At least they are worth a try.

And we will know if we are succeeding by the evidence all around us. Creation will let us know if we are rebuilding our house, restoring its foundations. Are species continuing to die out? Is the temperature continuing to climb? Our communities will show us if we are really changing. Are the numbers of absurdly rich and absurdly poor beginning to decline? Are we rebuilding institutions other than the mall, places like schools and parks and churches? The environmental crisis is so deep and so fundamental that our response will reveal who we most truly are.

3
Money & Misery

....

David Myers

It's pretty hard to tell what does bring happiness. Poverty an' wealth have both failed.—KIN HUBBARD, Abe Martin's Broadcast

Four *dramatic trends have marked American cultural life since 1960:* the sexual revolution, the decline of marriage, the diminishing well-being of children and the increase in violence. These trends have coincided with a fifth trend: the striking rise in materialism and affluence. Increasingly we value having more, and compared to 1960, most of us do have more. Let us examine our changing fiscal fitness and values, and see what they have wrought.

Increasing Materialism
Does money buy happiness? Few of us would say yes. But if asked a different question—"Would a *little* more money make you a *little* happier?"—many of us would reply with a smirk and a nod. There is, we believe, some connection between wealth and well-being. Asked in a Roper survey how satisfied they were with thirteen different aspects of their lives, including friends, house and schooling, respondents were least satisfied with the amount of money they had to live on.[1] When

interviewers from the University of Michigan's Institute for Social Research asked what hampers the search for the good life, the most common answer was "We're short of money." What would improve your life quality? "More money" was the most frequent answer.[2] According to a recent Gallup poll, one in two women, two in three men, and four in five people earning more than $75,000 a year would like to be rich.[3] Asked by the Roper Organization in 1992 to name an annual income they needed to fulfill their dreams, the average American answered $83,800. In 1995, the response was $102,000.[4] Think of this as today's American dream: life, liberty and the purchase of happiness.

A myth claims that such materialism grew during the greedy 1970s and 1980s. As my colleagues in literature occasionally remind me, myths can be deeply true, as this one is. The most dramatic evidence of this "greening of America" comes from the UCLA/American Council on Education annual survey of nearly a quarter million entering collegians (see figure 3.1).[5] Those agreeing that a "very important" reason for their going to college was "to make more money" rose from one in two in 1971 to nearly three in four in 1995. And the proportion considering it "very important or essential" that they become "very well off financially" rose from 39 percent in 1970 to 74 percent in 1996. These proportions virtually flip-flopped with those who considered it very important to "develop a meaningful philosophy of life." Materialism was up, spirituality down.

What a change in values! Among nineteen listed objectives, becoming "very well-off financially" is now ranked number one. It outranks not only developing a life philosophy but also "becoming an authority in my own field," "helping others in difficulty" and "raising a family." To young Americans of the 1990s, money matters.

Economist Thomas Naylor could sense this intense materialism during the six years he taught corporate strategy courses at Duke University. He asked each of his students to write a personal strategic plan. "With few exceptions, what they wanted fell into three categories: money, power and things—very big things, including vacation homes, expensive foreign automobiles, yachts and even airplanes. . . . Their request to the faculty was: Teach me how to be a moneymaking machine."[6] Little else mattered, reported Naylor, including concerns for one's family, one's spirituality, one's workers, or one's ethics and

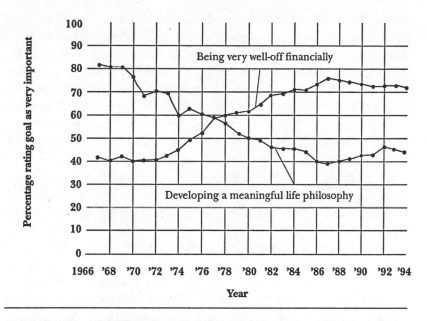

Figure 3.1. Rising materialism during the 1970s and 1980s appears in annual surveys of entering American collegians. Each data point represents 200,000+ students, yielding a total sample of some 6 million.

Source: Eric L. Dey, Alexander W. Astin and William S. Korn, The American Freshmen: Twenty-five Year Trends (Los Angeles: Higher Education Research Institute, Graduate School of Education, UCLA, 1991), and Alexander W. Astin et al., The American Freshman: National Norms for Fall 1991 (and ensuing volumes through 1996; Los Angeles: Higher Education Research Institute, Graduate School of Education, UCLA, 1991-1996).

social responsibility. Malcolm Forbes Jr. appealed to such values in marketing his magazine: "I want to make one thing very clear about *Forbes*, namely—*we are all about success and money*. Period."

Cornell University economist Robert Frank and psychologists Thomas Gilovich and Dennis Regan believe that economics professors are partly responsible for their students' materialism.[7] Their nation-wide survey of college professors revealed that economists, despite having relatively high salaries, were more than twice as likely as those in other disciplines to contribute no money to private charities. In responding to public television appeals, their median (and most common) gift was nothing. In laboratory monetary games, students behave more selfishly after taking economics courses.

Are today's collegians, Thomas Naylor's business students, Malcolm

Forbes Jr. and economics professors onto something? Does being well-off produce psychological well-being? Would we indeed be happier if we could exchange a modest lifestyle for one with palatial surroundings, Aspen ski vacations and executive class travel? Would we be happier if we won the American Family Publishers Ten Million Dollar Sweepstakes and could choose from its suggested indulgences: a forty-foot yacht, deluxe motorhome, designer wardrobe, luxury car and private housekeeper? "Whoever said money can't buy happiness isn't spending it right," proclaims a Lexus ad.

Would having more money, by enabling "the good life," buy us greater well-being? As our money goes up, does our misery go down? We can triangulate from this question, by asking three more specific questions.

Are People Happier in Rich Countries?

Surveys of several hundred thousand representatively sampled people—170,000 of whom were surveyed in one sixteen-nation study in the 1980s—reveal striking national differences in well-being. In Portugal one in ten people say they are very happy. In the Netherlands four in ten people say the same.[8] These appear to be genuine national differences, not mere variations in the connotations of the translated questions. For example, regardless of whether they are German-, French- or Italian-speaking, the Swiss report higher well-being than their neighbors in Germany, France and Italy.

Comparing the countries, we find some tendency for wealthy nations to have happier, more satisfied people. The Scandinavians, for instance, are generally prosperous and happy. But there are curious reversals. During the 1980s the Irish consistently reported greater life satisfaction than the doubly wealthy but less-satisfied West Germans. Belgians tended to be happier than their wealthier French neighbors. Moreover, national wealth is entangled with other happiness predictors, such as civil rights, literacy and the number of continuous years of democracy. So it is not just the wealth of the Scandinavians and Swiss that matters, but their history of freedom.

During the mid-1980s my family and I spent a sabbatical year in the historic town of St. Andrews, Scotland. Comparing life there with life in America, we were impressed by a seeming disconnection between national wealth and well-being. To most Americans, Scottish life would have seemed spartan. Incomes were about half of those in the United States. Among families in the Kingdom of Fife surrounding St. Andrews, 44 percent did not own a car, and we never met a family that owned two. Central heating in this place not far south of Iceland was, at that time, still a luxury.

During our year there and during three half-summer stays since, we enjoyed hundreds of conversations over daily morning coffee gatherings in my University of St. Andrews department, in church groups and over dinner or tea in people's homes. We repeatedly noticed that despite their simpler living, the Scots appeared no less joyful than Americans. We heard complaints about Margaret Thatcher but never about being underpaid or unable to afford wants. With less money there was no less satisfaction with living, no less warmth of spirit, no less pleasure in one another's company.

Are Rich Americans Happier?
Are rich people happier? In poor countries, such as Bangladesh and India, being relatively well-off does make for somewhat greater well-being. Psychologically as well as materially, it is much better to be high caste than low caste.[9] We humans *need* food, rest, warmth and social contact.

In affluent countries, however, where nearly everyone can afford life's necessities, increasing affluence matters surprisingly little. In the United States, Canada and Europe, the correlation between income and happiness is, as University of Michigan researcher Ronald Inglehart notes, "surprisingly weak (indeed, virtually negligible)."[10] Happiness is lower among the very poor, but once a person is comfortable, more money provides diminishing returns. The second piece of pie or the second $50,000 never tastes as good as the first. So far as happiness is concerned, it hardly matters whether one drives a BMW or, like so many of the Scots, walks or rides a bus.

Even very rich people, such as *Forbes* magazine's one hundred wealthiest Americans, as surveyed by University of Illinois psychologist Ed Diener, are only slightly happier than average.[11] With net worths exceeding $100 million, providing them with ample money to buy things they do not need and hardly care about, four out of five of the forty-nine people responding to the survey agreed that "money can increase *or* decrease happiness, depending on how it is used." Some were indeed unhappy. One fabulously wealthy man said he could never remember being happy. One woman reported that money could not undo misery caused by her children's problems. Examples of the wretched wealthy are not hard to come by: Howard Hughes, Christina Onassis, J. Paul Getty.

At the other end of life's circumstances are most victims of disabling tragedies. With exceptions, such as for victims of vicious child abuse or rape, most people who suffer negative life events do not exhibit long-term emotional devastation. People who become blind or paralyzed, perhaps after a car accident, thereafter suffer the frustrations imposed by their limitations. Daily, they must cope with the challenges imposed by their disabilities. Yet, remarkably, most eventually recover a near-normal level of day-to-day happiness. Thus university students who must cope with disabilities are as likely as able-bodied students to report themselves happy,[12] and their friends agree with their self-perceptions.[13] "Weeping may linger for the night," observed the psalmist, "but joy comes with the morning" (Ps 30:5).

These findings underlie an astonishing conclusion from the new scientific pursuit of happiness. As the late New Zealand researcher Richard Kammann put it, "Objective life circumstances have a negligible role to play in a theory of happiness."[14] A society in which everyone lived in 4,000-square-foot houses would likely have no happier people than a society in which everyone lived in 2,000-square-foot houses.[15] Good events, such as a pay hike, winning a big game or receiving an "A" on an important exam, make us happy until we adapt. Bad events—an argument with one's mate, a work failure, a social rejection—bring us down, but seldom for more than a few days.

Feeling the influence of short-term events, people use them to explain their happiness, all the while missing subtler but bigger influences on their long-term well-being. Noticing that an influx of cash feels good, they may accept the Hollywood-Robin Leach image of who is happy: the rich and famous.

In reality we humans have an enormous capacity to adapt to fame, fortune and affliction. We adapt by recalibrating our "adaptation levels," the neutral points at which sounds seem neither loud nor soft, lights neither bright nor dim, experiences neither pleasant nor unpleasant. In Michigan on a winter day, sixty degrees would feel warm, but not to someone adapted to the summer's heat. So it goes with things: Our first desktop computer, with information loaded from a cassette tape, seemed remarkable, until we got that speedier machine with a hard drive, which itself became pokey once we got a faster, more powerful computer. Yesterday's luxuries become today's necessities and tomorrow's relics.

The same is true with money. William Bennett, who has done much to alert us to the social recession and our need to renew values, is not exempt from the materialism of his age. In spurning a $125,000 offer to become chair of the Republican National Committee he remarked, "I didn't take a vow of poverty"—apparently what $125,000 felt like after making a reported $240,000 in speaking fees during the preceding four months.[16] But even $240,000 hardly feels like wealth to many professional athletes. "People think we make $3 million or $4 million a year," explained then-Texas Ranger outfielder Pete Incaviglia several years ago. "They don't realize that most of us only make $500,000."[17]

Does Economic Growth Improve Human Morale?
We have scrutinized the American dream of achieved wealth and well-being by comparing rich and unrich countries, and rich and unrich people. That leaves the final question: Over time, does happiness rise with affluence?

The answer, typically, is no. Lottery winners appear to gain only a temporary jolt of joy from their winnings.[18] Looking back, they feel delighted to have won. Yet the euphoria does not last. In fact, previously enjoyed activities such as reading may become less pleasurable. Compared to the high of winning a million dollars, ordinary pleasures pale.

On a smaller scale, a jump in income can boost our morale for a while. "But in the long run," notes Inglehart, "neither an ice cream cone nor a new car nor becoming rich and famous produces the same feelings of delight that it initially did. . . . Happiness is not the result of being rich, but a temporary consequence of having recently become richer."[19] Ed Diener's research confirms that those whose incomes have increased over a ten-year period are not happier than those whose income has not increased. Wealth, it seems, is like health: although its utter absence can breed misery, having it does not guarantee happiness. Happiness is less a matter of getting what we want than of wanting what we have.

For that matter, the pain of simplification may also be short-lived.

Cornell University economist Robert Frank had this experience:

> As a young man fresh out of college, I served as a Peace Corps Volunteer in rural Nepal. My one-room house had no electricity, no heat, no indoor toilet, no running water. The local diet offered little variety and virtually no meat. . . . Yet, although my living conditions in Nepal were a bit startling at first, the most salient feature of my experience was how quickly they came to seem normal. Within a matter of weeks, I lost all sense of impoverishment. Indeed, my $40 monthly stipend was more than most others had in my village, and with it I experienced a feeling of prosperity that I have recaptured only in recent years.[20]

Our human capacity for adaptation helps explain why, despite the elation of triumph and the anguish of tragedy, lottery winners and paraplegics usually return to their former level of happiness. It also explains why material wants can prove insatiable—why, for example, Imelda Marcos, living in splendor amid privation in the Philippines, could buy more shoes than she could conceivably wear. When the possessor becomes possessed by possessing, the adaptation-level phenomenon has run wild.

We can also ask whether, over time, our collective happiness has floated upward with the rising economic tide. Are we Americans happier today than in 1940, when two out of five homes lacked a shower or bathtub, when heat often meant feeding wood or coal into a furnace, and when 35 percent of homes had no toilet?[21] Or consider 1957, when economist John Galbraith was about to describe the United States as *The Affluent Society*. Per capita income, expressed in today's dollars, was $8,700. Today it is more than $20,000, thanks to increased real wages into the 1970s, increased nonwage income, and the doubling of married women's employment. Compared to 1957, we are therefore "the doubly affluent society." We now own twice as many cars per person, plus microwave ovens, big-screen color TVs and home computers. Moreover, we spend $200 billion a year in restaurants and bars—two and a half times our 1960 inflation-adjusted restaurant spending per person.[22] From 1960 to 1990, the percentage of us with dishwashers zoomed from 7 to 45 percent, while owners of clothes dryers rose from 20 to 69 percent and those with air conditioning soared from 15 to 70 percent.[23]

While looking through unsolicited mail order catalogs recently, my wife, Carol, remarked, "You know what's become big business? Stuff to put your stuff in." Such storage systems sell well in our neighborhood of century-old homes, built when there was less need for closets and shelving to store one's accumulated possessions. Now to store that shelving we are building bigger houses. In 1966, 22 percent of new homes had more than 2,000 square feet; in 1994, 47 percent did.[24]

Downsizing and recessions have contributed to the loss of 43 million U.S. jobs since 1973, with painful dislocations. But since then our economy has created 70 million new jobs. We have all heard of AT&T's laying off 40,000 workers, but fewer of us have heard that MCI's employment since 1985 has mushroomed from 12,000 to 48,000 or that Sprint's has risen from 27,000 to 52,000. People have lost jobs to corporate mergers, but found jobs in the growing smaller-company sector, including the many young technology companies. Thus, notes Zoe Baird, the combination of inflation and unemployment is at its lowest level in twenty-seven years.[25]

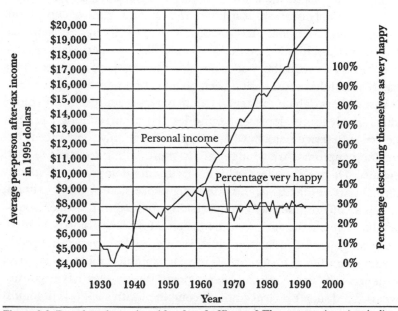

Figure 3.2. Does happiness rise with cultural affluence? The average American's disposable income (adjusted for inflation and tax changes) has doubled since the late 1950s. But happiness, as reported to the National Opinion Research Center, has not risen.

Source: Happiness data from Richard Gene Niemi, John Mueller and Tom W. Smith, *Trends in Public Opinion: A Compendium of Survey Data* (New York: Greenwood, 1989), and from personal correspondence with Tom Smith, National Opinion Research Center. Income data from *Historical Statistics of the U.S. and Economic Indicators.*

Believing that a little more money would make us a little happier, and having seen our affluence ratchet upward little by little over nearly four decades, are we now happier?

We are not. Since 1957, the number telling the University of Chicago's National Opinion Research Center that they are "very happy" has declined from 35 to 30 percent (see figure 3.2). People are twice as rich and a little less happy. In fact, between 1956 and 1988 the percentage of Americans saying they were "pretty well satisfied with [their] present financial situation" *dropped* from 42 to 30 percent.[26]

We also are more often downright miserable. Among Americans born since World War II, depression has increased dramatically: by tenfold, reports University of Pennsylvania clinical researcher Martin Seligman.[27] Today's twenty-five-year-olds are much more likely to recall a time in their life when they were despondent and despairing than are their grandparents, despite the many more years the grandparents have had to suffer all kinds of disorders, from broken legs to the anguish of depression. Similar trends are evident in Canada, Sweden, Germany and New Zealand, report psychiatric researchers Gerald Klerman and Myrna Weissman.[28] Everywhere in the modern world, it seems, more younger adults than older adults report having been disabled by depression.

Researchers debate the actual extent of rising depression. Do older adults simply forget depressive episodes that occurred long ago? No, the age difference persists when people report only their recent depressive symptoms. Are younger adults more willing to admit to such feelings? Or are they less willing to consider temporary despair a normal part of life? If so, then defining depression by other criteria, such as being hospitalized for depression and the duration of episodes, should eliminate the age gap. But no matter how depression is defined, the findings persist: today's youth and young adults have grown up with much more affluence, slightly less overall happiness, much greater risk of depression and a tripled teen suicide rate. Never has a culture experienced such physical comfort combined with such psychological misery. Never have we felt so free or had our prisons so overstuffed. Never have we been so sophisticated about pleasure or so likely to suffer broken relationships.

These are the best of times materially, "a time of elephantine vanity and greed," observes Garrison Keillor,[29] but they are not the best of times for the human spirit. William Bennett, no critic of free market economies, is among those who recognize the futility of economics without ethics and money without a mission: "If we have full employment and greater economic growth—if we have cities of gold and alabaster—but our children have not learned how to walk in goodness, justice, and mercy, then the American experiment, no matter how gilded, will have failed."[30]

How then can we avoid a startling conclusion? Our becoming much better off over the last four decades has not been accompanied by one iota of increased psychological well-being. The same is true of the European countries and Japan, reports economist Richard Easterlin.[31] In Britain, for example, sharp increases in the percentage of households with cars, central heating and telephones have not been accompanied by increased happiness.[32] The conclusion is provocative, because it explodes a bombshell underneath our society's materialism: *economic growth in affluent countries provides no apparent boost to human morale.*

We know this, sort of. In a nationally representative survey, Princeton sociologist Robert Wuthnow found that 89 percent of more than 2,000 participants felt "our society is much too materialistic." *Other* people are too materialistic, that is. For 84 percent also wished they had more money, and 78 percent said it was "very or fairly important" to have "a beautiful home, a new car and other nice things."[33]

But one has to wonder, what is the point? "Why," wondered the prophet Isaiah, "do you spend your money for that which is not bread, and your labor for that which does not satisfy?" (Is 55:2). What is the point of accumulating stacks of unplayed CDs, closets full of seldom-worn clothes, garages with luxury cars?[34] What is the point of corporate and government policies that inflate the rich while leaving the working poor to languish? What is the point of leaving huge estates for one's children, as if inherited wealth could buy them happiness, when that wealth could do so much good in a hurting world?

The Rest of the Story
Three hundred years ago, the philospher-mathematician Pascal observed that no single truth is ever sufficient because the world is complex. Any truth separated from its complementary truth is a half-truth. Since the late 1950s, average real personal income has

doubled. Moreover, we are having fewer children to spend it on, thanks to a birth rate that has been halved.

But it is true also that the real wages of hourly workers have *declined* slightly since the early 1970s.[35] Moreover, average real household income, though boosted by the increase in women's employment, has not increased as rapidly as individual income. This is because family divisions and declining marriage rates have spread personal income across more households. If all adults had their present income, but were as often married as in 1960, household income would be noticeably higher.

Inequality

There is another troubling truth. The rising economic tide has not lifted all boats equally. Although the economic pie has been growing, the rich (as usually happens during economic expansions) have been eating a progressively larger piece, the poor a progressively smaller piece.[36] And countries with large income inequality and much poverty, such as Brazil, India and Portugal, have populations that report lower psychological quality of life than countries such as Norway, the Netherlands and Belgium, where wealth is more equally distributed.[37]

Economists have some fancy statistical measures of income inequality. For us noneconomists, the simplest measure is the percentage of all income received by the richest fifth of the population (which in the United States in 1995 included 129 individual and family billionaires).[38] In 1980 the richest fifth received 41.5 percent, slightly under 1960's 42.6 percent. By 1994 they were up to 46.9 percent of income, while the poorest fifth earned less than one-tenth as much, 4.2 percent.[39]

Since 1970, the proportion of U.S. families earning more than $60,000 (in today's dollars) has increased from approximately 20 to 25 percent, as has the number earning less than $20,000. The proportion in the middle has, therefore, dwindled correspondingly, from 59 to 50 percent.[40] Expressed as household income, the rich/poor differences are visibly increasing (see figure 3.3).

In 1960, according to *Business Week,* the average chief executive of a major corporation earned as much as forty-one factory workers. In 1996, an executive of a Fortune 500 company was deemed worth nearly 185 factory workers.[41] If CEO Louis Gerstner of IBM worked six days a

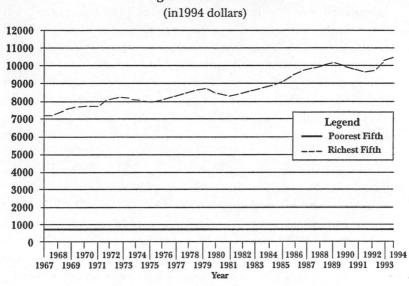

Average Household Income
(in 1994 dollars)

Legend
— Poorest Fifth
--- Richest Fifth

Year

Figure 3.3. The poorest fifth of households compared to the richest fifth.
Source: Data from the U.S. Census Bureau: http://www.census.gov/pub/hhes/income/incineq/pb60tb3.html Income in 1994 dollars.

week, forty-eight weeks a year, for his $4.6 million in 1994 salary and bonus, then he received a cool $16,000 a day—about what the average retail clerk who waits on him earns in a year.[42] Gerstner did manage to raise that meager stipend to $13.2 million in 1995, but got trumped by John Welch Jr.'s $22 million in direct compensation from the General Electric Co., which our $16,000-a-year clerk could match by working 1,375 years.[43]

Do big results justify big salaries? Consider the average income of America's physicians, which approaches $200,000. In Britain, which has less income inequality and a health care system that costs one-third as much per person, doctors earn one-fourth as much as in the United States. In the U.S., average life expectancy is 75; in Britain it is also 75.[44] Of course, rich doctors can point to richer CEOs, who can defend their salaries by comparing their societal contributions to those of professional athletes. Louis Gerstner's $4.6 million was one-tenth of Michael Jordan's $44 million in 1994 earnings.[45] But then Michael could look with envy on Disney CEO Michael Eisner's 1993 compensation of $203 million (which,

Business Week noted, was "nearly equal to the GNP of Grenada").[46]

Since 1980, wealth, like income, has been flooding upward, not trickling down. The richest one percent now own about half the country's net wealth (excluding their own homes).[47] In August 1997, *Fortune* magazine estimated Microsoft CEO Bill Gates's net worth at $42 billion.[48] How much is $42 billion? If Gates were to move to a town with 42,000 penniless people, his arrival would instantly make its average (arithmetic mean) resident a millionaire. If he could turn that wealth into cash and stick it between his mattresses, with no further interest or dividends from it, he could give away $10 million daily for a decade and still have $5.5 billion left over (more than enough to finance his new $40 million home and anything else he might desire).

As conservative political analyst Kevin Phillips has said, "The 1980s were the triumph of upper America—an ostentatious celebration of wealth, the political ascendancy of the richest third of the population."[49] Facing *Time* interviewers on being named 1995's "Man of the Year," Newt Gingrich was upfront about his mission "to maximize the creation of wealth and the acquisition of wealth rather than the redistribution of wealth."[50] (Note how Gingrich's philosophy differs from its alternative, exemplified by the professional sports leagues, which promote team equality by giving the lowest-ranking teams the first draft picks and by equally distributing league profits.)

Accompanying this growing economic inequality is growing economic segregation. More and more the rich live separated from the poor. Their children attend well-funded suburban schools, if not private schools. They live in enclaves with other rich. Rarely do they encounter the poor about whom they have many opinions. Old neighborhoods such as where I live—a neighborhood with blocks of beautiful historic homes interspersed with homes of the working poor, anchored by an elementary school where half the children are ethnic minorities—are being supplemented by new developments of homes and apartments at specified price levels.

Among African-Americans, the inequality between the richest and poorest fifths is especially great: 49 versus 3 percent of aggregate African-American income.[51] "There is more in common between two middle-class families one of which is black," notes Gertrude Himmelfarb, "than between two black families one of which is middle-class."[52]

The growing African-American middle class has, thanks to improved job opportunities and housing desegregation, been moving out of the inner city. Chicago's South Side in the 1950s, for example, had communal neighborhoods populated by the dictates of segregation with people of all classes and incomes.[53] The middle-class exodus from formerly stable neighborhoods has left an increasing concentration of poor African-Americans in underclass neighborhoods marked by persistent joblessness and poverty. Decreased racial segregation among the middle class has, ironically, led to increased economic segregation. For such concentrated poverty we all pay a price.

The Price of Poverty
The concentration of poor families creates high-risk settings for youth, notes a 1993 National Research Council report.[54] "Such neighborhoods are characterized by racial stratification, homelessness or very degraded housing, inadequate schools, a lack of recreational and employment opportunities, and in metropolitan areas, a high level of crime and violence. Constructing a family life that can guide children and adolescents into healthy constructive behaviors is a challenge of heroic dimensions in these settings." The challenge is exacerbated by the loss of resources needed to support churches and other community-building institutions. For family ecology, lack of money is the root of much evil.

The Children's Defense Fund, which relentlessly documents the links between poverty and children's pathology, concurs.[55] America's 15 million poor children, it reports, are much more likely to suffer malnourishment, family stress, inferior child care, frequent moves, adolescent pregnancy, overcrowding and death. They attend inferior schools and are more likely to drop out, to become delinquent and to approach life with little hope. With the sense of futility comes a loss of faith in the work ethic. The moral sense takes a back seat to mere survival, aided by an underground economy.

Money may not buy happiness, but it would buy the poor good food, decent shelter, opportunities to learn, reduced family stress, a healthy neighborhood, preventive health care, healthy recreation and improved economic opportunity. And, the Children's Defense Fund maintains, it would do so at less cost than the long-term price that society pays in escalating crime, welfare and unproductivity. Swedes pay more in the short run to ensure that few of their children live in poverty (proportionally, one-tenth as many as in the United States). But their child-friendly priorities are an investment in Sweden's national future.[56]

Poverty and single parenthood often go hand in hand, meaning that in social science studies each of these variables tends to be a proxy for the other. Although single parenthood is a major cause of poverty, family structure matters even when controlling for income. But the reverse is true as well: poverty matters even when controlling for family structure. One research team led by the University of Michigan's Greg Duncan followed 895 infants and preschoolers over five years. Their conclusion: "Family income and poverty status are powerful determinants of the cognitive development and behavior of children, even after we account for other differences—in particular family structure and maternal schooling."[57]

Moreover, poverty undermines marriage. One of the principal findings of the new science of evolutionary psychology is that females, worldwide, invest their reproductive opportunities carefully, by looking for signs of power and resources in potential mates. Men therefore strive to offer the resources that women desire, and women feel attracted to men whose wealth, power and ambition promise resources for protecting and nurturing offspring.[58] The high rates of unemployment and underemployment among certain groups of young men impede their odds of marriage.[59] African-American young women, some argue, face a serious shortage of similar-aged, employed African-American men. "A man who can barely support himself isn't likely to look forward to taking on the responsibilities of a wife and children," notes psychologist Lillian Rubin. "Nor is a woman apt to see him as a great marriage prospect."[60]

Is it a coincidence that the black family has weakened during an era when African-Americans have lost so many good jobs to automation and suburbanization? Here in Michigan, Detroit-area families have suffered the loss of thousands of unionized auto manufacturing jobs. Many of those jobs have moved to smaller cities such as Holland and Grand Rapids, where thousands of nonunionized workers have been hired in the last decade by newer companies that now manufacture plug-in mirrors, windows, electronic components and mechanical systems for assembly in Detroit.

Poverty-ridden Benton Harbor, Michigan, has led America's three thousand largest cities with 83 percent of its families headed by single parents. Ken Parnell, a retired mechanic, responds angrily when asked why Benton Harbor has so many single parents. "Because black men can't get no jobs. Because white men got all the jobs sewed up. . . . How can you take care of your family if you can't get a job? That's it in a nutshell."[61] More young men having a job with no future or, worse, a future with no job means more young women having no husbands, more children without fathers and more young men at loose ends without the civilizing responsibilities of marriage and fatherhood. Even among married couples, the odds of breakup are doubled in families where the father has no job.[62]

Such trends contribute to our present economic dilemma: over the last thirty years, total social spending by all levels of U.S. government has risen (in constant 1990 dollars) from $144 billion to $787 billion, more than a fivefold increase, reports the social science-oriented Council on Families in America.[63] Thus, at the very time that so many children are suffering the corrosive effects of poverty, the willingness of taxpayers to support children is being tested. Small wonder that organizations that care about children, including the Children's Defense Fund, advocate combating poverty both through child-friendly government priorities and through the renewal of marriage-supportive policies and values.

Home Economics

If we really want to get serious about nurturing children, strengthening families and improving our culture's prospects, we must turn from talking about family values to walking the talk, with government and corporate policies that actually value families. To praise parents who stay home to care for children and then veto a family leave bill that would have enabled new parents to stay home without pay for twelve weeks, as George Bush did in 1992, is to talk and walk in different directions.

If we set aside culture war issues such as abortion and gay rights, we see an emerging consensus among liberals and conservatives: government and corporate policies matter, and they have not made family welfare a priority. "No government can love a child and no policy can substitute for a family's care," acknowledges a pastoral letter from the

National Conference of Catholic Bishops. "But clearly families can be helped or hurt in their irreplaceable roles. Government can either support or undermine families as they cope with the moral, social, and economic stresses of caring for children."[64]

How might we, then, improve the economic ecology for families? Imagine that we were to start over on a lush new planet. We could take today's knowledge loaded in our brains and laptop computers, but we would need to create afresh our government, economics, educational systems and media. What sort of society would we wish to create?

Might it be in some ways like our own, yet different? Perhaps a pure democracy, uninfluenced by political contributions? Perhaps with tax-and-benefit policies that reward marriage? Perhaps with a socially responsible market economy that provides incentives for achievement while protecting the natural and social environments? Perhaps with a progressive consumption tax that encourages savings, investment and economic growth while putting a price on the accumulation of nonessential material goods? (Economist Robert Franks suggests doing this by simply taxing families not on what they earn but on what they spend—which is their earnings minus their savings and charity.[65])

As complete environmentalists, concerned for both natural and social environments, might we mandate "family-impact statements," including assessments of whether a new policy or program would tend to increase or decrease care by married biological fathers? Might we want government to consider its client to be not just the individual but the family system? Recall that having a job versus not having a job impacts marital well-being and personal happiness more than does high versus not-so-high income. Might a family-friendly new society therefore give less priority to increasing upper incomes than to providing full employment at livable wages? (That was part of the idea behind Jack Kemp's enterprise zones, which offer investors the carrot of zero capital gains tax on businesses built and jobs created in poor neighborhoods.[66])

By contrast, consider how we today award discounted fees, fares and prices. Although the wealth of today's average senior citizen greatly exceeds that of the average young parent, we give restaurant, airline and park fee discounts to senior citizens. Such discounts amount to an implicit penalty on financially strapped young adults who must therefore pay higher fees. At the gas station near my home, a sixty-year-old executive with grown children can buy gasoline at a discounted price below that paid by a struggling thirty-year-old parent of young children. The station could as well drop the price of the gasoline and add a surcharge for all those under sixty. Although this method sounds more tactless, it is simply another way of framing the same policy.

Thanks partly to favoritism toward the old over the young, including the indexing of social security payments, the poverty rate of seniors is now half that of children. Such favoritism may have made sense in an age when many more seniors lived in poverty. But do such policies express our priorities today? Starting afresh, would we choose to devalue younger parents by charging them more than older adults?

Family-Supportive Tax-and-Benefit Policies

As a general rule, what we tax we get less of, what we reward we get more of. If our highways are jammed and our air polluted, we create fast lanes that reward carpooling and penalize driving solo. Commentators from the conservative Family Research Council and Rockford Institute to the centrist Communitarian Network and liberal Children's Defense Fund agree on at least one thing: social policies can make or break families. Government tax policies can work either to provide incentives or disincentives for marriage and family life.

Without pretending expertise on family economics, here is a quick synopsis of proposals for how government might foster families.

Eliminate the marriage penalty. Better yet, reverse the antimarriage tilt in our tax and welfare policies. Under current law, an unmarried man and woman each with $30,000 taxable income would pay $1,000 less tax than they would on a combined $60,000 married-couple income. "This is terrible social policy," says Dan Quayle.[67] Eugene Steurle of the Urban Institute agrees: removing the tax penalty for marriage will increase marriage.[68] Economists James Alm and Leslie Whittington, noting that divorce rates have risen slightly following increased marriage tax, have estimated that a 20 percent reduction in the marriage tax would produce a 1 percent increase in the number of marriages.[69]

When allocating subsidized housing and housing loans, give priority to married couples with children. So advise the sociologists and public policy experts making up the nonpartisan Council on Families in America.[70]

Increase incentives for self-support. Reward at-risk teens, perhaps with a cash grant, for finishing high school (preparing them for decent jobs and marriage). By eliminating taxes on low-income workers or raising the Earned Income Tax Credit, increase incentives for jobless people to seek employment. In 1986 President Reagan called the Earned Income Tax Credit (which refunds taxes to the working poor) "the best anti-poverty, the best pro-family, the best job creation measure to come out of Congress."[71] To encourage marriage, a "marriage bonus" could be additionally offered to low-income families. For families on public assistance, such would reverse the current incentives, as described by Robert Rector: "The mother has a contract with the government. She will continue to receive her 'paycheck' as long as she fulfills two conditions: 1) she does not work; and 2) she does not marry an employed male. I call this the incentive system made in hell."[72]

Increase incentives for community and child support. President Clinton's 1996 proposal to reward adoption with a $5,000 tax credit supports adoptive families and their children. Senator Dan Coats's Project for American Renewal proposed similar incentives, such as a tax credit for married families receiving the Earned Income Tax Credit and a charity tax credit that would reward contributions to poverty-fighting institutions, even by those who do not itemize deductions.[73]

Index dependent exemptions to inflation. Some federal programs, notably social security, are automatically adjusted to keep the real payment constant, but not the inflation-gutted dependent exemption, which today would be worth more than $8,000 per child if indexed for post-World War II inflation.[74] To support families, the government could restore and index the dependent exemption.

Better yet, provide a child allowance. Increased exemptions would assist families, but especially rich families and parents who place a higher priority on income generation than dedicating increased time to children. The $400 per child tax credit, which begins in 1998, is a step in the right direction. Such family-supporting tax reforms will be expensive in the short run, but less in the long run, say child advocates, than the eventual costs related to increases in crime, welfare and drug use following the collapse of families.

Recouple reproduction with responsibility. Katha Pollitt of *The Nation* reports that "Newt Gingrich's Personal Responsibility Act is aimed against unmarried moms, but these women are actually *assuming* a responsibility that their babies' fathers have shirked."[75] Most teen mothers are impregnated by men over twenty years of age. There is therefore growing support for mandatory identification of fathers as a condition for receipt of government benefits.[76]

A Child Support Assurance System, articulated by Columbia University social policy expert Irwin Garfinkel, would create disincentives for hit-and-run fathering *and* increase support for single parents, only 40 percent of whom receive child support payments from the absent parent (usually a father).[77] Once paternity is established, in disputed cases by DNA testing, the absent father's (or mother's) income would automatically be taxed by the IRS at a rate such as 17 percent annually for one such child and 21 percent for two such children. This money would be transferred to the Social Security Administration and awarded, without means testing, to the custodial parent as $2,000 a year for one dependent child, $3,000 a year for two children and so forth.

The plan would make it harder for men to evade responsibility for their sexual behavior. It would tie men's payments directly to their income. It would transfer child support from the welfare system (which discourages work and marriage) into a self-funding social security program. And it would reduce bureaucracy, thanks to simplified mechanisms for collecting the money and distributing it without means testing. In this system the losers would be the men who now evade responsibility for supporting their children. The winners would be the single mothers and children presently receiving no support from deadbeat dads, as well as all of us who would benefit from a family-supportive policy that penalizes nonmarital fatherhood.

Family-Supportive Corporate Policies

In our new utopian world, family-impact analyses will also inform socially responsible corporate policies. Supported by government incentives (without which the competitive market economy necessarily limits corporate generosity), businesses will value their workers' families and will invest in the *social* capital—family and community networks—that nurture the civility and trust required for a productive market economy. A strengthened corporate focus on the family could do the following:

Minimize the uprooting and relocation of families with children. Companies will recognize that stable communities enable the family supports that flow from kin networks and from the social bonds formed in stable neighborhoods, churches and schools.

Provide greater opportunities for parental leave. There is evidence that long hours of low-quality day care that begins in the first year of life and continues through the preschool years produces children who tend to be more insecure, disagreeable and aggressive. This research leaves Pennsylvania State University developmental psychologist Jay Belsky arguing "for support for quality infant care for those who absolutely must have it, for policies of paid parental leave, and for occupational opportunities that turn once full-time jobs into part-time jobs during the infancy years and then revert to their full-time status with . . . health benefits preserved."[78]

Some European countries offer either new parent up to a year of paid leave. The United States now offers ninety days of possible unpaid leave to those in companies with fifty or more employees.[79] Such could be expanded to include some pay and health coverage and gradual reentry into the workplace.

Offer flextime, compressed time and part-time work schedules. Create new incentives for a thirty-hour work week. Flextime work allows a parent to come early or late (and leave late or early) if a child is sick or the other parent is unavailable. In my community, the Donnelly Corporation, the world's largest manufacturer of auto mirrors, allows parents to stay with a sick child or attend a daytime school activity and make up the time later. Along with nineteen other local corporations, Donnelly also funds a Children's Resource Network that provides referrals to child-care providers and consultation and emergency backup services.

Compressed time schedules allow for the working of more hours in fewer days, as might suit family needs. Job sharing and part-time arrangements, another Donnelly practice, would become more attractive if the United States, like most other industrialized countries, would mandate proportionate fringe benefits to part-time workers. As it is, low-income people (often women and minorities) often must work temporary jobs or two part-time jobs, neither with benefits, so that employers can evade responsibility for their benefits, pensions and vacations. Other corporations may force employees to work overtime, also in order to save on the fringe benefit cost of additional workers.

Redistributing work would simultaneously reduce overwork and underemployment. Better to downsize the workweek than the work-force, says Jeremy Rifkin; better to increase leisure and family time than unemployment.[80] For example, why not have two parents combine for sixty hours a week of employment with, say, either two thirty-hour jobs or one full-time and one half-time job? A recent survey of randomly selected workers nationwide also revealed a corporate benefit to fam-ily-responsive policies: regardless of whether they personally expected to gain, workers at companies with such policies felt a higher level of commitment to their company and were less inclined to leave.[81]

Spreading the available work among more people working fewer hours, re-creating a culture in which people work to live rather than live to work, would have multiple benefits: less jobless poverty and associated social pathology, less of an income gap between haves and have-nots, more relaxation, less stress and more time for parenting. Although those who might now be working fewer overtime hours may need to simplify their lives, most will do so with no long-term cost to their well-being. To encourage a more equal distribution of work, some European countries such as France are offering employers reduced payroll taxes as a incentive to reduce the work week. Mandating proportional fringe benefits to all would also encourage a more even distribution of work by eliminating the incentive employers now re-ceive to work employees overtime.

With technology-aided productivity increases, corporate restructur-ing, and the shift to a global economy, the working world is undergoing a new revolution that will likely entail social consequences on a par with those of the industrial revolution. Now is therefore the time to ask: What sort of communities do we want for tomorrow? What level of joblessness and associated poverty and crime are we willing to tolerate? What priority do we wish to give children and family life in the twenty-first century? And, in view of our answers, what sort of tax and incentive policies will move us toward the social world we want rather than a world we dread?

Allow increased work at home. Where feasible, a flexible work policy would give family-oriented workers more say not only in when and how many hours they work but also in where. The team of people who produce my introductory psychology textbooks are a case in point. Supported by fax machines, e-mail, telephone and overnight express, my editor, who formerly worked with the publisher in New York, now works thirty hours a week from a home office in Anchorage. She suffers no lost time in daily travel and incurs fewer expenses for clothing, meals and transportation, while her employer saves on New York City office expenses. At home she is free to be at work at 6 a.m. while her preschooler sleeps, and to adjust her daytime work hours around her childsitter. Much the same has been true for the book's photo editor, supporting freelance editors and copyeditor, all of whom also gain increased time for their children. The resulting products emerge from the coordinated efforts of a team of home-based and office-based workers in at least a half dozen cities. Government could support this home work movement by eliminating zoning restrictions on in-home labor and easing restrictions on deductions for home office expenses.

Equitably compensate workers and executives. The socially responsible marketplace will also seek to balance the need for lucrative incentives to attract and reward outstanding executives with the need to preserve fairness and equity among employees. In my community, Herman Miller, Inc., one of the world's three largest office furniture manufacturers and periodically one of America's ten most admired companies in *Fortune*'s annual survey of executives, has been known for such policies. Workers share in company profits and over time become invested in its success as stockholders. The CEO's salary and incentive bonus compensation is limited to "20 times the average annual compensation earned by the Company's regular full-time employees."[82]

Poverty of the Spirit

Economic growth has given the average American a standard of living that is the envy of the world, and a social recession that is the envy of no one. Despite economic growth, our morale and social ecology have waned. The poverty that plagues us is less absolute material poverty than a relative poverty that breeds spiritual starvation. To languish ruddlerless without prospects for meaningful work, surrounded by others' affluence, is a recipe for hopelessness, purposelessness and futility. For such reasons, Martin Luther King Jr. reminded us that "a true revolution of values" will be troubled by "the glaring contrast of poverty and wealth."[83]

We humans have thrived under conditions of equal or greater

absolute poverty. Depression-era families may have lacked the television, refrigerator, hot water, flush toilets and food stamps of today's poor, but their families were largely intact and their neighborhoods safe. African-Americans faced worse racism, poverty and slavery-spawned disadvantages fifty to a hundred years ago, yet their two-parent families were overwhelmingly intact. (From 1890 to 1960, four out of five African-American families with children were headed by married couples.[84]) Immigrant families have typically been close-knit, despite having fewer material resources.[85] Calcutta's families are more wretchedly poor than America's, yet more intact.[86] The problem is not racial genetics (which have not significantly changed) or absolute poverty (which is not greater today than sixty years ago) but a spirit strangled by broken attachments and surrendered hopes.

Marian Wright Edelman recalls, from a more poverty-ridden time, her father, a Baptist preacher:

> He was not elegant, but he was educated; not rich, but richly read. He didn't care about things, he cared about thinking and thoughtfulness. He didn't care about status, but about service. He and my mother didn't leave their children any funds, but a more lasting legacy of faith. He didn't own guns because he knew goodness was more powerful, was never greedy, and was always grateful for God's amazing grace. He never hid the ugly realities of our segregated and unjust world from us, but he, my mother, and other community elders never left us children to confront that world alone. They tried to right the wrongs and teach us that the ways of the world were not the ways of God or of a purposeful life. They didn't promise us we would win all the battles we would face but instead we had to try to fight them. So we never lost hope and learned to struggle and take responsibility for ourselves and our communities because adults loved us enough to struggle with us.[87]

The novelist Thomas Wolfe was right: "You can't go home again." We cannot drive backwards to that kinder, gentler (though also more impoverished and prejudiced) world of Edelman's childhood. We can only move forward from today's realities into the next millennium. If we assume all is hopeless, we will be right. But if we can agree that prosperity must be seasoned with purpose, capital with compassion and enterprise with equity, then maybe, just maybe, the best is yet to come.

4
Catholic & Protestant Ethics
••

Competing or Complementary Conceptions of the Public Good?
John E. Tropman

F_{or} *about a century, Max Weber's "Protestant Ethic"[1] held sway on the* consciousness of scholars and the public. Everyone knew what the Protestant Ethic was, and even if the details were a little fuzzy, the uncertainty was within that very construct.[2] No one, it appears, thought of other religiously based ethics. Recently, however, the concept of a Catholic Ethic has emerged, parallel to the Protestant Ethic and based on the formal and informal teachings of the Catholic Church.[3] The Catholic Ethic is, of course, a precursor to the Protestant Ethic, having existed for about fifteen hundred years before the Reformation. Perhaps it was the very commonness of the Catholic Ethic that led the public and scholarly community to ignore it in favor of the newer Protestant Ethic. Simply put, the Catholic Ethic has a more communally oriented conception of the public good than the Protestant Ethic, which is more acquisitively oriented.

In Europe the Catholic Ethic, with its variations, was predominant. The Protestant Ethic was the intruder. In America, however, the reverse is true. The Protestant Ethic was dominant for two hundred years or more (from 1620 to the 1840s) until larger numbers of Catholics (and Jews) began to immigrate from Europe. Now the Catholic Ethic holds a vital but subdominant position. (And, by extension, there is likely to be a Jewish Ethic as well, with its perspectives and orientations.)

The worldviews according to the Catholic and Protestant ethics have important implications. Take, for example, the conception of capitalism itself. Lester Thurow's ideas of "Individualistic Capitalism" and "Communalistic Capitalism" fit very well into Protestant and Catholic ethic orientations.[4] Other areas in which the difference in worldviews matters are attitudes toward helping, toward the public good (each tub on its own bottom versus a rising tide lifts all boats) and toward ownership and consumption.

Looking at American society today, a central question for discussion is this: How can Americans, singly and severally, blend individualistic and collective approaches to thinking about resources, needs and assistance in order to form a truly just society?

The Catholic Ethic

While older, the Catholic Ethic has been discussed less.[5] It is communal in orientation, emphasizing family and community as vital parts of life. Its perspective on work and money is instrumental; both are important, even necessary, but should not be overdone and do not have any positive mutating properties (especially money). (A positive mutating property is something that changes you for the better because you do it or have it.) The Catholic Ethic emphasizes the human cycle of sin and forgiveness. Compare that view with Weber's description of the Protestant Ethic: "The God of Calvinism demanded of his believers not single good works, but a life of good works combined into a unified system. *There was no place for the very human Catholic cycle of sin, repentance, atonement, release, followed by renewed sin.*"[6]

Within the umbrella of such an ethos, the presentation of need is taken as natural, and the offer of help is similarly something only to be expected. There is no distinction between the "needy" and the "rest of us" or between the "worthy poor" and the "unworthy poor." Need is need. You need help today. Tomorrow I might need it. Indeed, poverty might be embraced as being a situation of closeness to God.

In an article for the *Journal of Business Ethics,* Charles Curran expresses the core values of the Catholic Ethic, especially those that the attitude of sharing encompasses:

First, the Catholic understanding of society in general and the state in particular proposes a middle ground approach between the extremes of individualism and collectivism. . . .

Second, the principle of subsidiary [is] . . . to transfer to the larger and higher order collectively functions which can be performed and provided for best by lesser and subordinate bodies. . . . The state thus exists as a help *(subsidiu)* for individuals. . . . [The idea here is that functions should be performed at the level closest to them; in organizations this is called "decentralization."]

Third, the Catholic tradition has insisted that the principles of justice must govern economic life in society. The tradition has recognized three different types of justice—commutative, distributive, and legal or social. Commutative justice governs the relationship between one individual and another. Distributive justice governs the relationship between the community as a whole or the state and individuals. . . . Social justice or legal justice governs the relationship of the individual to the common good. . . . Social justice recognizes the contribution all must make to the common good, but especially emphasizes the right of the marginalized to participate in every way in the life of society.

Fourth, Catholic social teaching in more recent times has developed a theory of human rights including so-called economic rights . . . grounded in the dignity of the human person. . . .

The understanding of private property in the Catholic tradition has always included an important social dimension. . . . In early Christianity the social aspect of the goods of creation was strongly emphasized. The very existence of private property was often understood as resulting primarily from the fall or the presence of sin in the world, and not resulting from a demand of human nature as such. . . .

[Fifth], Catholic social teaching has recently insisted on a preferential option for the poor.[7]

In sum, from the perspective of consumption and stewardship, key elements of the Catholic Ethic might be capsulated as follows:

☐ Need is collective in cause and remediation.

☐ Adequate resources for consumption is a human entitlement.

☐ Acquisition is acceptable up to a point, but not too far beyond what one needs.

The Protestant Ethic

The Protestant Ethic is broadly understood to be centered on work, its importance, and, through work, the acquisition of money. Work becomes a kind of sacred ceremony and money a sacred product. Unemployment, especially in America, is a "fall from grace."[8] From this perspective, one can never have too much money, any more than one can get too many "A" grades in school. Possessing money is reassuring and shows others that one is a success.

In this cultural system, need could become something of a disgrace. It indicates a distance from God's favor, and poverty might be even an occasion for sin, if, for example, it led to theft. Providing help just discourages the energy and enterprise needed to "get it together." Some help, though, to the worthy poor who need assistance through no fault of their own might be offered, but not indefinitely.

For the Protestant Ethic, its perspectives on consumption and stewardship might be summarized as follows:

☐ Need is individual in cause and remediation.

☐ Individuals must earn their "right" to the pool of resources.

☐ Acquisition is necessary and prudent.

Three Caveats

Presenting the big picture has drawbacks; in generalizing, one risks overgeneralizing. Thus it is important to pause for a moment to note some cautions.

Archetypes. The big picture presents views that are, of course, archetypical, or ideal-typical. Individual Protestants and Catholics are rarely, if ever, pure types. We are all approximations and mixtures.

Dominance and subdominance. Simply stated, *subdominant* refers to that which is important, but not as important as that which is dominant. In this context, where Catholic Ethic ideas are dominant, Protestant Ethic ideas are present but subdominant.

Foreground and background. Within any ethic, different elements may be more "up front" or more "in the back." Some versions of the Protestant Ethic, for example, may emphasize work more than others.

Secular Versions

While obviously religious, these Protestant and Catholic ethical value systems also have secular applications. One does not have to be Catholic to act out of a Catholic Ethic base, anymore than one needs to be Protestant to act out of a Protestant Ethic base. Indeed, secular manifestations of these ethical systems are important in helping us understand how one can operate out of a Catholic Ethic/Protestant Ethic mixture. These two belief systems take positions on important concerns facing all societies: How is the self constructed and understood? How do I act toward others? What are the basic rules governing this society? How fixed or fluid are the status categories? How do I approach goal achievement? When does my responsibility kick in? On what basis do I help others? Figure 4.1 illustrates this.

Value	Alpha Attitude (Protestant Ethic)	Omega Attitude (Catholic Ethic)
Nature of self	Solo self (I am therefore I am)	Ensemble self (I am my community)
Relationship to others	Competitive	Cooperative
Key rules	Fair play (I get mine)	Fair share (Everyone gets some)
My status is	Either up or down (More or less fixed) (OK or not OK)	Up and down (Changeable) (Depends)
To pursue goals I	Seek the best	Accept the adequate
In assessing responsibility for events I ask	Whose fault was it?	Was anyone hurt?
Basis for help	Worthy	Needy
Availability of resources	Draining pond	Replenishing spring
Resources are	Constrained	Plentiful

Figure 4.1.   Two basic value packages

Basically, the Protestant and Catholic Ethics have different answers to these questions. The Protestant Ethic has an individualistic self, a competitive approach to others, a heavy emphasis on fair play and status, an optimizing attitude, an emphasis on cause or fault with respect to responsibility, and a stress on the worthy poor as deserving of help. Resources are constrained.

The Catholic Ethic, on the other hand, constructs a self defined through and in family and community (e.g., the ethnic self), approaches life more cooperatively, wants to be sure that everyone has enough, sees status as malleable, seeks enough rather than "the most" and provides help based on condition and need. Resources are plentiful.

When we see these ethical systems through a secular lens, it is easy to understand that we operate out of both. Once we take off the religious nameplates and generalize the orientations, both ethics fall into a values dualism framework; still we can, and do, have *more* of one than the other. That is dominance and subdominance. Figures 4.2-3 provide another form of display.

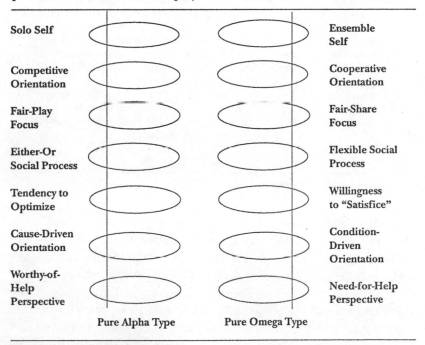

Figure 4.2.   Archetypical presentation

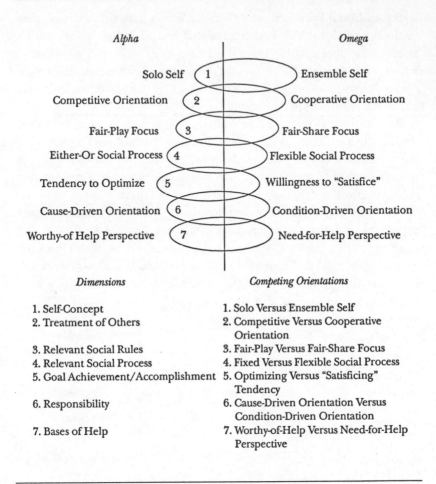

Figure 4.3   A sample of a "real" person

Societal Implications

Welfare versus poorfare state. These two value systems—Catholic Ethic and Protestant Ethic, Omega and Alpha—have different implications for social helping and prosocial behavior. One way to look at this might be as the difference between Social Catholicism in Europe versus the prevalent American attitude of "God helps him who helps himself."

In the Catholic Ethic tradition, collective definitions of need and help are dominant. In Europe, for example, a tradition of social helping developed early and continued through the Middle Ages to this day. Catholicism was one of the moving forces behind this approach, says Paul Misner, defined as "the particular pattern of . . . public presence and activity that developed after the French Revolution in the Catholic parts of Europe."[9] Recently the term "social Catholicism" has come to be one expression of this old tradition. According to Misner, "the term 'social Catholicism' refers heuristically to Catholic responses to *economic modernization* in particular, and hence to the industrialization process and its consequences in the social classes."[10] Ultimately, the programs supported by this orientation came to be called "the welfare state."

This approach is in contrast to the path taken in America, which relied on private, more minimalist assistance, heavily oriented toward ascertaining if those in need were among the worthy poor. Governmental aid was frowned upon. For example, a mid-nineteenth-century attempt by Dorothea Dix to interest the federal government in assuming a greater caretaking role by setting aside ten million acres of federal land for the care of the indigent insane was vetoed by President Pierce. His 1854 veto message has become an important document in U.S. social welfare history.

> If Congress has the power to make provision for the indigent insane without the limits of this District, it has the same power to provide for the indigent who are not insane and thus to transfer to the federal government the charge of all the poor in all the states. . . . The whole field of public beneficence has been now thrown open to the care and culture of the federal government. Generous impulses no longer encounter the limitations and control of our . . . fundamental law.[11]

Two previous helping programs, the Freedman's Bureau and the Civil War Pension system, each of which had the potential for transformation into larger helping programs, were canceled. As Walter Rauschenbusch commented in 1911,

> To accept charity is at first one of the most bitter experiences of the self-respecting workingman. Some abandon families, go insane, or commit suicide rather than surrender the virginity of their independence. But when they have once learned to depend on gifts, the parasitic habit of mind grows upon them, and it becomes hard to

wake them back to self-support.[12]

It took a depression to get American society moving toward governmental, prosocial helping, but even then there were questions and hesitations. Illustrative of the tensions within American social policy is the Nichlos plan, developed in Oklahoma in the 1930s.

Thus John B. Nichlos of the Oklahoma Gas Utilities Company wrote to his friend Patrick J. Hurley, the Secretary of War, about an idea he was trying out in Chickssha, Oklahoma. By the Nichlos plan, restaurants were asked to dump food left on plates into five gallon containers; the unemployed could qualify for these scraps by chopping wood donated by farmers. "We expect a little trouble now and then from those who are not worthy of the support of the citizens," Nichlos wrote philosophically, "but we must contend with such cases in order to take care of those who are worthy." Hurley was so impressed by the plan of feeding garbage to the homeless that he personally urged it on Colonel Woods. . . .

Anything was better than the dole, a word invested with every ominous significance. . . . It was better, Calvin Coolidge said philosophically, "to let those who have made the losses bear them than to try to shift them to someone else." "Unemployment insurance," said Henry Ford, "would only insure that we always have unemployment." "If this country ever voted a dole," said Silas Strawn, now head of the United States Chamber of Commerce, "we've hit the toboggan as a nation."[13]

Such suspicion of those in need, and hesitancy toward helping, is different from the orientation in Europe. The United States is not really a welfare state; it could perhaps be called a "poorfare state." I coined this term to connote a society that, on the one hand, provides help but, on the other, does not really like it.

While in the United States we have spent large sums on welfare state expenditures, there is still a negativism and suspicion of the poor that pervades American daily life. When we do help out, we do so often with suspicions and concerns about why the recipients are so needy and what they might do with the resources provided. As Montgomery suggests, we may be more generous outside the country, with foreign aid, than inside the society.[14]

In the poorfare state there is the sense that the needy will "rip us off." Here is a small example of the attitudes we see. In a column in the *Detroit News,* Kate DeSmet wrote:

> The Central Business District Association recently handed out 1,200 flyers in Detroit asking people to stop giving money to panhandlers. "Avoid supporting what in most cases is an alcoholic and destructive lifestyle," the posters say. "You need not feel guilty when saying no." Many business owners applauded, but others question the morality of such a move. In a conversation overheard among several Metro Detroit businessmen, one said, "You know, it's never bothered me to give money to someone who walks up to me on the street. If it's because he wants to go and get drunk, I figure that's his problem, but if the guy is hungry and I don't give him anything, then that's what bothers me."[15]

In Berkeley, California, merchants tried a different strategy. They sold chits, which could then be given to street people. Chits were redeemable only for food and essential items. This approach seemed to solve a problem for those who wanted to be helpful but had doubts about how monetary help might be used.

The two capitalisms. One implication of the influences of the Protestant Ethic and the Catholic Ethic for America can be seen in Thurow's discussion of individualistic capitalism and communalistic capitalism. The former, the American version, is an "each tub on it's own bottom" approach, emphasizing each firm and each worker. Business is strictly business. The latter, the European version, takes a somewhat greater view of the good of all into account. Thurow illustrates the difference:

> Germany, the dominant European economic power, sees itself as having a *"social market"* not just a "market" economy. Codetermination is required to broaden the ranks of corporate stakeholders beyond that of the traditional capitalistic owners to include workers. . . . Social welfare policies are seen as a necessary part of a market economy. . . . In contrast, in the United States social welfare programs are seen as regrettable necessities. . . . In the ideal Anglo-Saxon market economy, social welfare policies would not be necessary.[16]

These orientations stem from deep value structures. As Thurow explains:

> America and Britain trumpet individualistic values: the brilliant entrepreneur, Nobel prize winners, large wage differentials, individ-

ual responsibility for skills, easy to fire and easy to quit, profit maximization and hostile mergers and takeovers—their hero is the Lone Ranger. In contrast, Germany and Japan trumpet communitarian values: business groups, social responsibility for skills, teamwork, firm loyalty, industry strategies, and active industrial policies that promote growth.[17]

American society is, on a worldwide basis, more individualistic than we perhaps imagine. Businesspersons traveling abroad comment about this factor all the time. And Geert Hofstede, in his global study *Culture's Consequences*, reports that the United States ranks highest on the individualism index.[18]

The differences in social welfare orientation and the links of that orientation to the culture of business extend further than just support for government action. The business itself becomes a sort of social welfare center, with substantial fringe benefits, extra vacation days, national holidays and other "social" benefits. To an extent, fringe benefits are a sort of private social welfare program, existing parallel to the public ones, and of importance to the individual worker.

Global stewardship. Let us now return to the question with which we began: How can Americans, singly and severally, blend individualistic and collective approaches to thinking about resources, needs and assistance in order to form a truly just society? In the light of global concerns, we may wish to change "Americans" to "world citizens."

To begin, perhaps we should define a just society. For me such a society is one with minimal social exploitation. By this I mean the securing of resources—human, animal or environmental—for free or cheap. In human society, needs and wants will always exceed current resources; this is the law of rising expectations. Hence, there is always a gap between available cash, as it were, and enhancements we seek. One way of handling this situation, of course—and one definition of stewardship—is simplicity. Trim those desires and strive for the simple life. This has been a popular solution over the ages for some groups.

A second approach, also a definition of stewardship, is thrift. Thrift is related to simplicity, but it is more a "making do with the leftovers" approach. (Some might call it being cheap.) At its best, thrift uses all resources carefully, eliminates scrap and waste, and is a good trustee of resources.

Both simplicity and thrift are appropriate approaches to balancing wants and available resources. A great threat, however, comes from the third approach: exploitation. There are many examples, such as slavery and child labor. Animals are also victims of exploitation, through cruelty and the destruction of the environment. The common theme is that users of resources are not paying the full cost.

Stewardship in this context requires us to blend the two views—the Protestant Ethic, or draining pond perspective, and the Catholic Ethic, or the replenishing spring perspective—to achieve harmony and balance. The image of the draining pond suggests caring for resources but perhaps hoarding them as well. The image of the replenishing spring suggests that there will always be plenty; thus we do not need to take too much care of our resources. On the other hand, it also suggests a community view with respect to the access to these resources. An individual is more of a community trustee than a sole proprietor of a resource.

Obviously too much individualism means that resources may be sequestered far beyond reasonable need, perhaps leaving others without enough. The drift in American society into two economic classes, the well-to-do and the poor, may be emblematic of this approach. On the other hand, a strong communal view may sap ambition and diffuse responsibility. Hence stewardship requires us to recognize our own orientations and to acknowledge that if pushed too far, every strength becomes a weakness. It also requires us to respect the approaches of others. Finally, it invites us to consider that in spite of our dominant orientation, each of us may have a bit of the other ethical system within us in a secularized, subdominant form.

Conclusion

Existing with the historical Protestant Ethic is an equally historical, but only recently discussed, Catholic Ethic. Each of these belief systems is vigorous and powerful and has withstood the test of time. Each has secular versions, here called Alpha and Omega, that allow us to look at them in a context that is not exclusively religious. This permits us to understand the ways in which each of us may have a bit of both ethics within us, one dominant, the other subdominant.

These two ethics have important implications for stewardship. Each may have downsides if pushed too far, but each has, in its own way, great strengths. A just society—defined here as one with minimal levels of social exploitation—can be achieved and maintained through stewardship. Stewardship, then, which moves us toward this kind of justice, requires a blending of the two perspectives through mutual respect, a tempering of our own possible excesses and a recognition that, within each of us, the other ethic exists in subdominant form.

Part 2

Consumption & the
Theological Traditions

5
After Eden

The Search for the Holy
in a Consumer Society
Tsvi Blanchard

In the Garden of Eden, Adam and Eve were able to consume safely, and, we assume, joyfully, almost anything they wished, so long as they did no harm. They inhabited an abundant biosphere that they as humans and G-d's partners were meant to complete. In order to play their role in this biosphere, the first couple had only to work the garden and to watch it.

What was the meaning of Adam and Eve's consumption? Was consumption simply one part of a divinely ordained, biologically balanced design? We know that one act of consumption meant eating of the Tree of the Knowledge of Good and Evil. It meant following what was "good for eating . . . a delight to the eyes . . . desirable to contemplate" (Gen 3:6) instead of obeying G-d. From the human point of view, this act of consumption had ecologically disastrous consequences. The dream of a foraging society, with unending, effortless consumption, became the nightmare of an agricultural society: painful, unceasing and poorly rewarded labor on the land. After Eden the primary meaning of consumption was subsistence.

But Eden, or for that matter the Bible as a whole, does not represent the last Jewish word on the relationship of humanity to the biosphere. For much of rabbinic Judaism, a Jewish view of ecology and consumption is rooted in the following three beliefs:

1. The world is created by G-d. Hence, the world is holy, good and filled with creative possibilities.

2. Humanity is responsible for the right use of and completion of divine creation.

3. Being fully human (i.e., being in the image of a creating G-d) can be realized only by life *within* the biosphere.

In this picture, who is the ideal consumer? The ideal consumer is one who, in consuming (as well as producing), completes creation *(tikkun 'olam)*.[1] He or she is fulfilled as a human being through the responsible appropriation and use of a world understood as holy at its origin. For this interpretation of Judaism, human beings, individually and in social groups, must view consumption as both expressing and embodying who they think they are, how they see themselves as connected to one another, and what their imaginative vision of an ideal world, a world "made whole," is.

In the next three sections of this essay, I will use this picture of the ideal consumer to examine the relationship of consumption to the three Jewish concepts indicated above. While the context of our exploration is spiritual and rooted in the Jewish religious tradition, we shall not stray far from an economic and social theoretic analysis of the consumer culture.

Sacred Consumption: Acknowledging the Holiness *(kedusha)* of the World

In the Babylonian Talmud, we read:

Our Rabbis taught:

"It is forbidden for you to enjoy the use of something in this world without first reciting a blessing *[b'rakha]*. . . . Anyone who enjoys something in this world without reciting a blessing has misappropriated sacred property *[me'ila]*. . . .

Rabbi Levi posed a problem:

it is written: "The earth is the L-rd's and all that it holds." (Psalms 24:1)

and it is also written: "The heavens belong to the L-rd but the

earth was given over to human beings." (Psalms 115:16)
[To whom does "the earth" belong?]
the first verse applies before a blessing is made, while the
second applies after the blessing has been made. (B'rakhot
35a-b)[2]

The principal operative concept in this text is *me'ila,* the misappropriation
or misuse of sacred property. To be sure, the world belongs to its Creator.
But, more important, because of its divine origin, the world is primally
kadosh (sacred, holy). *Me'ila* derives its meaning from the Temple and its
sacrificial system. When someone sets something aside as belonging to the
Temple, and therefore consecrates it, it can now be used exclusively for
Temple purposes. To derive personal benefit from a consecrated object is
misappropriation, or *me'ila.*

The wider meaning of *me'ila* derives from the Temple system. At least
in the ideal, the Temple is the point at which the divine and the human
meet. The Temple is where the Jewish people, and indeed all humanity,
encounter G-d. Israelite life derives from the people's covenantal
encounter with its G-d. The Temple, being the site of this encounter,
is understood as the spiritual center of Israelite life and even of the
cosmos as a whole. The Temple is at the center of the "spiritual ecology"
of the Israelite system in which the otherwise mundane activities of
both agriculture and commerce find their higher meaning.

Our rabbinic text compares the created world to the Temple. To
understand this comparison, we should remind ourselves of the rabbinic belief that creation is holy. For the rabbis, G-d renews the work
of creation daily, and hence, everything in our world is either created
by G-d or made from materials themselves created by G-d. Everything
traces its meaning back to G-d's creating power. In this way, every
moment, every object and every person is a point at which the divine
creative power and the human being may meet.

The rabbis recognized that the products of human labor may still
retain the stamp of their divine origin. For example, although a loaf of
bread is the product of human activity, before eating it a blessing is
made that speaks of G-d as bringing forth bread from the earth.[3]

For this rabbinic text (B'rakhot 35a-b), any personal use of created
things is initially a misuse because it uses that which is holy (i.e., the
divinely created world) for profane purposes. Conceptually, such mis-

use occurs whenever the transcendent is taken solely for one's particular needs. But how are we to live if we cannot make use of creation? To make it possible for humanity to benefit from the world, the rabbis created a system of blessings acknowledging the divine origin of the things that give us pleasure, while at the same time accepting the finite limits of their human use.

In the world of this rabbinic text, what does consuming mean? It means taking that which is intrinsically holy and, to a limited extent, desacralizing it, making it ordinary or profane. To compensate for this desacralization of things, the activity of consuming them is sanctified. A particular piece of fruit, a part of the created world, loses its special holiness, but by reciting a blessing, the eating of the fruit becomes holy. Within the rabbinic culture, then, objects of consumption are understood as possibilities for sanctification. This is accomplished not just by dedicating these objects of consumption to the sanctuary or its substitutes but, as we have seen, through the act of making a blessing *(b'rakha)*. This blessing transforms the act of consumption itself from the search for personal pleasure and benefit into a sanctified activity whose scope is theoretically as cosmic as that of the Temple system itself.

Blessings are, of course, part of the larger rabbinic transformation of Judaism that took place in earnest after the destruction of the Temple. In that transformation, the possibilities for *kedusha* were spread out into heretofore quite mundane spheres of Jewish life. For example, the family table is now reconceived as an altar, the family meal is thought of as a replication of Temple sacrifice and the ordinary Israelite now performs mealtime rituals previously reserved for priests.[4]

Now let us allow our imagination to work on contemporary popular culture. Consider the use of automobiles.[5] For many, the automobile is one of the ultimate consumer objects whose misuse should be likened to the oppressive luxury excoriated by the prophets. Some have even adopted the view that the use of automobiles is, for the most part, irredeemable. With this view, the best we can hope for is setting limits to the use of private cars and the pollution they create. To stretch the analogy a bit, the private use of automobiles is, like the private use of Temple property, a form of misappropriation *(me'ila)* that pollutes the public realm much as *me'ila* pollutes the communally sacred realm created by the spiritually central position accorded the Temple.

I think we are better off if we begin by making "the rabbinic move" and asking: What can be done to sanctify the use of cars? Contemporary American culture understands automobiles and the mobility they provide as symbols of much the same individual power and freedom that are primary values in both our political institutions and in American civil society. To be sure, we are beginning to recognize that limits need to be set on our commitment to individual power and freedom. But in my view, individual power and freedom should remain central values within our society. If we wish to recognize and take advantage of the real opportunities afforded us in the present situation we must ask: What rituals, ceremonies and institutions can we develop that can transform the use of an automobile from a mere private benefit and pleasure to a socially meaningful act embodying our ideas of holiness?

Consider the following real example.[6] We, at the National Jewish Center for Learning and Leadership (CLAL), asked a group of Jewish high-school sophomores to name the most important event of their upcoming year. They unanimously agreed: getting their driver's licenses. During an extended discussion, we explored their sense of the meaning this special event had and should have for their parents and community. We then asked them how they would make the act of driving holy *(kadosh)*.

They understood driving as about more than extending their personal power. For them, getting a driver's license meant being granted more freedom and responsibility by their family and community. It meant that they were being recognized as "more adult." It indicated that other adults would now hold them accountable for the safety and well-being of others and themselves. The students perceived these values as an important part of their Jewish identity.

The students could now sketch out a response to our question: How can driving be made holy and Jewish? They suggested that the car itself should reflect the communal and ethical concerns that constituted their Jewish identity. Perhaps, they proposed, there should be a prayer for travelers in the glove compartment or on their key chain. Somewhere a national or communal symbol might be displayed, such as an Israeli flag or the logo of their own Jewish community. They should make sure that the cars had dual airbags and working seat belts. Biblical verses about the value of safety and self-protection could also be displayed in the car.

Sometime during the year there would be a ceremony at a centrally located parking lot. Together with their families (as on Passover), the students would stand next to their cars. They would then celebrate by reciting the blessing over wine (as at the sanctification of the Sabbath). They would, however, use "bubbly" grape juice, which feels as special as champagne and expresses their responsible commitment to avoid drinking and driving. After this, they would read personal statements of their views on "sacred driving." These statements would explain how they connected their being Jewish with the meaning that freedom, responsibility and adulthood had for them. Finally, they would enter their cars, circle the lot seven times (a symbol from the traditional Jewish marriage ceremony, which for them expressed the covenantal nature of driving), and having taken responsibility for the serious implications of being a driver, they would drive off (symbolizing their increased adult independence from their families as well as their joy at driving the car).

The students' sanctification of using a car has all the features we derived from our rabbinic text. Inherited symbols of holiness are employed in a new context. Appropriate boundaries are acknowledged and connected to personal as well as communal identity. Jewish values (freedom, power, responsibility, conscious awareness of the meaning of actions) are expressed by the way in which consumption occurs. (Holiness is more often in how we act rather than in what we do.) We have even found a good definition of one important aspect of Jewish stewardship: sacred consumption is an act of joyful responsibility.

Responsibility and the Social Ecology of Stewardship

We have been focusing primarily on the expressive function of consumption, or on the ways in which the consumer is able to sanctify cultural objects by endowing them with spiritual significance.[7] Producers as well can take advantage of the human ability to endow cultural objects with meaning. Their motives, however, may not be quite so positive. How so? In our consumer culture, consumption is not always expressive. It is also about meeting perceived needs.

This can be misleading. To be sure, there are basic human physical needs met by consumption. But contemporary consumption principally addresses our anxieties far more than it meets basic needs. We worry about our social presence: How are we perceived by others? Are we valued by them? We worry about our power, or more often about our impotence. We fear our vulnerabilities—sickness, aging, being isolated and alone. These anxieties fuel much of our consumption.

Moreover, we must also remember that our anxieties are exploited, augmented and sometimes even created by producers in order to sell products. Contemporary consumption often means trading our resources for temporary relief from our fears. It primarily derives from the producer's need to control and expand markets. But to successfully exploit our anxieties, the world of advertising must win us over to its fundamental "theological" dogma: We are flawed, broken and missing something important, but we can be made whole if only we buy something, namely, the product they are advertising.

Note that this view provides our version of capitalist consumption with an almost salvific function. This is cheap grace. Teenagers cannot become adults simply by smoking and drinking. We cannot become sexy merely by the cosmetics we use. And we cannot keep our promises if all we do is buy insurance.

Our values are not necessarily off base. Being adult, being attractive or keeping our promises are all worthwhile, and it is not even that many of these products are irrelevant to these values. It is rather that anxiety-driven consumption will not in fact help us fully realize these values. On the contrary, it diverts us from accomplishing this. We can only achieve what is most profoundly significant to us by placing consumption, and our anxieties as well, within a wider web of beliefs and practices that allows us to possess a deeper, more spiritual notion of our flaws, our brokenness and our finitude than contemporary advertising provides.

Let us turn to a Talmudic text about consumers. Although not the last word on this subject, it still affords us a helpful look at the deeper cultural values of rabbinic Judaism.

It has been taught:

R. Judah said, "The sale of a Torah scroll . . . is not subject to [the prohibition of] *ona'ah* [price gouging, or more precisely, charging ⅙ more than the market price], because its value can not be assessed [literally: no end can be fixed to its monetary worth]; an animal or a pearl is not subject to [the prohibition of] *ona'ah* because one [often] desires to buy them to match [ones he already possesses].

Said they [the Sages] to him [by way of objection], "But one wishes to match up everything!" [i.e., almost everything one buys is meant to be suited for some particular purpose.]

And R. Judah? [What might he reply to the objection? He might say] These [items] are particularly important to him [the purchaser], others are not.

[The text continues by asking:]

And how much more may be charged [than market price]? [Assuming that even R. Judah insists on some limit.] Said Amemar: [One may add] up to their value [i.e., charge double the market price].

Mishna: Just as there is *ona'ah* in buying and selling, there is also *ona'ah* done by words. [For example,] one may not ask another "What is the price of this article?" if there is no intention of buying. If someone is a repentant sinner, we may not say "Remember your former deeds." If one is a convert, we may not say "Remember the deeds of your ancestors!" because it is written "Thou shalt not abuse a stranger and you shall not oppress him, [for you were strangers in the land of Egypt. (Ex 22:20 [21])]. . . .

[After deriving the same law from verses in Leviticus, and providing examples, the Talmud adds:] If one is afflicted by suffering or buries his children, one must not speak to him as his companions spoke to Job. . . . If donkey drivers seek [to buy] grain [from a person who has none], he must not say to them "Go to such and such a person who sells grain," all the while knowing that this person has never sold any [grain].

R. Judah said: One may not pretend to be interested in [making] a purchase when he has no money, for this is a matter which is known only within one's own heart [literally: given over to the heart] and of such matters it is written "and you shall fear your G-d" [Lev 25:17].

(b. Baba Metsia 58b)

This passage comes at the end of an extended discussion of *ona'ah* in the context of business dealings. In the rabbinic era, local markets were stable enough to generate market prices. As the Talmudic discussion indicates, *ona'ah*, selling far above market price, is fraud and deception, since a buyer knowing the true price of the item in the market would never pay a grossly inflated price. The seller is, then, prohibited from taking advantage of the buyer's ignorance. The seller is also prohibited from acting as if the price is fair and true when in fact it is not. Hence, a Torah scroll cannot have a true price because it is beyond monetary evaluation.[8]

To study this text about buying and selling is to study the social nexus of production and consumption. In this system we encounter the created world as a product of human labor, at the very least of the labor of bringing the item to market. What we consume is, then, the joint project of G-d and human beings. Humanity is a partner *(shutaf)* with G-d, and human completion of the world demands productive activity.

However, in a monetary market economy, to consume means to place a numerical value on products and to do so in relation to the many other products available to consumers. But what of things that can not be so evaluated? If you want to "use" them you will have to agree to the placing of a monetary value on that which is beyond value. But within the legal system, you can mark these items as different in some way. Here the tension is between the consumer's agreement that "everything has a price" and the consumer as free agent whose humanity can never be given a monetary value.[9]

Producers, then, are G-dlike *(shutaf)* because they create value through labor. By forming ethically responsible relations with other members of the economy, consumers too become G-dlike. This requires the exercise of free, informed choice based on the wishes, purposes and interests of both producers and consumers.[10] This is seen in the Talmudic text's discussion of finding a match, suiting an item to a particular purpose, the item's importance to the consumer and the setting of some limit to the seller's right to exploit the particular needs of the buyer.

In the contemporary situation as well, consumption may also be seen in part as the expression of the systematic and ethically regulated interconnection of persons who are understood to be G-dlike by virtue of their ability to act freely on their choices. Stewardship in this context demands more than the ethical use of resources. It also requires the consumption of resources in ways that express the human ability to be G-dlike by enhancing human power, consciousness, freedom, relationship and will.

Without ethical direction, however, the informed exercise of free will in order to fulfill one's purposes may become, at best, a mutually agreeable hedonism and, at worst, a domination of the vulnerable by the cleverest and most powerful.[11] Indeed, this has been the source of the most incisive critiques of capitalist economic systems. While market systems significantly increase human choice, power and knowledge, they also destroy them. As contemporary experience shows, downsizing, the decline in real wages and executives fixated on short-term profits are far more likely to diminish human power and freedom than to augment them.

The second part of our Talmudic text moves in just this direction. It broadens its conceptualization of the production-consumption nexus beyond the merely economic. *Ona'ah* now applies not only to setting the price of goods but to the speech, behavior and inner intentions of the consumer as well. Just as there is deception in selling, there is deception in buying. But true to the biblical use of this Hebrew root *(ynh)*, the text moves beyond a commitment to truthfulness and honesty in speech to the avoidance of oppressive speech.

Is there a family resemblance among these examples of abusive speech and behavior? I suggest that they are all examples of exploiting an objective vulnerability. They are often accompanied by subjective emotional pain. But this need not always be the case. One can imagine a store owner so vulnerable in the market that nearly any abuse would seem tolerable and even preferable to being ignored. One can easily imagine a convert or repentant sinner so desperate for acceptance that verbal abuse might seem a small price to pay for being included. But in all the cases, the objective distribution of social (or situational) power leaves these individuals (or classes of individuals) open to being exploited.

For purposes of our discussion, this means that we need to acknowledge our destructive as well as constructive power as consumers. We must take responsibility for the way in which how we consume, including the way in which we interact with others as we consume, may take advantage of other people's objective vulnerabilities. Given the social nature of production and consumption, we are thus required to ask how our system of production and consumption disadvantages some participants relative to others. In addition, we must take care not to use any privileged position we may hold to exploit the weaknesses of other participants.

Obvious examples of our failures in this regard spring to mind.

Western countries consume the lion's share of the world's energy, medical and food resources at a significant cost to the other disadvantaged participants in our global economy. Corporations as consumers of land may take unfair advantage of those unable to resist having toxic waste dumped on them. The expansion of western markets by creating new product needs driven by underlying anxieties costs those in other areas of the world who have yet to meet basic needs.

Let us return to our example of students and the automobile. I believe that, for all the value of their plans and celebrations, certain important questions went unaddressed. Were they aware of the social cost of the automobile? Of the cost to those poor who must spend money they do not have to buy cars in order to get to work? Did they attend to the ecological and health cost of auto-centered transport? Of the social inequalities of auto-centered transport?[12] How might they integrate paying the real social cost of a car, rather than merely its price, into their understanding of the responsibilities that come with a driver's license?[13] Without asking these questions, the students merely celebrate their own advantages without taking any responsibility for the cost to others.

The Jewish tradition already possesses examples of the ritual acknowledgment of how our individual satisfaction is sometimes compromised by its cost to others. Take the Passover Seder, for example. In the recitation of the ten plagues, Jews remove a drop of wine from their cups for each plague. At the moment of celebrating the paradigm of G-d's redemption of the Israelites, the cost—the sufferings of the Egyptians—is acknowledged with regret. (Note that it is *how* consumption takes place that sends this message.)

What we need now, I am suggesting, is the kind of ritual symbolization that, by the very way in which we consume resources, acknowledges the pain and deprivation of others. Such rituals should serve as consistent reminders of the wider questions raised by the painfully unequal distribution of resources.[14]

To be sure, there has been and continues to be significant resistance to the acknowledgment of the social costs of consumption, both global and regional. Much of this resistance is motivated by the fear that we will not have enough resources for ourselves. But for upper-middle-class Americans, "not having enough" is as much an issue of quality as of quantity. The experience of consuming has itself become more

SELLING LUXURIES

superficial. We rush through life, eating and drinking far too quickly. We dress for success, more aware of our impression on others than of the colors and textures of our clothes. We are so busy listening for information that we miss the deeper tones and more subtle nuances of our conversations. No wonder that no matter how much we possess, we still fear that we will not have enough to truly satisfy us.

What would happen if we were to "consume our world" with the kind of profound gratitude and deep awareness of its holiness that I suggested at the outset of this essay? Having deepened and intensified the experience of consumption, we might find that the celebration of the jointly created "goods" of our world makes it easier to then acknowledge and accept responsibility for the costs that are part of the social ecology of consumption. We have imagined stewardship as the way of sacred consumption, and we have conceived sacred consumption as acts of joyful responsibility. May we not hope that students who have accepted this joyful responsibility, and reaped the fullness of experience it provides, will be more likely to acknowledge the real costs to others? May we not hope that as we experience our world with qualitatively greater satisfaction, we will also learn how to do with quantitatively less of it?

Imagining Ideal Stewardship: The Meaning of Consumption in a Completed World

Where are social ideals and global visions in this picture of responsible celebration? The idea of a responsible use of resources, sensitive to the real cost to others, keeps celebratory consumption from being merely self-serving. However, in the face of entrenched interests and ideologies, it also takes a well-developed moral imagination to motivate and direct the work needed to transform the existing arrangement of production and consumption. We must be willing to dream.

The following text reflects the early rabbinic imagination about these issues. To the extent that we share the ideals emerging from this passage, they may help inspire, direct and regulate our present efforts by imagining goals and ideals toward which we work.[15]

We . . . find ten things which the Holy One . . . will renew in the Time to Come.

The first is that He will illumine the whole world. . . . When someone gets sick, G-d will order the sun to heal him. . . . The second thing is that He will bring out living water from Jerusalem and heal there with it all those who have a disease. . . . The third is that He will make trees yield their fruit each 'month and when one cats of them he will be healed. . . . The fourth is that they shall rebuild all the cities which have been laid to waste so that there will not be one waste place left in the world, even Sodom and Gomorrah will be rebuilt in the Time to Come. . . . The fifth is that He will rebuild Jerusalem with sapphire stones. . . . These precious stones will shine like the sun, and the heathens will come and see the glory of Israel. . . . The sixth is that *The cow and bear shall feed; their young shall lie down together* [Is 11:7]. The seventh is that He will gather all the wild beasts, birds and creeping things and make a covenant with them and with all Israel. . . . The eighth is that there will be no more weeping or wailing in the world. . . . The ninth is that there will be no more death in the world. . . . The tenth is that there will no longer be any sighing, wailing or anguish, but that all will be rejoicing. (Midrash Rabbah. Sh'mot 15:21)

The relevant themes are clear. The text is saying that in our use of the world we have damaged it and ourselves along with it. To complete this inhabited world, we must also repair it. Natural resources that have been squandered must be replenished. In the world of human cultures, devastated cities must be rebuilt. Conflict over resources needs to be replaced by mutual cooperation. We have begun to imagine a world of complete healing and restoration. The total ecology of the world (natural and social) no longer works through strife and competition but instead through mutuality, reciprocity and collaboration (i.e., covenantal relationships). Although the human world of the messianic imagination is far more complex then the paradise of Eden, it nevertheless is infused with what we imagine to be Eden's pristine joy and delight.

But can a world of multinational capitalism really be transformed by a vision stemming from the dreams of a far more simple society, perhaps even of a simple foraging society? Is such visioning in the realm of primal fantasy and wish fulfillment and not a genuinely constructive exercise of the human moral imagination?[16] Such a conclusion is, I think, hasty.

Simply consider how appropriate the issues of this passage are in the

REVELATION / REASON / POWER
pre   modern   post

present situation. Are we not wrestling with the ongoing damage our present systems of production and consumption do to the world and ourselves? Do we not need to find ways to replenish the natural resources we have squandered and continue to squander? Are not our cities devastated? How many human cultures need support and rebuilding? To complete our own lived-in world, must we not also repair it?

Moreover, consider the problems of our own social ecology, in which powerful individuals, corporations and societies dominate and exploit those with less power. Do we not need to find ways to enhance collaborative problem solving and a sense of human solidarity? How will we do this without replacing the existing belief that conflict over resources is productive with a commitment to concrete processes of mutual cooperation?

The focus of this sacred effort will have to be, as in the past, at the intersection of the divine and the human. But our vision will now have to go beyond biological systems and encompass social and economic structures as well. If anything, the sheer size and global interconnectedness of our world demands that we seek linked environmental and social solutions. Our postindustrial world does not make it helpful to fully separate the "natural" world from the one made by human efforts. For better, and also for worse, our world is the result of a partnership between G-d and humanity. Solutions to those problems will require a similar joint effort.

Here, too, we have inherited ideas on which to build. For example, the radical social, economic and agricultural redistribution of the Jubilee year may serve as the kernel of a comprehensive restorative vision. The emergence within Judaism of vegetarianism as a religious ideal may signal the possibility of revisioning our relationship to other sentient beings. The rabbinic insistence that the corners of the field, or the gleanings, already belong to the poor might open discussion about the meaning of ownership of resources. In these examples, we begin to ask the questions that address the transforming of the human world as a whole. The issue of consumption and stewardship has now gone beyond the level of individual concern and become both societal and global.

I am not suggesting that utopian messianism alone is the agent of moral change. Its grand vision is only one part of a dynamic process in which both the celebration of existing realities and also the acceptance of the limits set by existing, legitimated rules, rituals and imperatives also have important roles to play. A utopian vision is far more helpful in raising questions and guiding discussion than in producing detailed programs.

To return once again to our automobile example: What questions can the messianic imagination raise for the students? We start with the broadest question: Are there cars in the messianic era? To respond to this question will require us to balance the values of individual freedom and power with the values of health, safety and the appropriate use of land and energy. Because we are asking this question from a messianic perspective, however, we are not limited to narrow solutions. We may imagine radical, across-the-board changes in societal systems and structures.

We can ask: In the messianic world, do people need to derive their sense of personal freedom through the ability to drive? And what if the only responsible use of energy means that cars can no longer be available for use whenever individuals want them? While in my twenties and living in the Midwest, I sometimes felt trapped by the demands of family and academic life. As a result, I did on occasion feel the need for the freedom to simply get in my car and go exploring. Somehow, now older and living in New York, I feel no loss in not owning a car. I have learned to experience and express my freedom in other ways. Am I wiser or simply more exhausted? Can we imagine raising children to feel at sixteen as I do now? We need to ask young people: Do you imagine that in the messianic era, teenagers will think of the most important event of their year as getting a driver's license? Why or why not?

To guide the discussion in this messianic way allows and also requires us to think of the problem of the automobile as a social and even global problem. Using our "messianic imagination" allows us to seek long-term strategies for system-wide change, while at the same time making short-term compromises. When it works, this process takes us one or two steps forward toward the ideal. It pushes the limits of our physical, moral, legal and religious realities. To be sure, it does not transform these realities all at once. There is a wisdom in this. Those of us uncomfortable with apocalypse see no wisdom in rushing the world to its completion.

Can we say anything about the ecology of a "new Eden"? I think that, at the very least, we can say that it will not be a mere repeat of the original. That primal garden was a relatively complete biosphere whose harmony derived from its static nature. In contrast, given our present beliefs and values, we need to imagine an ecologically dynamic Eden. We must imagine the interplay of environmental forces. We must imagine more fluid, shifting socioeconomic arrangements. I believe that the most interesting long-term questions will come from thinking less about specific issues about consumption and more about the structures that will influence how decisions about consumption are made, individually, regionally and globally. In sum, to ask about the meaning of consumption in a messianic era means to ask about the kind of consumption that is created by and also embodied in a social system that expresses our most profound values, even our ultimate values.

What then of our search for holiness in a consumer society? I have suggested that we must do three things at once. First, we must acknowledge the existing structures of consumption and find ways of sanctifying both the objects and the processes that form those structures. Second, we must critically probe those structures using our best existing system(s) of values, principles and narratives. Our critique guides, limits and, in part, transforms the given system of consumption. In doing so, it sometimes diminishes and sometimes enhances our celebration of that system and its sacred possibilities. Finally, we must engage our utopian-messianic imagination to generate a long-term movement toward the completion of the world. The first steps in this movement become our immediate next steps. In this way, our persistent repair of the world is informed by our constantly self-renewing vision of an ideal society. Here is the paradox of sacred consumption: we must at one and the same time both celebrate and work to radically transform the consumer society. But this is the paradoxical nature of all living holiness. It exalts and sometimes even venerates the very institutions it is in the process of morally reconstructing.

6
Stewardship, Sabbath & Time

John D. Mason

*A*s *economists are quick to remind us, the world is beset by scarcity. Scarcity* gives rise to competition between households, and to tradeoffs, even sacrifices, within households as well as within the larger society. The tradeoffs and sacrifices within the household require *personal* stewardship, just as competition and societal tradeoffs mandate the difficult task of *social* stewardship. It is not surprising, therefore, that the Greek word for economic *(oikonomia)* is that used in the New Testament for stewardship and means proper care of one's household. What may be more surprising is that the majority tradition in economics offers little formal discussion of stewardship.[1]

The discussion of stewardship in economics, as in society, is so difficult because it requires the specification of norms, a task continually confounding our attempts to live peaceably with one another amidst the competing values within our diverse society. One might hope that within the community of earnest Christians and Jews who find the biblical traditions authoritative (the primary audience for this essay), we might hope for greater success. Stewardship, we could say, bespeaks the character of our response to God's initiative in the scarce worlds of our households and surrounding communities. God owns all property and we are to use his property as he desires (Deut 10:12-22), to walk, as the text says, in all his ways.

Sabbath Time and Sabbath Mercy

When faced with perplexing social realities and wondering what, if anything, should be done, the test I have developed is to ask what the elders of an early Israelite community seeking to apply God's laws would have done. This test betrays my working hermeneutical principle: that God offers in the Pentateuch provisions intended to guide all nations, and the remainder of the Bible applies, refines and helps us see the true meaning of the pentateuchal foundations. Led by the biblical testimony, and aided by commentary from the Jewish and Christian traditions over the millennia, we are given a light to the nations, for all nations will stream to God's holy mountain and the Law will go out from Zion to settle disputes between nations and peoples (Is 2:2-5).[2]

So far, so good. But stewardship, like the command to love our neighbor as ourself (Lev 19:18; Mt 22:39) or the general biblical admonition to pursue justice and righteousness, is a broad norm and requires specification for it to be usable. One set of specifications we may use to approach stewardship practically is that offered in the Deuteronomy text cited above and its concern for the fatherless, widows and aliens. Herein lies one emphasis of the Sabbath: its humanitarian concern, seen most particularly in the various provisions relating to the release of debts and slaves and the use (and return) of lands during sabbatical years.[3] The detail of these provisions and the outcomes sought offer guidance to our contemporary quest for proper stewardship, finding expression in the private and public measures a society uses to assist its poorer and weaker members.[4] The intent of this essay is to explore Sabbath's other preeminent value, time.[5] How, in our attempt to give specification to stewardship, are we to understand time?

Abraham Heschel wrote a wonderful little tract[6] that can help us grasp the significance of time surrounding the weekly Sabbath, that realm of society where we are not to have but simply to be; where, like eternity, time stands still; where we experience a day to enjoy rest, tranquillity, serenity, peace, repose, and not be bothered by matters of efficiency (or "measuring" time), where we set aside a day for joy and the celebration of life. Given such emphases, is not the very notion of stewardship, with its practical attention to measuring time and efficiency, a fundamental affront to the Sabbath notion of time? I don't think so, and I offer the reflections that follow to suggest why.

The seeming presence of contesting norms for the Sabbath has puzzled me: God has a clear desire that we rest and let time stand still, but this desire coexists with humanitarian concerns that seem to require busyness and strategic action so that all fellow households are able to enjoy the regular freedom to rest and repose and simply be. On the one hand, the Sabbath is the seventh day and not the first, implying that rest should dominate and not hard thinking about how best to assist poorer and weaker households. But then the prophets lament how our celebrations of Sabbath weary God (if not worse) when we fail to seek justice or plead the widow's case (Is 1:13ff). Jesus saw fit to heal on the Sabbath and reminded his critics of the earlier prophetic warning that mercy and not sacrifice should control our understanding of Sabbath (Mt 12:7). On the surface of things such seeking and pleading and healing seem of the order of stewardship rather than rest and tranquillity, thrusting us into the familiar world for economists and ethicists of conflicting norms, with the need to calculate tradeoffs and offer unpleasant counsel. But could it be that we have become so caught in a modern sense of the economic value of time and organizational solutions that we fail to grasp something more profound at work? That the importance of rest and tranquility are not meant to conflict with the humanitarian burden (what Christ calls mercy, I think) for seeking and pleading and healing

Most who have struggled to give contemporary relevance to the sabbatical provisions (including myself) talk primarily of socioeconomic measures. How best can we help each household today maintain a personally controlled productive base (my sense of the thrust of the Jubilee provision in Leviticus 25)? What steps might we take to assist the poor in our midst to achieve the purposes of gleanings in an earlier era? Could the seven-year release of debt mean something today other than bankruptcy laws? Not many have attempted to understand these biblical provisions in terms of of the contemporary significance of time. Have we missed something? As one who has struggled hard to understand poverty in our midst and to use biblical materials to guide our response to it, I am beginning to think so.

Let us then wonder about these provisions and the use of time. Debt forgiveness and release of bond slaves created time: the actual time otherwise spent working to repay loans, along with whatever time benefits accrued because one was less anxious about the forgiven or released contractual obligation. Time for what? To maintain regular celebration of the weekly Sabbath, to be sure! Perhaps also to become more involved in family life, offering one's children the Sabbath detachment from things and the experience of their parents' time focused on them that confirms for them how important they are. Perhaps also to spend quality time with a sick friend in just "being there" (as if time were standing still). In the sabbatical year fields were to lie idle, freeing their owners from seeding and tilling and harvesting. To do what? Perhaps to protect a sojourner family from demeaning dependency in a way that no bureaucracy could because they know from the time you spend with them how much you care for them? Perhaps to become a mentor to the son or daughter of a local widow (a time-intensive process if done well)?

We were deeply touched when we heard Mother Teresa tell of tending leprous men and women; the reason, I am coming to discern, is that we see here a blending of the sabbatical values of time and mercy. Could it be these two normative elements of Sabbath complement rather than contest? We can picture Jesus and Paul spending great amounts of time with the disciples and young churches, building relationships sufficient to establish accountability and, when necessary, exercising a form of tough love. Could it be, then, that a truly effective humanitarian concern requires the quality of time we see in the Sabbath?

My quest to grasp better the dimensions of stewardship by exploring Sabbath and time will be enhanced by grounding my reflections in three contemporary realities: first, the family; second, the current call for private charities to replace state welfare assistance; third, the needed response to the troubling circumstances of our inner cities.

The normative social unit assumed in the Bible is the extended family,[7] which contemporary society too often has allowed (if not encouraged) to erode.[8] Analyzing the damage done by the change in family structure has become today a major growth industry, with the focus largely upon the impact of broken nuclear families for the economic and psychological well-being of children.[9] Far less attention has been paid to developments among extended families (except possibly among immigrants) and whether we are served well or poorly by what appears to be a practical breakdown at this level as well.

As noted, the Sabbath's blending of time and humanitarian concern or mercy appear very natural when applied to family life, as much as we might neglect this practice today. Though we too often try to raise healthy children through the purchase of goods and the time of parent-surrogates, there simply is no good substitute for the Sabbath-like, timeless attention of a parent and grandparent to a child, whether beside the crib or at a piano recital or listening to the experiences of that first year of college. Simply being there is the name of the game for raising a healthy child. What has been less appreciated is the same reality surrounding the nurturance of aging parents and grandparents. Can we imagine anything other than just being there—as if time had stopped—as one of the best medicines when someone is sick or dying or feeling obsolete and left out?

We hear a growing cry in the land for devolving the existing welfare system to lower levels of government, if not for elimination of government-mediated assistance altogether. In 1996 the U.S. government enacted the most sweeping reforms in welfare since its inception in the 1930s, placing far greater responsibility on individual states to administer welfare programs, mandating that most recipients prepare for and then take employment in order to continue receiving assistance. Christian commentator Marvin Olasky even has encouraged the complete elimination of welfare. In both cases, we are told, these steps should be taken to satisfy our humanitarian obligations more effectively.[10] An understandable and appropriate response to such calls is inquiry into the adequacy of the private alternative. Given what seems to be a growing spatial segregation within society of late along economic (not necessarily racial) lines, which breaks the locational proximity between poor and nonpoor that contributed to a commendable charitable response earlier in our history, it is unlikely that a charitable response to poverty will be as great today. Moreover, given the all-too-human tendency for individual households to engage in what economists call "free-riding"—to lessen one's gifts of time and resources on the presumption that others will rise to the occasion—the sufficiency of private response to the existence of poverty in our midst is brought into question. I am prepared to argue that a basic reason God gives us government is to correct for the free-rider potential.

This train of analysis, however, does not encourage us to peer into the *character* of assistance to the poor, particularly the importance of spending time with poorer and weaker households in order to help them achieve that standard of subsistence that God desires of all households. As much as I find Professor Olasky's perceptions of the harm done by welfare to be grossly exaggerated, as well as his presumption that charity was in the past and would be in the present an improved alternative, he serves us ably by rehearsing measures that seem to have marked effective assistance earlier in our nation's history, thus pointing the way to a more humanitarian response than we have at present.[11] What strikes me in his accounts is the importance of men and (especially) women spending considerable amounts of time with the poorer households: sufficient time to discern the precise measures of assistance needed, from stern admonishments for irresponsible fathers in some cases to pressure on city hall to address harmful social conditions in others; time spent teaching the Word of God and time spent finding suitable employment; time spent, as he emphasizes, to "suffer with" the poor. Time becomes the ointment to make assistance truly compassionate and effective.

In his historical analysis Olasky too often emphasizes the use of volunteer time to achieve restrictive ends, seeking to discern who among the poor was deserving and thereby setting necessary conditions on assistance. Whether he recognizes this or not, what he may in effect have chronicled is the crucial importance of Sabbath time at work. This is the time spent as one sits with a single mother struggling emotionally to stay on top of her difficult situation, and the time that supplies an absent father with critical encouragement to resume his family responsibilities and pull his life together. In this we see once again that proper stewardship requires time blended with mercy, those values that lie at the heart of Sabbath.

Seen in terms of young lives lost, potential labor power wasted and an attack on the American dream of opportunity, the presence of numerous pockets of concentrated poverty in or near many of our central cities must be seen as one of society's most pressing problems today. When we think things could not possibly get worse we pick up the morning newspaper and read of one more tragic loss. Princeton crime expert John Dilulio has described a condition of "moral poverty" in such settings to help explain the increasingly youthful and increasingly dangerous face of violent behavior.[12] Urban specialist William Julius Wilson has described these settings today as "socially isolated" in a way they never were earlier in our history. They lack good job information networks and the presence of socially stabilizing nuclear and extended families.[13] In a working paper, Harvard economists David Cutler and Edward Glaeser have found that

> blacks are significantly worse off in segregated communities than they are in non-segregated communities. If we measure success with high-school graduation rates, not being idle, earnings, or not becoming a single mother, then integration is intimately associated with success. . . . Our instrumental variables results suggest that segregation leads to adverse outcomes, not that adverse outcomes result in more segregation.[14]

What could stewardship mean today for these complex social realities? What would the elders of an early Israelite community do were they confronting the realities of the American inner cities in the late twentieth century? Would they have allowed the amount and character of concentrated poverty to reach the levels we know today? In the political checkerboards we call metropolitan regions, would they have allowed the extent of local municipal autonomy (and the freedom from tending to the problems of the metropolitan regions within which they reside) that we allow today? Would they have allowed suburban communities considerable freedom to erect land-use restrictions that effectively prevent development of housing that could help relieve the problems of the inner cities? Most tellingly, would they have allowed the conditions of the inner cities to fester as long as we have, with such loss of life and hope, without taking more action than we have? In each case noted, I believe the answer is no.

In an otherwise commendable concession to local autonomy, allowing each household (as it were) to sit under its own vine and fig tree (Mic 4:4), I do not believe the U.S. has strategically, as in some form of conspiracy theory, constructed the spatial economic realities within metropolitan regions that exist today.[15] Our failing, rather, is the sin of omission, of not acting to redress these realities with greater earnestness once their horror became clear to us.[16] My purpose here is to investigate neither the causal linkages giving rise to the current situation nor the range of feasible responses, as important as both these steps are to a complete analysis of moral obligation. I want rather to wonder once again about the interweaving role of time and mercy, and struggle once again to discern the outlines of proper stewardship.

We know the elders of early Israel would have counseled us to build strong (extended) families. I believe they would tell us as well that the contemporary application of Jubilee would be community assistance with human capital accumulation (i.e., a good education), thus requiring educational processes that work. I believe they would have inquired into the structures of employment that would allow inner-city households to work their way out of poverty, assuming that the loans at issue in the Sabbath year most likely were related to employment. Because the concentration of poverty appears clearly to have harmed family stability and made human capital attainment more difficult, I believe they would have taken steps to deconcentrate the poverty.[17]

These suggestions may help define proper social stewardship, but how, if at all, do they embody the sabbatical interest in time? One obvious example is the importance of significant adult mentors in the lives of many of the young men and women who manage to escape the lure of the street and succeed in conventional social and economic ways.[18] One suspects a good part of the dynamic at work here is that the young men and women realize the mentor is sacrificing valuable time to be with them, an important element missing where the older adult is paid to spend time with them (whether through publicly or privately funded programs). Experts continue to debate the causes of higher poverty rates and lower labor force participation rates among inner-city households, vacillating between an inadequate supply of jobs and welfare-induced dependency, which inhibits them psychologically from searching out and taking available jobs. The answer surely is some of both, and the presence of men and women willing to spend Sabbath-like time with these households should help chip away at either set of circumstances, whether harmful psychological patterns or inadequate access to good labor market information. Given all the harmful and hope-destroying realities that we have allowed to fester in our inner cities, from gang-related violence and insufficient schools to employer reluctance to gamble on employees from these areas, far more than Sabbathlike time is needed. But once again, Sabbathlike time becomes one of the necessary elements for a stewardship that hopes to have any chance of success in attacking these deadly conditions.[19]

The Sacrifice of Time

Sabbathlike time then emerges as a necessary component of a steward-ship that will yield healthier households and a healthier society. How likely is it, however, that we will receive gifts of this time? Compelling economic realities suggest that it is not very likely. Scratch an economist and she will tell you about opportunity costs, that everything (and especially time) has a cost. As earnings have increased substantially for most workers over the past century, the value of time away from work has become more costly.[20] As more and more women earn advanced degrees and compete in labor markets, households face even greater time scarcities, leading couples to substitute for their time the use of purchased goods and purchased time from others to carry out the normal tasks of the household. Time, it turns out, is precisely what more and more households simply do not have.

Possibly offsetting this dismal assessment is what economists call the "income effect" of greater earnings, the desire to spend higher income on activities away from work. This potential most likely will be realized among those whose income is less tied to current earnings, and hence those either approaching or already in retirement. As the baby boom generation ages, a growing number of households will move into this category, portending the possibility of more volunteer time.

The question then becomes how much of time spent away from work will be provided as Sabbathlike time, whether offered to God in the weekly Sabbath or to other households in a quest for greater mercy within society. The likely answer is not nearly enough, unless a moral foundation to elicit sacrifice has been laid. To enlist men and women and children to offer "just-being-there" time at the weekly Sabbath or in missions of mercy requires a motivation to set this time apart. Sacrifice surrounds Sabbath as much as time and mercy. Otherwise the prophets and Jesus would not have issued the warnings they did.

I return to the opening paragraph of this essay and its claim that scarcity requires sacrifice. Working as they do with their Enlightenment-driven calculus, economists typically treat this in terms of *individual* sacrifice: if I forgo current consumption and use my time to achieve a higher level of education today, then I can reap higher income later. The sacrifice at issue in our inquiry, however, is sacrifice for others: for God and for fellow households. Economics, as with most systems of moral obligation, today offers little on this front. This type of sacrifice requires an unusual motivating force beyond appeals that ultimately reduce down to what makes me better off.[21] The God of the Bible offers what must be seen as the most compelling motivational basis to sacrifice for others: the fact, painful beyond comprehension (Is 53), that God in Christ sacrificed to save us from our sins. This reality, already rehearsed in different form over and over again in the motive clauses sprinkled throughout the presentation of the Law, is that God had acted in history to save Israel from slavery in Egypt (Ex 19:4, among many other citations). As we come to realize and rehearse and see modeled what great sacrificial steps God has taken for us, then we should be willing to sacrifice our time for others.[22] Herein lies the motivational impetus for the wedding of mercy and time that Christ and the prophets said should mark the Sabbath.[23]

Hence, the church of Jesus Christ must take the lead within society in offering Sabbathlike time in the pursuit of mercy. Christ instructs us that the world will know we are his disciples by the love (time?) we have for one another (Jn 13:35), offering us a paradigm of the way we should respond to non-Christians as well (Gal 6:10). Jesus healed many, showing mercy upon them and taking time, in opposition to his disciples' protestations, to attend to children and a hemorrhaging woman, among others. We are about serious business here. We bear a covenant obligation (Gen 18:18) sealed in blood (Ex 24:8; Mt 26:28) to lead the nations. In part that means leading by using our time in Sabbathlike ways for merciful ends, particularly to assist the poor and needy among us, which is the major objective of the various sabbatical provisions.

The world needs to see more case studies from Christians like Mother Teresa. We should be teaching and encouraging one another more than we do that to forgo potential earnings and other uses of our time in order to offer Sabbathlike time is the prophets' and Christ's call upon us for mercy. Perhaps we should make a "time tithe" along with our resource tithe.

Conclusion

I have made an attempt here to understand the sabbatical interest in time and to show how time and mercy complement more than conflict. We have seen some sense of the importance of "time-stands-still" time and "all-my-time-is-focused-on-you" time for achieving mercy. Ultimately time and Sabbath remain, in part, a mystery. Mercy and Sabbath time appear to me far too often in tradeoff terms. But I am coming to realize that the blessed and profound shalom we all desire is wrapped up in some way in Sabbath time and not only in the frenetic quest for mercy that has compelled so many of us to this point.[24]

7

ΘΕΩΣΙΣ in Freedom & Love

The Patristic Vision of Stewardship
Kenneth Paul Wesche

The Christian patristic vision offers a coherent metaphysic in which to interpret and to address issues of ecology and global consumption; that is to say, how human beings are to understand their role relative to the world and the use of its resources in a manner that is consistent with the world's own nature according to the Christian vision. This metaphysical vision is indicated in the biblical and patristic application of the term "stewardship," οικονομια.

In its mundane setting οικονομια designates the management of a household and is the activity assigned to an οικονομος, a steward. When brought into the sphere of Christian confession, the household being managed is the world, and the steward who is doing the managing is the divine itself. The way in which God manages the household of the world is by sending his Son not to condemn the world but to save the world (Jn 3:17). The Incarnation, then, is the comprehensive plan, the οικονομια, by which God manages the salvation of the world.

Already in the first generation of Christian thought, in the Pauline epistle to the Ephesians, the term οικονομια has received a christological content:

In Christ we obtain redemption through his blood and forgiveness of sins according to the riches of his grace which he has so lavishly poured out upon us. For he has made known [γνωρισας] to us in all wisdom and understanding the mystery of his will—which is in accordance with his good pleasure which he has set forth in Christ— which is to unite, in his οικονομια of the fullness of time, all things in Christ: uniting in him everything in heaven and on earth. (Eph 1:7-10)

God's οικονομια is the mystery of the Incarnation and this is how it is taken in patristic literature. The term οικονομια is a common one in christological texts where, distinguished from theology, which properly speaking refers to the dogma of the Trinity, it may be translated "Incarnation."[1]

Towards a Christological Vision of Stewardship
The patristic identification of οικονομια with the Incarnation brings the term into the mystical setting of the divine's union with humanity that humanity might be united to divinity. Study of this divine οικονομια accordingly belongs to *gnōsis,* that mystical knowledge that has to do specifically with penetrating the veil of externality to the divine mystery within that gives meaning to human existence and that conditions the world's nature and destiny. The connection of οικονομια and γνωσις is made by St. Paul, exemplified both in the passage just cited and in the following:

To me this grace was given . . . to make all men see what is the οικονομια of the mystery hidden for all ages in God who created all things; that through the church the manifold wisdom of God might now be made known [γνωρισθη] to the principalities and powers in the heavenly places. (Eph 3:8-10)

Inasmuch as the Incarnation has to do with redeeming and divinizing the world of materiality, it should be clear that identifying stewardship with the Incarnation in no way diminishes the term's significance for issues of ecology. Quite the contrary, it deepens our approach to those issues by providing us with a *gnōsis* of the world's true meaning and reality, by which we are enabled to manage the world and its resources in a manner that is responsible to the world's true nature because it is informed by a *gnōsis* of its Creator's intention, which is its salvation.

To discover the basic outlines inherent in this *gnōsis* I propose to lay before you a philosophical account of the christological vision articulated in the seven Ecumenical Councils of the patristic period (A.D. 325-787). The heart of this vision can be introduced by tracing in broad outlines the intellectual history of *essence* both in "pagan" philosophy and in the christological vision of the Ecumenical Councils.

Essence in the Thought of Pagan Philosophy and Arian Theology

Around the year 318, when Arius began putting forth his ideas about God and the Son, he compelled Christian thought to rise to a higher level of philosophical discourse. Arius claimed that "there was a time when the Son was not," that he was the first of the unbegotten Father's creatures, the concretization, as it were, of the Father's will and thereby the agent of creation. Eunomius, the most articulate and prodigious apologist of Arian theology in the fourth century, articulated the nub of the Arian position when he reasoned that

Divine essence is first.
Unbegotten is that which is first.
Therefore, the divine essence is unbegotten.
The Father alone is unbegotten essence.

Therefore, the Father alone is God.
What is second is created essence.
That which is begotten is second.
Therefore, that which is begotten is a created essence.
The Son is begotten.
Therefore, the Son is a created essence.[2]

Although philosophically coherent, Arianism was not acceptable to Christian thought ultimately because it is not acceptable to pagan experience or the experience of the human soul. In explaining the second part of this assertion, I intend to set the patristic vision of stewardship in its properly christological setting.

The dispute between the Arians, who asserted that the Son was of a different essence from the Father, and the several orthodox parties, who eventually rallied around the Nicene formula of the ομοουσιος to refute the Arians, centered on the notion of essence as it pertains to the existence and character of the particular. On this same concept of essence, represented by the formula of the One and the Many, the philosophical program of the Hellenistic world was based. Arianism assumed in its theology the philosophical structure of essence given in Greek philosophical thought insofar as it identified absolutely the particular with its essence. The orthodox, in seeking to give expression to all that was contained in the Church's vision of Jesus as the Christ, the Son of God, were led to bring forth a deeper vision of essence that is, in fact, implicit or latent in mythology and in the vision of the Hebrew prophets. Let us trace briefly this notion of essence as it was applied particularly in Greek philosophy.

The concept of essence—from the Latin *esse* and the Greek ουσια, both of which come from the copula "to be"—in Greek philosophical thought is conditioned by the program of the pre-Socratics who inquired after "the what it was for a thing to be what it was" (το τι ην ειναι). The terms of this program led to the distinction of two general kinds of being, or essences: phenomenal essence, characterized by constant change or "becoming," and real essence, which is Being itself, incorporeal and therefore changeless and eternal. This distinction of essences led to the discovery of the soul's immortality. "Soul" is the incorporeal life-giving force of the cosmos and everything in it and as such is shown to be unaffected by change, by birth or by death. Its immortal and incorporeal character follows logically and reveals the naturally divine quality inherent to its essence.

The distinction of two kinds of essence provides the metaphysical structure that produces the philosophical program: to awaken oneself to the presence within of that particle of the divine essence that constitutes one's soul or real self. Philosophical analysis of the soul's various parts and capacities has as its immediate purpose the task of identifying that part of one's soul that is from the divine, in order to liberate it from the mesmerizing stupor and shackles of egoistic and corporeal, or phenomenal, essence. The philosophical program's final purpose is to reunite one's divine self with the primal divine essence from which it somehow fell away.

real essence Being itself / incorporeal / eternal
phenomenal essence change / becoming

Directly pertinent to our subject is the fact that although the two essences are very much connected with each other—the phenomenal derives ultimately from the real—the goal of the philosophical program is the soul's abandonment of the phenomenal realm, the world and everything in it. This constitutes "salvation," which means, literally, "being healed" of the phenomenal.

This is a significant departure from the earlier, much more ancient cult of the Goddess, the Great Mother, worshiped for millennia as the *mysterium tremendum* that seems to permeate nature, emanating from some profound, invisible depth and manifesting itself in the living, throbbing, potent forces of nature that bring creatures into being, animating and agitating them, inspiring them with uncanny powers that enable them to thrive. In this earlier, more primordial experience all things are united in the Great Round: the *uroboros.* The world and all its creatures are experienced as numinous since they are incarnations or epiphanies of the divine. All of life is a unity, every particular is integrally connected in the living whole. The inner is manifested by the outer, the body is merely the outer shell or final extension of "spirit." Death and life go together: to be buried in the tomb of the earth is to be planted in the Great Mother's maternal womb. As surely as day follows night and the green of spring follows the death of winter, so each death is the prelude to a new life in the Great Round of the divine.

In the Greek philosophical program, by contrast, the inner self is distinguishable in essence from the outer body and its accidents. Salvation is realized when one's inner divine self has finally transcended its attachment to the outer body and is reunited with the divine. Plotinus's "Bring the god in you back to the divine in the All!" echoes Socrates' "Know that you are immortal, capable of attaining wisdom, goodness, and righteousness"—all attributes of the divine essence, which the soul is, in its inmost self.

From this, it may be easy to see why many of those anxious about the fate of our earth would find a return to the primordial Goddess so appealing; her religious experience honors the soul's sense of the earth's sacred character and gives to that intuition a metaphysical orientation that serves also as a comprehensive guide for action. The metaphysical framework of Greek philosophy, on the other hand, together with Christian theology, which has adopted that framework in large measure, is easily caricatured as indifferent to the world, offering no religious program compelling enough to generate a venerable regard for the world and its resources as something truly sacred. The caricature is not without historical foundation in fact, but it need not be allowed to stand as truly representative if a deeper, more wholistic vision of Christian dogma can be demonstrated.

Although the conceptions of the divine in the program of Greek philosophy and the primordial experience of the Goddess are clearly different and lead in turn to different attitudes to the world, beneath the differences there is manifest a common yearning to be united with the divine. The presence of this common yearning in such wide and varied religious contexts I take as indication of an essentially human desire, which the gospel claims to consummate.

Union with the divine is at the heart of the Christian vision: St. Peter looks to our becoming "partakers of the divine nature" in Christ (2 Pet 1:4). In different ways, beginning with Ignatius of Antioch (d. 110), the fathers of the church describe the mystery of the Incarnation as "God becoming man in order that man might become God." Against Arius, Athanasius of Alexandria (d. 363) writes:

> If we wish to know the advantages we attain by this [Incarnation of God] we shall find them to be as follows: that the Word was made flesh, not only to offer up this body for all, but that we, partaking of his Spirit, might be made gods, a gift which we could not otherwise have gained than by his clothing himself in our created body. And as we, by receiving the Spirit, do not lose our own proper essence, so the Lord, when made man for us, and bearing a body, was no less God; for he was not lessened by the envelopment of the body, but rather deified it and rendered it immortal.[3]

Arianism is disproved not simply on the grounds of Christian dogma but on the grounds of universal human experience. By identifying absolutely the particular with its essence, such that the Father *is* unbegotten or uncreated essence and the Son *is* begotten or created essence, Arius's Christ is not simply different in essence but is essentially separated from the Father. He is the first of all God's *creatures*, and as such cannot promise union of the created in *itself* with the *uncreated* in *itself*. Arius's Christ can bring one no farther than to the borders of one's created essence, where one is able only to gaze at the divine splendor in stupefaction from the other side of the chasm that still separates one's inmost self from God's inmost self. For the "self" in each case is identical with its essence by which it is distinguished and separated from the other. There is here no θεωσις, no union with the divine in which God becomes human that humans might become God. The deepest yearning of the human soul, from one's inmost self, is betrayed.

In seeking to give expression to this human yearning for union with the divine, however, Christian thought is saddled theologically with the same difficulty that landed Arius in his Arianism, a difficulty not present in pagan thought. Christian theology takes from Judaism the distinction between the one uncreated God and the rest of creation, so that in its appropriation of the pagan distinction of essences, Christian thought presents a God who, in his uncreated essence, is altogether different even from the human soul which, though incorporeal in its essence, is still created. How, then, can Christian thought express coherently humanity's union with God, humanity's deification, while remaining true to this fundamental axiom of its religious heritage and without falling back into Arianism? Tracing out the philosophical implications of the Church's christological confession leads to an understanding of being not in terms of essence but in terms of personality and freedom. One of the principal keys opening up this deeper vision of being as a mystery of personal union is precisely the notion of created essence.

Toward a Christological Vision of Essence

The first step leading to a deeper vision of being is the refutation of Arianism in which it is shown that divine essence can neither be named nor known. In the fourth century Gregory the Theologian expressed it most clearly: the term divinity itself does not refer to God's nature in an essential way. Every name is indicative of our conceptions of the divine nature, but does not signifiy what that nature is in itself. The term divinity does not signify a nature but an operation (ενεργεια) which emanates from and manifests the supracomprehensible divinity.[4] Arius, rigidly following the pattern of pagan philosophy, had identifed the Father absolutely with his essence; in knowing the Father he knew the Father's essence, for they are one and the same. Orthodox theology places divine essence altogether outside human knowledge or philosophical discourse. Yet although divine essence, which makes the divine persons what they are, is unknowable, it does not prevent the divine hypostases from being knowable. In this philosophical conception the particulars are not comprehended or embraced by their essence—they are not particles broken off from some primordial essence—but they are "those *in whom* divine essence exists [τα εν οις θεοτης ειναι]."[5] The particular transcends and embraces the essence. The essence does not make the particular exist but the particular, the person or hypostasis, makes the essence exist and determines the mode of its existence. This model presents a vision in which the divine is altogether free, for the divine is a Trinity of Persons who can be known because they exist, by nature as it were, "outside" the unknowable essence. The Word of God is therefore free to become "what he was not," namely human, even as he remains "what he is" in order that humanity might become what it was not, namely god, even as humanity remains "what it is."

The hypostasis is presented here as the foundation of being; the world is grounded not in an impersonal essence but in a Trinity of divine Persons who create the world not out of essential necessity but out of their hypostatic, personal freedom. Their unity is a unity of essence, but more than that, because they exist personally outside of their essence, their personal unity is a unity of love in which each Person exists in the other even as each Person exists hypostatically as himself. This means philosophically that being is a mystery grounded in personal freedom and love, not essential necessity.

The second step leading to a deeper vision of being in patristic Christology was the refutation of Apollinarianism. Apollinaris was a staunch opponent of Arius and strong defender of Nicaea, but like Arius, though in a different way, he was unable to break out of the pagan identification of the particular with the essence. Accepting the psychological assumptions of Hellenistic philosophy in which the real self is the soul, Apollinaris taught that the divine Logos took the place of the human mind and soul to create an enfleshed Word, who is one essence, one nature, one hypostasis, one *prosōpon*. For Apollinaris, self and soul were identical; Christ was but one self, and that was the essence of the divine Logos. To preserve the integrity of Christ's personal unity, Apollinaris taught that the Christ's identity was one because "inside" the flesh was not a human soul or self in conjunction with the Logos (as taught by Theodore of Mopsuestia, Apollinaris's chief opponent on the christological front) but the divine Logos alone.

In his refutation of Apollinaris's Christology, Gregory the Theologian identifies the soul as "the most essential part of man that needs saving," but he does not identify the soul with the real self. The τις or "who" of Christ is not a man but the divine Logos: the Christ is two "whats" but not two "whos" (αλλο μεν και αλλο, ουκ αλλος δε και αλλος).[6] "He bore in himself [εν εαυτω] the whole of me that he might consume in himself my inferiority."[7] "The Icon of the archetypal Beauty, the immovable Seal, the unchangeable Icon, the Definition and Word of the Father, came to his own icon, and took on flesh for the sake of my flesh, and mingled himself with an intelligent soul for the sake of my soul, purifying like by like."[8]

As in the refutations of Arian triadology, so here in the refutation of Apollinarian Christology: Orthodox thought distinguishes the particular from the essence by distinguishing the "self" of the Logos from the human "soul" he assumed and united to himself. Christology thereby introduces soul as an integral part of *created* essence, or nature, which it distinguishes from personhood or the real self. As in the triadological model, so also now in the christological model: personhood is not embraced by or comprehended by essence but transcends its essence, determining how the essence exists even as the essence makes the person to be what he is.

Thus human personality in its christological realization is called to transcend its created essence through a personal εκστασις, a going out of oneself, out of one's created essence, to unite with the divine uncreated essence in the person of the Son. This ecstatic movement of an "I" that is not exhausted by its essence is what makes union with the divine in Christology a union of persons—an "I" and a "Thou"—conditioned not by the attributes of essence, whether created or uncreated, but by personal freedom, on the basis of which alone genuine loving communion is possible. In this union of personal love in the Person of the Son, human persons are given the power to determine how created essence shall exist, that is, in union with the divine, permeated by the divine energies by which it is transfigured, becoming by grace all that God is by nature. Personal εκστασις, transcending essence, is the term of personal freedom, personal freedom is the term of communion in love, and communion in love is the term of the world's deification.

Implications for Stewardship

In the christological vision of the Ecumenical Councils the Church acknowledges and confirms the ancient wisdom of the human soul, reflected in the religious experience of the Great Mother and in the philosophical thought of the Greeks. But under the rubric of created essence, inherited from its Jewish ancestry, the Church teaches that the world is holy, sacred, an epiphany, an icon of the divine because the whole of creation is rooted in an act of divine, personal love and freedom. The christological content of stewardship teaches that humanity's essential yearning for the divine does not mean the abandonment of the phenomenal world or an indifference to it, but its transfiguration through personal union with the divine in which creaturely essence is made to exist in a manner that embodies and manifests the mystery of being as a loving communion of free persons. Assuming the responsibility of stewardship of the world is thereby a response to the divine call to bring oneself and one's world to authentic being, which is personal communion with the divine in love and freedom. The possibility for such a reality is given, according to the Christian confession, already in the Incarnation, in which God has already united himself with humanity. What remains is for humanity to unite itself to God through responsible stewardship.

If humans are the stewards of creation, this can only mean, in the context of the christological vision, that they must transcend their creaturely essence so that they are governed no longer by biological instincts and psychic libido but rise to become free, "gnostic" governors of their natural energies and impulses. In this process humanity is called to bring the world with itself in order to transfigure the world by governing it in accordance with the mystery of being revealed in the mystery of God's οικονομια: the Incarnation.

This gives to our understanding of stewardship a metaphysical orientation that teaches us to treat the world with loving care, since its salvation—transformation through union with the divine—is inseparable from ours. It teaches us, I think, that the cause of our present ecological disasters is humanity's failure to pursue the capacity for the divine that makes us to be what we are. When governed by essence—by the egoistic impulses of biological instinct and psychic libido—we approach the world as though asleep, consuming its resources in a blind compulsion to satisfy the egoistic desires of our own narrowly constricted egoistic world. We consume and consume and consume some more, treating the world as though it were made for us and for the satisfactions of our bodily and spiritual lusts. Oblivious to our deeper depths, we do not know (γιγνωσκειν) that the insatiable desire that agitates us is for the divine, and in our egoistic blindness we violate the natural integrity of the world that has been given us. We fail to see that our desire and the world's essence can never be fulfilled until we undertake the journey in the Logos of our being—whom the church identifies as Jesus Christ—toward full individuation, full personhood in communion with the divine in the Divine Logos incarnate.

The christological vision of stewardship also teaches us, however, that those of us who would like to identify with the ecological movement in one form or another cannot succeed in our efforts to remedy our destructive consumption of the world's resources until our ecological solutions themselves are genuinely informed by the gnosis that comes from the "journey of the soul," or in Christian terms, the "way of the Cross." By the way of the Cross, men and women are able to unite with the divine bridegroom—Christians identify him with Jesus of Nazareth and understand his "becoming flesh" as the consummation in history of the mythic sacred marriage—whose penetration of our soul transforms and deifies us and gives us the wisdom and power to direct the world and all its essential energies toward its true end: union with the divine.

8
On New Things
....

John R. Schneider

O*ur present subject of Christianity and wealth is certainly not new. In times* following Pentecost, the first Christians strove for goodness in the marketplaces of the world as though their eternal lives depended on it. For over a thousand years, Catholic pastors and theologians made economic life a primary subject of church theology and moral teaching.[1] In later centuries, the leaders of Protestantism reminded all of Europe that Christian faith is dead without works of the right economic kind.[2] And so it is in the present age that we worry intensely over the matter of God and mammmon. Rightly so, for to use H. Richard Niebuhr's famous term, it is a question of "Christ and culture" that grows from the very soil of Christian experience on earth in every age.[3] That we struggle is hard, but it is a sign of spiritual health. In that larger historic sense, then, the good fight somehow to "make friends with unrighteous mammon" is the same as it has always been.

The economic world in which we live and move and have our modern Christian being is not the same, however. For, perennial as it is, mammon takes on new forms in every age. The advanced economic systems of today are unlike anything ever imagined in the cultures of ancient Rome and medieval and early modern Europe. In the last two centuries, industrialized market economies have grown and spread like vast sprawling vines all around the globe, and their fermenting fruits have caused many an old wineskin to burst in our churches' cellars of tradition. Safe to say, we are not nearly finished making the new ones we so desperately need.

This essay is devoted to finding a model for seeking personal Christian vision in the culture of modern capitalism. It has two main, complex theses. The first is that we cannot very well operate as Christians within the economic *system* known as capitalism without also having grounds in our theology and ethics for affirming involvement in the *culture* of capitalism. It seems that those Christian thinkers who are unfavorably disposed to that culture, but nevertheless wish to operate in and to use the cash-making power of the system, have not taken that point as deeply to heart as they should. This leaves them without the theological justification and force they need in order to be the strong presence for justice in the culture they wish to be. On the other hand, the most comprehensive and compelling Christian defenses of market systems (as human cultures) are largely grounded in the cosmology of the Old Testament. Their understanding of human purpose, in the economic context, is much less obviously guided by New Testament teaching than it is by a certain general doctrine of creation. This leaves them open to the serious criticism that their theories are not truly and radically enough Christian, especially in view of the profoundly antimaterialistic life and teachings of Christ.

In that light, the second thesis of this essay is that this use of creation theology as a context for affirming Christian involvement in the market culture is correct, but limited. For it to blossom into a fully Christian view, we must have some convincing means of making Christology the final measure of human identity and purpose in the economic world. In this essay I shall offer some proposals about the integration of these two great realms of biblical teaching.

Let us begin with a review of historic teaching on economic life. This look backward will help us to know better how to go forward. It will give us the constant points of reference we need to understand our own situation in all its newness.

Historic Christian Teaching on the Use of Wealth

To be sure, we should not flee to the past for refuge from the complexities of the day, as we may well be tempted to do. Nevertheless, history is indispensable as a guide. Before entering this forest, overgrown with modern questions as it is, we had better first study the work of those pioneers in the faith who have gone before us. The value of their hard-won experience to our own quest cannot easily be overstated.

As a broad perspective on the issue, the best teachers in times past preached from the rooftops their deep belief that the norms for personal piety were also norms for life in society. They understood that the Christian life was not to be lived in compartments but as an integrated whole, both inside and outside the private sphere. That eternal life really comprises economic life in this world was for them, whatever their disagreements on other matters, a bottom line. There will be no debate about that in this essay.[4]

But furthermore, as we shall see, these great teachers mapped out the entire realm of economic life as a category of human culture. In good rhetorical fashion, which they revered as essential to clarity in all things, they established the analytical distinctions preliminary even to forming the right questions. They also identified the primary framework of Christian doctrines that is appropriate to answering them. In doing so they forged something that grew and matured during the centuries into a synthetic Christian view of the economic culture as they knew and experienced it.[5] Let us take some time, then, to see how this map of theirs might give us the orientation we need today.

One primary matter of dispute that church theologians had to settle in the beginning was whether Christians, as individuals, should own property at all.[6] A great deal was at stake, since without justification of ownership no real involvement in a human culture of ownership, as with Rome, would be possible beyond active, communal asceticism. (Of course even that might become unjustifiable by the implication that ownership in any form is sinful.) They sensed that this outcome would be bad for both the church and the world. It would also make life hard to the point of denying basic human desires that seemed less fallen in nature than just normal and were commensurate with sustaining life. In thinking things out they came to realize that a complete moral view must include perspectives on the different possible specific modes of ownership. A person did not just own something in a neutral or fixed sense. Ownership, they realized, had a contingent, organic and living quality about it, so that it could not very well be treated in the abstract. As they recognized, there were always circumstances, and attitudes and actions within those circumstances, that gave ownership different possible moral and spiritual connotations in a fallen world. In their treatises for the rich they commonly identified those morally relevant circumstances as three: acquisition, use (and abuse) and enjoyment.

Should Christians have property at all in any of these various modes of possession? With these distinctions in view, moral teachers applied their Christian theology to the economic culture. They understood early that the doctrine of creation was the most fundamental and necessary place to begin. During the fierce battles with Gnosticism in the second century, the emerging church leadership established as a major premise of orthodox teaching that the physical realm was not evil, as Gnostics believed, but that it was good in the strongest religious sense of that term.[7]

When taking up the cultural question of material property, they intuitively realized that this assertion about the cosmos was momentously important to their moral discourse. The basis for this realization may seem obvious now, but it is nonetheless profound for its simplicity: the physical realm is God's good creation. This simple intuition guided theologians to agree that it was, under proper conditions, a basically good thing for Christians to have property and also to be actively involved as a presence in the marketplace.[8] The economic world, they reasoned, partook of the goodness that belongs to the material world generally as God's good work.[9] Largely for this reason, the strategy of mainline Christians ever since has not been one of separatism, but one form or another of that complex expression of wishing to be *in* the world but not *of* it.[10]

Theologians of the past, however, looked beyond creation and recognized the importance of Christ's person and teachings to economic life. They understood that their principles of creation had to be shaped coherently by a moral understanding of Christology. The primary example to Christians of how to live as human beings, after all, was Jesus. In the economic realm of life, his incarnation, life, death and resurrection seemed to integrate and then to give moral shape to all that we have just reviewed about the creation and human purpose within it. On the one hand, the astonishing *bodily* character of these events gave powerful redemptive approval to the creational realm of the physical.

On the other hand, however, theologians could not but be struck by Jesus' own life of poverty (as they mainly believed his condition to have been), by his blessings upon the poor and by his many dire warnings and critical judgments against becoming and being rich, hording and satiating oneself on riches. Weighing all these things together, the common opinion was that poverty was indeed a higher spiritual way of life, but that it was not required of everyone. Furthermore, theologians broadly opined that having possessions was permitted under certain moral conditions regarding attitudes and actions of proper usage. The common judgment was that proper usage was determined by order of need, so that evil lurked not in the mere having of things but in the selfishness that came with enjoyment of that which was clearly superfluous to meeting one's own real needs. The excess of wealth must not be so *abused* but instead *used* to meet the most pressing needs of others, especially the poor.[11]

However wise and good this consensus may have been, we must realize that it was to a considerable extent the product of its times. This simple fact is one of the main points of this essay. As a rule, the distribution of wealth and power in premodern economies was (as it is today in economies that are not yet modern) top-heavy in the extreme. A very small minority of people were rich in relative terms (had more than they needed), and the vast majority were either poor or facing poverty (did not have, or barely had, enough to live on) as a constant danger.[12] Of course there were also those pockets of trade and commerce where many enjoyed the benefits and even occasional periods of broad economic growth. But on the whole, premodern societies generally endured economic extremes; that is part of what makes them *pre*modern.

This state of affairs was also largely true of the world in which the events and teachings recorded in the New Testament occurred. The oppressive economic world of ancient imperial Rome, especially as it was experienced in satellite economies such as the Palestine of Jesus, also gave context and shape to the economic teachings of Jesus and the early church.[13] Not in the least to avoid the most prominent message of the New Testament, which is undeniably negative toward the enjoyment of excess, we must presume that this state of affairs had to have a great effect on the entire direction of moral teaching in the early church.

In such social economies it would be extraordinary, even bizarre, to find moral theologians seeking elaborate justifications for the acquisition and enjoyment of superfluous wealth, since this represents everything that the Law and the Prophets inveigh against. To acquire wealth in abundance usually required impoverishing someone else, and to enjoy such wealth was damnable. No wonder that almost all the rhetorical stress among theologians was upon the proper *use* of wealth. Apart from monastic asceticism (which could not support civilization if advanced as a norm), the utilitarian approach seemed the only viable moral path available for the few wealthy and powerful Christians.

However, on this point the contrast with modern market economies could not be greater. Apart from whatever social, political or environmental evils we might name, one of the most extraordinary features of modern free market economies is that they have inverted these fundamental conditions in the distribution and movement (or lack thereof) of wealth. Moreover, they have done so by what are apparently quite morally sound mechanisms of acquisition. In spite of new and terrible social evils that have accrued, it is nevertheless true that in these systems the vast majority of ordinary people have become rich by any literal or historic measure, while the small (by comparison) minority are materially poor. But even the majority of the remaining poor have realistic hopes that one day soon they too will escape the grip of poverty. This is an amazing hope, unthinkable in earlier centuries.[14] As Michael Novak has never tired of pointing out, this system, for all its faults, has been the primary means of liberation for millions of human beings from those ancient enemies of humankind: tyranny and poverty.[15]

A closer look at the mechanisms and patterns of market activity helps explain the novelty of the moral situation that modern economies have brought into being. Democratic market systems operate by processes that cause the *creation* of wealth. People acquire wealth in fair abundance, generally, not by taking it from others but by engaging in productive activity and by benefiting from the productive activity of others. As Walter Lippmann astutely observed in *The Great Society,* for the first time in history, with democratic markets human beings have constructed "a way of producing wealth in which the good fortune of others multiplied their own" and "the golden rule was economically sound."[16] A new species of acquisition has been born that not only does not naturally oppress other human beings but actually liberates them. Primarily due to its power to liberate masses of human beings from the grip of poverty, growing numbers of theologians, after a long struggle of conscience and ideas, are affirming the superiority of market systems to those of the statist variety.[17]

Serious questions remain, however, about the integrity of this preference within a truly Christian worldview. As Craig Gay has observed, in spite of the victory of capitalism over socialism in the global struggle for power (especially after 1989), many Christian writers protest that capitalism is not at all ethically superior in terms of environmental, political and cultural concerns.[18] Among those cultural concerns, obviously, are matters of personal consumption and lifestyle issues related to the enjoyment of wealth. One problem with this position is that we cannot very well have the system without its culture of enjoyment. The attempt to affirm involvement in and with the system of capitalism without imbibing its ethos of delight in material happiness is not unlike affirming modern science while asserting ancient caveats against doubting a literal six-day creation. It invites images of the person who saws off the limb on which he sits.

Meanwhile, stalwart Christian proponents of market systems present defenses that vary considerably in theological acumen and quality.[19] Perhaps the most convincing have come out of Roman Catholicism. Nevertheless, the skepticism of many is not entirely unwarranted, for even the best of these defenses seem wanting in that delicate requirement to integrate the doctrines of creation with that of Christ's person. For reasons given previously, it is still in that relation that truly Christian answers must come.

Vindicating Capitalism in Theology
A monumental step forward in this process was the encyclical published in 1891 by Pope Leo XIII under the title *Rerum novarum (Of New*

Things).[20] In this document Leo XIII commented impressively on the revolutionary "new things" that modern industrial, free market economies had by then already brought into being in severely testing forms for Christians. Among them were new concepts of property (capital) and work (labor), and with these whole new societal problems and debates.[21] There were many Christian intellectuals then being swayed by the arguments supporting state control of capital and markets. The swelling masses of exploited labor and the spread of worsening conditions for many (including many children) in the newly industrialized societies seemed too high a price to pay for the prosperity of many others. They cited Old Testament social law, especially the Jubilee, and they revived sensitivity to the radical message of the prophets and of Jesus.[22] Well aware of these new evils, Leo XIII nevertheless strove to counteract this growing movement away from property rights and toward Christian socialism. The pope and his magisterium sought mightily, with great things at stake, to find a theologically and morally sound way of affirming the new and triumphant market systems, but then also of placing them under critical view.

The whole argument of *Rerum novarum* cannot be summarized in this space. Other theorists have built ably upon the economic and theological reasoning of this encyclical. Today, under the influence of their arguments, it seems that something like a consensus is emerging among Catholic authorities in favor of a morally shaped market system over that of Christian socialism.[23] As noted, that consensus (especially since 1989) seems to be spreading to include many evangelical and Reformed theologians who have previously differed markedly, and still do so, in their ethical teachings. For example, Ron Sider observed at the Oxford conference that produced the Oxford Declaration on Faith and Economics (1990) "liberation-oriented theologians affirming free-market strategies and conservative market economists demanding a special focus on justice for the poor."[24]

This consensus, if it is genuine, is welcome. Nevertheless, agreement that market systems are the best alternative for ordering societies has by no means brought about accord over matters of social and personal ethics. That division remains in part because the terms of the consensus have been more pragmatic, especially on the side of "liberation-oriented" theologians, as Sider has called them, than they have been solidly grounded in theology. As critics from the left have themselves objected, the concession to free market strategies of liberation is much less principled theologically than it is expedient.[25] The vast power and success of capitalism, by themselves, no matter how wonderful the results for Christians and the poor, do not suffice to make it the rod of Moses.

To restate the point, there has to be some meaningful sense in which we can with integrity affirm just that kind of power, and make a distinction between its successes and those wonders we are told that the antichrist will perform, to deceive even the very elect. On the other side, however, those "market-oriented" theologians who have made a clear and unequivocal theological case for affirming capitalism as a kind of human vision for culture make many points that seem questionable, especially in the light of Christ's life and teachings.

Before going further into this complex of problems, perhaps it will be useful to review the clearest case that has been made for Christian affirmation of market economies. Searching for the right theological language to express the religious and moral value of this kind of economic activity and its effects, the ablest Christian defenders of market economies have, like the ancients, turned instinctively to the doctrine of creation. In this context, they have sought to construct a fresh approach to the existential matter of human teleology. They have rightly pointed out that in Genesis human beings are made in the image and likeness of God, and that part of what this means is that divinely ordained human purpose is about having dominion over the earth and thus being free for creative and productive work in the context of property.[26] Being in the image and likeness of God is about flourishing creatively and productively in the material world, under God and in the context of absolute moral norms that lead to principles of love and justice.[27] It seems then, they argue, that the ideological vision animating modern democratic capitalism (always with stress on the term *democratic*) makes such systems, in spite of imperfections, something like cultural mirrors of the cosmic design. "Humans become co-creators through discovery and invention, following the clues left by God."[28] More than merely human, these systems express (if variously and imperfectly) a divinely created system of truth that is universal and good for all human beings in any culture.[29]

From these apologies for capitalism as a philosophy and cultural system, the outline of certain principles for governing social and personal economic life begins to emerge. However we state them, they will be affirmations of individual freedom, enterprise, competitiveness (of a certain sort), creativity, productivity and flourishing with dignity, while seeking justice for all, in the material realm, under God. Furthermore, it is hard to see how anyone may accept capitalism as a system without also accepting philosophical and cultural principles of some similar kind. To adopt ascetic principles as universal norms, for instance, such as Augustine did with Neo-Platonism, is obviously to reject the cultural core of capitalism as deeply alien to God's spiritual designs. But to come to our own focus on consumption, the person who decries the enjoyment of wealth beyond necessity, as John Wesley apparently did, and at the same time adopts capital as his primary source of help for the poor, is in a very awkward position.[30]

Again, the quintessential workings of market systems require a culture of enjoyment that is active on every level and part of every economic action performed by anyone within it. It should be obvious by now that utilitarian ethics, no matter what their virtues in moral reason or in the historic teachings of the faith, are not compatible with the workings of market capitalism. Likewise, they are not compatible with a Christian view that aims at working redemptively within the culture of capitalism. The utilitarian cashing in on capitalism, as Wesley advised (and as others seem to do by holding up his example) in order to promote an end to poverty, is most confusing.[31] It seems not very different from a virgin taking admissions at a bar, which she believes in fact to be a brothel, in order to finance revival meetings that she leads for the prostitutes inside. This is no model for people inside the system. The virgin had better get out, or else revise her judgment of what is actually going on in the establishment of which she is a freely and deliberately assenting part and beneficiary.

Nevertheless, before she revises things too much in the interest of keeping herself in the business of morality, she had better be sure that her revisions are grounded in the existence of something more than money. The justification for involvement had better be immune from charges of the sort of self-serving rationalization that leads to Babylon. This seems to me to be a part of the liberationists' legitimate worry.

They are pressed into acknowledging that Adam Smith's god is stronger and does more material good than Marx's, but they are concerned that the available theological justifications of capitalism are somehow not quite Christian. They fear that these justifications are more rationalizations than truly biblical authorizations.

This fear is not altogether unwarranted, for our sense of vocation as human beings comes at last not from James Madison, Adam and Eve, Isaiah or King David. In the fullest and deepest teleological sense, it must come from identification with Jesus Christ. If the readings of Genesis are true, as I believe they are, and if they correlate nicely with the ideological elements of our democratic market culture, which they do, it is not at all clear that they are in keeping with the human vision we have received in Jesus Christ. In what remains of this essay, we shall see how this fresh cultural doctrine of creation might be integrated with an equally fresh approach to Christology. We will then have made some progress toward gaining the model of Christ and culture that we all need if we are to be involved as Christians in the culture of capitalism. Both liberationists and market-oriented theorists will have a more broadly biblical and better integrated common framework in which to conduct their work and debates. And all of us will be a little less vulnerable to the secular cynicism of our day, which says that theories drawn from sacred texts are nothing more or less than expressions of our personal and social preferences.

Christ and Adam, and Economic Vision

Creation, Law and the Prophets. In Genesis, the vision of human purpose breaks forth unashamedly in the language of royalty. In biblical idiom, to have made the man and woman God's very own image and likeness is to have made them a king and queen, monarchs to rule the earth.[32] By itself the text makes this connection as God blesses them with dominion over the earth and over all the earth's creatures. The royal stature of human beings carries over into Genesis 2 with its picture of them tilling and flourishing in a garden of delight, in freedom to eat of every tree of the garden save one. That this royal standing and domain must conform with the quality of God's own life-giving and redemptive character does not in the least reduce the scope of their freedom or the story's intense affirmation of extravagance. By itself this vision of true shalom must mean that enjoyment of material things in excess is basically something good, since it was built into the order of creation itself.

On the other hand, the fruit of "knowledge of good and evil" bitterly warns that some actions of pleasure are not good. Of course it is a story primarily about the spiritual realm and of how humans are not to behave in relation to it. It is about what happens when we seek to become autonomous and thus to use the creation without deference to any power greater than ourselves. In that event we curve in upon ourselves, to use Luther's metaphor, and our godly dominion turns to something dark, deadly and evil in the way of the serpent. While the lesson is spiritual, its points obviously materialize in the world. Whatever the genre of literature, the action of eating is portrayed as physical, and so is the ruin it causes for humans and the curse it brings on the earth. If in their role of dominion and delight, the man and the woman were made in the form of the servant, by their own act they are translated into the form of the serpent. This simile comes very close to expressing the quality of enjoyment that is not good but evil. Perhaps it is better described by narratives, as in the writings of the prophets, than through denotative definitions. Its root, however, is sin conceived primarily as making oneself the equal of God. In this spiritual state our actions of enjoyment are bound to deviate from true delight in endless ways. Just how they do emerges in many other texts that are concerned directly with economic questions.

Because the main burden of this essay is to integrate the older vision of biblical Judaism with that of Christ in the church, we shall only briefly examine the (less controversial) view that this vision of human purpose is developed continuously throughout the various documents of the Old Testament.

In reference to the narratives and laws connected with the exodus, scholars of the Old Testament seem universally to agree that the narratives of the land are at once metanarratives on creation. Through this land we behold the original Land, which God shaped into a garden of delight for royalty, and vice versa. If we miss this telescopic typology of canon, as it were, we miss the fullness of vision: no mere place, the Land is to be for Israel a royal place, and in that way, sacred.[33]

Careful study of the important Jubilee texts in Leviticus 25 reveals similar patterns of integration between themes of creation and redemption in economic moral life. Far from providing a vision of liberty to the captives through weakening property rights in the way of socialism, or a more ascetic-minded and morally utilitarian-shaped capitalism, these texts (as part of a re-creation story) reestablish the royal man and woman as godly lords over the land, who become the agents of liberty and justice for the poor and powerless. Contrary to much that is written, these texts actually *strengthen* their ownership of the land to the point of making it absolute and immutable. Indeed, the clearest logic of the Jubilee is not that Israel's families must give away or share what they own—quite the contrary. That God gave them the land implies directly that they may not liquidate their claims in perpetuity. Even if they have sold it, they get it back after what really amounts to a lease has run its course (in the fiftieth year).

All this is supported and made clearer by the parallel verses in the book of Exodus, where their inheritance of the land, not their existence as sojourners, makes them "a priestly kingdom and a holy nation" (Ex 19:5-6). From the conviction that God, who is King of the universe, gave them this land in perpetuity as their domain (for his purposes), it follows theologically that they who journey with this God are likewise kings and queens on earth, as God is royal in heaven. Likewise, it follows that as God is holy, so must they be holy. This voice of creation and law, as it were, which puts Israel's flourishing and delight in the strongest possible ontological terms, also gives the perspective we need on the terrible warnings, judgments and even cursings against the rich that occur in the Prophets.

In the Old Testament these voices of cursing against the rich are loudest in the Prophets. However, we must be careful not to presume that the principles beneath their preachings were ascetic or utilitarian. They were neither. First, prophets such as Amos were not by natural bent disposed to disparage material accomplishment of a culture committed to the production and enjoyment of good things for people. Their entire tone is rather one of thoroughgoing, wrenching lament over what is about to happen to the nation. Their vision is that the Lord God is going to reverse the mighty blessing of the exodus. The forthcoming descent from a position of royal liberty and delight, in a land flowing with milk and honey, is comparable in its terribleness perhaps only to the great flood. For it is (to the prophets) the unmaking of God's very own good creation, and that is lamentable only to prophets who deeply love the very thing God must destroy. Theirs was not the emotion of *Ressentiment,* in Nietzsche's sense of it, but of the deepest sorrow and sickness of heart. However we classify their principles, they stem from this view of the land and its grounding in God's good creation.[34]

This does not mean that the prophets have nothing to say to today's rich Christians. They certainly do. However, we will not see just how they do until we are clearer about the principles that animate their tirades against the rulers of their time. For just as we can be too easy on ourselves, we can also be too hard on ourselves and, worse, on others.

One way of identifying their moral principles for application is to isolate as specifically as possible the evils they addressed. Was it in the enjoyment of luxuries alone? Few would so argue. Was it in the enjoyment of luxuries while other (in theory) reachable persons went without? That seems not quite precise enough, for the whole tragedy of the coming exile entails the goodness of godly delight. Was it in the enjoyment of extravagance while others under their divinely appointed care went without? Now we are getting closer, but still not exactly to the mark. For we must reasonably judge that had they been celebrating in the larger moral context of working at just policies and doing their job of looking out for the poor (as David and others had done), and certainly had they not been destroying them on purpose, nothing like the exile would be justly warranted. Amos gives the clue to the essence of the evil. It is not the finery that Amos judges as evil, but the horrible hardness of the rulers toward the poor, even as they crushed them underfoot. As they ate, sang and danced on the battered bodies of widows and orphans, they celebrated their royal lineage and connection with the great King David. One thing they lacked, however. They did not "grieve the ruin of Joseph" (Amos 6:6).

If Amos is a good example, the prophets do not condemn the rich in an ascetic way, or in the utilitarian way for enjoying luxuries while others elsewhere (anywhere within reach) go without. They condemn the rich, in the context of clear-cut obligations, for falling to seductions of power and privilege. We must take note of the frightening ease by which they apparently crossed over from God-given delight into wanton hedonism and hardness toward the poor under their care. Utterly self-absorbed and without empathy, their unconnectedness and lack of grieving for people serves as a warning of what can happen to people with more than enough wealth, even to good Christian people. In this crossing over of the spirit, translated into actions of unbelievable oppression, the very same wonderful delights of wine, food, music, song and dance that David enjoyed became self-destructive evils of the worst kind. The prophets knew how to tell the difference between the one form of enjoyment and the other. A lack of grieving was at the bottom of everything. Of course, with the merrymaking, all-out oppression was the conspicuous fruit at the top.

We will not go on to discuss applications of the norms we have suggested are there. Enough has been said for the careful reader to construct an outline of what our approach might look like, with its models of "delight" on the one hand and "not grieving" on the other. Exactly how to state the principles that seem to emerge from those narratives is better left to moral theologians and trained ethicists. Nor will we go on to examine texts within the Psalms and writings of wisdom, which in their own different ways give shape to very similar notions.[35] Our concern remains to explore the Scriptures for roots of a unified human vision between creation in the Old Testament and Christology in the New Testament.

The character of Christ. All Christians not only believe in the incarnational nature of Christ's personhood but also seek to identify with Christ's truly human nature. Here "truly human" does not refer primarily to that Chalcedonian truth of Christ's ontological status as being "of one substance" with the human species. Instead it means something more like what the philosopher Sartre understood by the teleological sense of being human. For just as there is a teleology of being human in our cultural system and in the Old Testament that is rooted in a view of creation, so there is such a vision in the narratives of Jesus Christ, rooted in the story of his whole life. In this part of the essay, we shall examine a division of Christ's identity into his character identification and his character development. The meaning of these terms should become clear enough in context.

First, it follows that if we take literally the incarnation claim that in Jesus the eternal Word or Son of God deliberately decided to become human flesh and to dwell among us, we believe that Christ (unlike us) deliberately chose his human identity as a person. While this reveals and at once accomplishes God's solidarity with us, it also establishes a special oneness between God and a particular cultural identity. When the Son of God becomes human, he also becomes a first-century Jewish man, who was born of Mary and Joseph, grew up in their home in Nazareth of Galilee and became an adult working as a carpenter or builder. In all this there is what we may call character identification on God's part with a gender, race, religion, social and economic class, family structure, geographical environment—all of which shaped his character as God chose to have it shaped. Fair to say, the Word came in the likeness of sinful flesh, but he did not become that which was evil. The ancient premise holds that whatever he identifies with is not just redeemed, it is good.

Furthermore, in the history of Christianity, theologians have widely regarded the chosen social and economic class identity of Christ to be more or less normative for working out a general Christian economic identity in the world. The idea seems to be that his way of choosing and thus identifying with a human social and economic character is a model for Christians who, in following Jesus, must also choose where to identify their social and economic "incarnations" in the culture.

In contemporary moral theology many writers attempt to show (or merely assume) that the character of Jesus' incarnation is exclusively one of identification with the economic poor. They argue by continuation that Jesus was himself born to poor parents, that he thus lived in poverty, that his main associates and supporters came from the classes of poverty and that through this character *identification,* he evolved by what we may call narrative character *development* into one who lived ascetically, blessed poverty and generally cursed the rich.[36] As we shall see, however, the incarnation of Christ comprises a much larger field of economic class identity and culture than this view indicates.

It is undeniably true that Christ's incarnation was the deliberate expression on God's part of passionate love for the world of human beings. It is also of great theological, moral and spiritual urgency that Christians ponder the terrible downward movement of this cosmic event. For like all great actions, it is an act of character, and with that a hard commentary on our own pride. In a sense it is an act of socioeconomic character identification with a cultural mode of being human.

When Jesus was born his parents had but enough for the barest of sacrifices—two turtledoves—and the whole narrative of his birth is a gentle but clear rebuke against the arrogance of wealth, position and power. To have come from the glory of heaven to the manger of Bethlehem is a long way down. To have left the constant presence of adoring angels and archangels for the unspeakable humiliation of death on a Roman cross is truly to have descendend into hell. The contrasts speak for themselves on the larger issues. Nevertheless, when it comes to character identification of the economic kind, especially when such important judgments are being made about people in its light, we must form our classifications with delicate care.

The Palestine of Jesus' day was by all accounts strained to the breaking point by economic extremes. The political presence of Rome was felt everywhere, especially by the majority of people who were really poor. That is to say, they had no land and no steady way of making a living, and they rightly blamed their condition on the Roman system of trade and taxation. They were not merely poor, they were poor largely because they were oppressed.[37] On the other extreme were the very rich, and they (generally) owed their wealth to alliances made with the Roman powers. Political alliances spilled over into upward mobility in the religious institutions (rather like the Russian Orthodox Church under Soviet rule), so that religious leaders were not merely rich, they were rich largely by way of being oppressors of the most profane sort to the religious mind. In such an environment it almost follows that to be righteous is not to be rich, and thus to be poor is a blessing. However, the complexities of real life (as distinct from narrative life) obviously make that more a rhetorical than a moral or logical truth.

In the clearest possible economic terms, where do we locate Jesus on this spectrum? The truth is that the Gospels' Jesus belonged neither to the class of very richest people in Palestine nor to that of the very poorest. The most comprehensive evidence shows beyond much doubt that the Jesus of the New Testament belonged somewhere in between; he belonged to that often overlooked sector of the Jewish economy that constituted the middle. While people of his day would not have called him rich in economic terms, they would not have called him poor either.[38] The economic position of Jesus, growing up in the home of a builder and then working in that trade himself until about thirty, proves that he enjoyed a certain amount of economic security during the formative years of his life. Had his act of incarnation literally identified him with the poorest of the poor, he should have become one of those tens of thousands of homeless children who roamed the streets of the ancient world like small scavengers and, if they survived, grew into adults with the psychic damage that can only result from poverty. But by the tender care of his Father in heaven, Jesus did not grow up that way. He grew up in an environment conducive to innocence and consistent with the culture in which his sort of world-winning and soul-winning righteousness becomes humanly possible. Perhaps we have not reflected enough on the connections between his character identification with simple goodness (which is what it comes to) and the traditional doctrine of his own sinlessness.

Moreover, something of the same pattern of character identification emerges from careful reflection on Jesus' basic associations. All came from the trade classes in the Galilee. Peter, John, James and Andrew were not poverty-stricken. The brief descriptions in the Gospels are enough to indicate their relatively solid grounding in the economic culture. Furthermore, their action of leaving behind "everything," which radical Christian theorists like to stress, is not itself very impressive if everything they abandoned amounted to little.

Sociological historians of the New Testament such as Martin Hengel rightly observe that one circle of Jesus' followers did their "following" at home and at work.[39] Peter's mother-in-law, the family of Lazarus and the women of means (Lk 8:3) who supported Jesus and his disciples all indicate the existence of a secondary circle of propertied people who, like the righteous rich of the exodus, identified with God, and God with them. Of course there was also that third sprawling circle of supporters, which the text classifies generally as "the multitudes." Sick, lame, blind, deaf, mute, possessed by demons—these poor, too, heard the good news and rejoiced. It seems that the larger event of character identification in Jesus' earthly station was, in different ways, identification with all different economic classes. In a sense, his presence brought all together into a kind of creative and redemptive harmony in which all gave what they had and all received what they needed and then some.

With respect to our debate over the Christian existential vision, the character identity of Jesus, while its primary movement is a dreadful downward spiral of "becoming poor for us," strangely elevates rather than diminishes us in our ordinariness of economic existence. Perhaps the teleology of that spiral, "that we might become rich" (2 Cor 8:9), corresponds to the blessed affirmation of human beings that is the incarnation (Jn 3:16). This affirmation is not in the abstract terms of "humanity" but in the earthy terms of productive work, craftsmanship, building an economically secure home life. All these primary enjoyments of wealth (even as others do not enjoy them, and even as much of it comes unfiltered through the auspices of Rome's oppressive colonialism) are once again, nevertheless, pronounced *good*. Of course they can become evil, but they are not evil by themselves, no more than the Garden was, or the Promised Land or the wine and song of royal David. Therefore, in respect to the relevant theories of economic infrastructure (capitalism versus socialism) and vocation (downward versus upward mobility), the incarnation affirms and challenges both, albeit in different ways and on different levels, by integrating them. This opens the way for considering that an affirmation of enjoyment in our contemporary sense may be possible.

In the narratives, we may also think of Jesus undergoing character development in his economic life. Moral theologians have helped us to discover Christ's revolutionary character, in contrast to the "gentle Jesus, meek and mild" of Sunday-school lore. His demand that his disciples abandon everything to go forth in prophetic procession to proclaim the coming kingdom of God is downplayed. This Jesus confronts the rich young ruler with implied charges of materialism and loss of salvation. In the presence of rich people who came for a different sermon, he tells parables that portray one rich man as a (literally) damned fool and another as suffering in the torrid fires of hell. In apparent reversal of all godly wisdom, he pronounces his "poor" followers blessed and then declares curses upon the "rich." Radical Christians rightly challenge rich Christians to stop looking away, to look this Jesus straight in the eye and to respond with integrity to his demands, blessings, curses and commands of promise.

Many more questions arise from Jesus' radical demand of divestment—what at first looks like an ascetic vision and strong support for deconstructing the existential ideology of our materialistic consumer culture—than we can grapple with here. Nevertheless, we can see, as already suggested in the foregoing section, that things are not so cut and dried as they might seem with the character development of Jesus in the Gospels. As with the prophets, we must very carefully seek to discern the principles that gave shape to his character, life and teachings. In this search we must try to avoid ascribing to Jesus an entirely new vision of human purpose, alien and contrary to that of his Jewish antecedents. That would amount nearly to denial of the very things that made his religion what it was and which connected that faith with our own. While the cosmology of delight and flourishing may not be the most conspicuous theme of his life, in an almost Kierkegaardian sense of repetition, it is powerfully present. Perhaps we can state with confidence in the Old Testament view of creation, and in concert with the ancient adversaries of Gnosticism: "Once a cosmos, always a cosmos."[40]

Close reading reveals that Jesus did not generally demand literal divestment and liquidation of all property. When he called Peter, John, Andrew and James, their leaving amounted to putting their capital in storage. Moreover, I have already mentioned the second circle of disciples who "gave everything" by keeping everything, albeit in redirected modes of having and using it. The example of Zacchaeus also shows that, unlike with the rich young ruler, more than one pattern of economic life was possible.

Second, we must be very careful how we read and apply the middle sections of the Gospels where Jesus does command almost total divestment. These radical demands and actions come at that extraordinary time when Jesus transfers his powers of healing and casting out demons to his followers.[41] As his sayings in the Upper Room suggest, that situation was clearly momentary and certainly not normative for the church (Lk 22:35-36). Finally, even at the center of these far-reaching demands comes that almost paradoxical promise (again Kierkegaard) that this trust leads not down the path of the ascetic or of the utilitarian. It oddly evolves, by repetition, into getting back ten, twenty, even a hundredfold, the very things they gave away (Lk 18:28-30). It is that most mysterious and truly sacred sort of enlargement by reduction. As with his own being exalted to the right hand of the Father, the end of that trust (in this world *and* in the age to come) is a glory greater even than the great Solomon ever knew.

Amid their wandering, the lives of Jesus and his followers displayed this theme of celebrative delight in the good things of the world. As Richard Horsley, in defense of very different points, has observed, not only did the second circle of disciples remain propertied in the economic culture, but even the first circle of followers, while they were itinerant, did not live in poverty. On the contrary, their life together with Jesus was marked conspicuously by festive merrymaking, eating and drinking.[42] This last observation leads to my final main point: the same Son of Man who had "nowhere to lay his head" was also, always and to the end, the celebrative Christ of delight, the one who came "eating and drinking," the Royal Man of God's first vision in the beginning.

If we consider the three "offices" of Christ in traditional Christian theology as those of Prophet, Priest and King, then we may fairly judge that in discussions of materialism and human identity under capitalism moral theologians have stressed the prophetic and priestly character of Christ (and obligations arising therefrom for Christians), but it seems we have not reckoned very directly with his kingliness. Nevertheless, there is much in the narrative to encourage making just that connection, and when we do, the whole picture of Jesus as an economic person becomes fuller, more liberating—but in some sense more demanding— because it really hits home.

We must note the royal effect of Jesus' own personal identity in the narratives as one "who came eating and drinking." This theme is among the most profoundly revealing descriptions we have of his character as it developed. In Jesus' own deepest personhood, it seems, was a joy that could not be contained, not even by powerful and intimidating legalistic convention. It burst forth constantly in celebration with friends and followers (some of them unsavory) through food and drink. Moreover, there was a real sense in which this image, eating and drinking, was what defined him to the public as the royal figure that he truly was, in spite of what Barth liked to call the "veiling" of his royal power. That royal identity is "unveiled," as it were, in the protomessianic feasting he and his followers enjoyed.[43]

Again, as Jesus' confrontations with the scribes shows, this is a deep theme in the character development of his identity in the Gospels. It shows that in his profound joy, even as the shadow of the cross advanced ominously upon him, the voice of creation triumphed over all the evils around him. He lived life as if it really was that great royal banquet of victory for shalom that he spoke about so very often. Jesus' eating and drinking was an intense commentary on the goodness of the *abundance* of what is good.

Abundance is good, not in spite of suffering all around, but because of it. In Jesus' eating and drinking is eschatological hope for all human beings, especially for the ones who presently hunger and thirst for shalom. Furthermore, in his eating and drinking, those of us who do not suffer want may find freedom from guilt for what we have got and vision for our devotion, in great and small ways, to making possible for those who have not. His eating and drinking of the superfluous did not make him a "drunkard and a glutton," as his enemies claimed, any more than his permitting the woman of shame to pour pure nard (worth a good year's wages) on his head made him the outrageously self-serving degenerate that some judged he was (Mk 14:4-5).

Conclusion

A great deal more must be done to complete the job of forging a Christian view of economic life in the midst of "new things." Nevertheless, it seems clear that the resources do exist within the Scriptures for containing the most actively fermenting new wines. In both doctrines of creation and Christology the resources are there, just as they were at the wedding feast at Cana, for developing principles by which to affirm the enjoyment of wealth while seeking spiritual health and social justice. That is exactly what prophetic Christian involvement in the culture of capitalism requires. Although there is no space here to demonstrate it, this same conclusion is supported by careful and studied reading of the details of Jesus' commands, sayings and parables on wealth.[44] Hopefully, other Christian thinkers, especially those who lead the way in the cause for the poor, will help outline strategies for the rich (in a comparative sense) that encourage neither assimilation into nor separation from the culture that God has placed us within as his agents of redemption.

9
How a Christian African-American Reflects on Stewardship in a Consumer-Oriented Society

Clifford A. Jones Sr.

How Christian African-Americans reflect on stewardship in a consumer-oriented society is colored by numerous variables and the level of commitment to Jesus Christ as Lord in principle and/or praxis. This was evident during various historical periods: the era of slavery, the Black Renaissance, the eras of segregation and of integration, and the post-Civil Rights era. The economic status of Christian African-Americans—poor, middle-class, wealthy, employed, underemployed, self-employed—and their educational level also will be reflective in stewardship patterns. These areas will have significant impact on African-Americans as Christian stewards in a manipulating consumer-oriented society where the theme is "Buy Baby Buy."

This essay will not allow an exhausting exploration of all the aforementioned issues. However, there are four areas this writer will present to expose, inform and stretch our minds. The first area of discussion will be history, in order to observe how Christian Negroes responded to and thrived in a segregated society. Throughout this essay the words

Negro, colored, black, Afro-American and *African-American* will be used to reflect historical periods. These words have distinct historical significance. It was not until the utilization of the word *black* during the Civil Rights era that people of African descent used the word of their choice (knowing that *black* was not universally accepted even among people of African descent). However, the significance was in no longer allowing others to use imposed negative words to describe us. In the initial part of this essay, I will use the word *Negro*, knowing that it has no descriptive value or intrinsic significance related to personhood that is not captured in adjectives.

The second area focuses on advertising's appeal to our visual sense instead of to our intellect. The third area examines the problem of racial disparity in the allocation of economic resources. The final emphasis is on empowerment, and moving from seeing to thinking as Christian African-American consumers.

W. E. B. Du Bois concluded that "any study of economic cooperation among Negroes must begin with the church group."[1] As the only institution available for spiritual nurture and affirmation, the Negro church was all things to all its people. It created schools, homes for the aged, secret societies to keep in touch, banks, insurance companies, benevolent and burial associations, black cemetery associations, mutual and benefit societies, and more. It organized charitable and relief efforts in the community, disseminated news and information, led movements for social betterment, and provided members with an extended family.[2]

Money was always limited and the church encouraged members to "make sacrifices for the Lord's work," to "make do" and to always expect a blessing from God, for "God loves a cheerful giver." Negroes were encouraged to save in order to have a nest egg for hard times. This mentality is expressed by Ida Wells: "Let the Afro American depend on no party but himself for his salvation. Let him continue to education, to character and above all, to put money in his purse. When he has money, and plenty of it, parties and races will become his servants."[3] The reverend sought to elevate his congregation not only through preaching salvation, community responsibility and the wise use of money but also through personal example, for he was usually in the forefront.

Alonyo Herndon, a former slave, said, "We can spend all our days shaking our fingers at capitalism or we can make it work." This call was amplified by the Reverend Dr. B. F. Johnson when he was pastor of the Metropolitan Baptist Church in Newark, New Jersey. He was fond of saying, "We need to put overalls on our money and let it work for us."

Economic Development in the Negro Community and Church
The following are some notable pioneers:

Bishops Richard Allen and Absalom Jones founded the Free African Society in 1787, which attempted to meet both religious and social needs.

Benjamin Tucker Tanner, editor of the *AME Christian Recorder* from 1868 to 1884, urged black people to imitate the economic advancement of Jews in Europe.

John Merrick founded North Carolina Mutual, one of the two largest black life insurance companies, in Durham, North Carolina, in 1898.

Alonyo Herndon founded Atlanta Life Insurance Company in 1905.

The Reverend J. Milton Waldron founded a mutual benefit society in a Baptist church in 1901 that later became the Afro-American Industrial Insurance Society of Jacksonville.

Booker T. Washington preached a gospel of wealth that espoused the major values of the Protestant Ethic: thrift, industry and self-help. He called for "Negro support of Negro business."

Robert Wesley Morgan, a black dentist and leading AME Zion layman, taught classes in economics and household finances at both the Catherine Street AME Zion Church and the Ebenezer Baptist Church of Poughkeepsie, New York, in 1936.

The Reverend Adam Clayton Powell Jr. took more radical and publicly visible measures by leading civil rights protests on economic issues in the 1950s.

Father Divine fostered economic self-help programs, economic development of the Negro community through housing and employment, and feeding programs during the 1950s.

The African ancestors of American Negroes had developed an economic orientation around agriculture and bartering and selling (fruit, clothing, beads, wood carving, tools, meat) that far exceeded the narrow, paternalistic, cyclic and racist economic structures on the plantations. Cultivation of crops, domestic services, crafts, pottery and basket weaving all played an essential role in the worth of the Negro slave. Although plantation life took advantage of all these skills, opportunities were not afforded to the Negro slave to participate in the profits. While they strengthened the economy by providing these goods and services, they were thought of and treated as among the expendable commodities.

In the slave environment the Negro church struggled in a society where for them freedom was nonexistent and health protection was herbal medicine and prayer. Their society did not provide a buffer to abate trauma and personal travesty. This is perceptibly demonstrated in the rearing of children, where an elder matriarch was daycare for their children who were fed from a trough like young suckling pigs. The quality of housing was inferior to huts; employment was one hundred percent from can't to can't—"can't see the sunrise until you can't see when it sets." However, in the midst of this catastrophe the Negro church provided a place of praise, empowerment and temporary peace. The congregants owned literally nothing—not even themselves—and their owners sought to control their awareness of God and faith for their own economic gains, which took precedence over the spiritual interest of *their* Negroes. Yet cultural black pearls of truth found their way through small crooked cracks in this sickening society, and progress was accomplished. Kinfolk and community filled in the gaps during this historical transitional period through sharing, borrowing a cup of sugar, lending money, giving and receiving hand-me-downs, and continuously taking burdens to the Lord. "Nevertheless, as important as the stage of survival economics was for poor people, it was inevitably marked by extreme dependency, uncertainty and insecurity."[4]

In the mid-nineteenth century, Booker T. Washington spearheaded the development of the National Negro Business League to encourage enterprise. The League was founded on certain assumptions that were designed to generate high character, develop racial respect, cultivate economic stability and lay the economic groundwork for future generations.[5] Washington developed these assumptions knowing that the most severe forms of racial discrimination against Negroes were economic in character. By keeping the Negroes landless and without allowing them to accumulate wealth, white racists controlled their physical and social destiny. The everyday economic strategy of the Negro became one of "survivin' one day at a time," "eking out a living," "just makin' do," "gettin' by," waiting for "my ship to come in," working and praying "till my change comes." This demonstrated tenacity was not an otherworldly mystical encounter but a this-worldy experience that found support from and in the Negro church and preacher. These economic practices conditioned and systemically manipulated realities, causing the historical and social transition from Negro to colored to black to Afro-American to African-American consciousness. It ushered to the forefront conscientious religious leadership, leading fresh soldiers in an old battle for dignity and economic stability with renewed vigor. Among the leaders:

The Honorable Elijah Muhammad created opportunities and promoted racial pride and dignity through the Black Muslims of America. He stressed the necessity of "so called Negroes" to establish businesses to purchase farms and control their own economic destiny.

The Reverend Dr. Gardner Taylor, while serving as pastor of the historic Concord Baptist Church in Brooklyn, spearheaded the development of a church-operated credit union to provide loans and opportunities for investing, a state-of-the-art nursing home that provides jobs and housing for the elderly in the church and community, and a private school to provide alternative educational opportunities.

The Reverend Leon Sullivan, pastor of Zion Baptist Church in Philadelphia, recognized the need for a community-based employment training facility and helped to found in 1964 the Opportunities Industrialization Centers of America. This organization quickly became a nationwide phenomenon, operating in seventy cities within five years and handling federal government contracts worth $18 million. Sullivan also was responsible for the "10-36" plan, initiated in 1962. This plan called for persons to give ten dollars each month for thirty-six months to support the Philadelphia community Investment Cooperative; $200 of every $360 subscription was invested in the for-profit Progress Investment Associates, while the remaining $160 was donated to the nonprofit Zion Charitable Trust.

The Reverend Dr. William A. Jones, senior minister of the Bethany

Church of Brooklyn, developed the Harvest Manor restaurant, which has created jobs and provided culinary arts training within this inner-city community.

The Reverend Floyd Flake, Allen AME Zion Church in Jamaica, Queens, set up a church-sponsored housing cooperation that rehabilitated ten stores in the neighborhood and created a housing development fund, a home care agency, three hundred housing units and an $11 million complex for senior citizens.

The Reverend Dr. Charles Adams, pastor of the Hartford Avenue Baptist Church in Detroit, established a multipurpose social service agency that handles everything from medical needs to nursing care. The church family has created a vocational program to provide persons with marketable skills.

The Reverend O. T. Tomes, senior minister of the New Mount Olive Baptist Church in Asheville, North Carolina, has developed and nurtured a unique partnership for the past twenty-five years with the Asheville Buncombe Community Christian Ministry (ABCCM). They jointly built and manage a health clinic in the African-American community that specifically confronts health-related issues germane to African-Americans. The church also sponsors Project Kutana Outreach, the result of a grant from the state of North Carolina to provide services to reduce infant mortality through education. Project Kutana Outreach provides medical health services to mothers and a strong mentoring program to young single mothers with older parents. Probably the major economic success of this church family of under three hundred members has been the growth in home ownership. Some twenty-five years ago Tomes said, "When I came here most of the members were tenants. I proceeded to teach financial management through tithing, debt management and saving. I'm proud to say that the majority of this membership are home owners."

The Reverend Jason Barr, pastor of Macedonia Baptist Church in Pittsburgh, has led this inner-city church to establish the Macedonia Faith Endowment Center, which has received over $300,000 in grants over a four-year period, as well as several million dollars to run an adoption and foster care agency over a five-year period. The church began a Spirit of Entrepreneurship Ministry to teach teens to start and operate businesses so that they can practice production as an alternative to consumerism.

The Reverend Dr. John D. Fuller, pastor of Lewis Chapel Baptist Church in Fayetteville, North Carolina, has led the effort to build fifty units of housing for low-income persons and is preparing to develop eight acres into an educational and recreational complex in a rural area.

The Reverend Dr. Robert Murray is pastor of the historic First Baptist-Bute Street Church in Norfolk, Virginia, which has provided services for the past seventy years through Shepherd's Way, an adult housing ministry funded in part by the church. Presently a $3 million family life center is under construction to provide child development, K-6 private educational opportunity and other community development partnerships. Also, this area provides space for a flea market where ten to twelve vendors can sell items at reasonable prices.

These examples are only a few of the economic success stories of religious leaders who take seriously the necessity of intentional involvement in the empowerment of African-Americans through economic interdependence. These examples represent churches in the Northeastern and the Southern parts of the United States, from large inner-city churches to small rural churches in retirement cities.

Becoming Critical Consumers

Our consumer-oriented society does not promote critical thinking, so we have not learned as consumers to use critical skills. Taking advantage of this, advertisers appeal strongly to the ocular sense of their targeted market, not to the intellect. Two very popular magazines that are widely distributed in the African-American community are good examples of this very thing. I will refer to them as *Alpha* and *Omega*.

Alpha is a widely circulated magazine in the African-American community, with a targeted market of persons with annual incomes between $27,000 and $50,000, especially college-educated, working single women. In a sample of this magazine consisting of 178 pages, 102 pages contained consumer-oriented messages.

Judging by its content, *Alpha* is more of a quasi-consumer guide than a magazine. Its theme is spend and charge, not manage and save. There were no ads encouraging home ownership or the purchase of land, nor about IRAs, 401(k) plans or investments in stocks or bonds. There is no strong appeal to thoughtful financial management but sharp, colorful, instant gratification ("Don't postpone for tomorrow what you deserve today"). In this issue were advertisements for a host of products and services: 18 cosmetic products (African Pride, Avon, Estyle, Maybelline), 9 vehicles (Ford Explorer, Cadillac, Chevrolet, Aurora, Dodge Caravan, GMC Van, Saturn, Lincoln, Buick), 5 foods and drinks (Coca-Cola, Sunny Delight, grits, Lowrey's seasoning, milk), 5 cigarettes (Capri, Kool, Misty, Newport, Virginia Slims), 5 liquors (cognac, Seagram's Gin, Miller, Coors, Busch), 4 household products (Pepto Bismol, Tide, Pine-Sol, Morton's Salt), 4 financial businesses (American Express, Herd House, GMAC, H&R Block), 2 insurance companies (Allstate, Prudential), 2 restaurants (McDonald's, Denny's), 2 cereals (Cheerios, Frosted Flakes) and others (Shell, Amway, KMart, birth control, DisneyWorld, HBO and Luvs diapers).

Omega is a monthly magazine with a wide circulation among African-American professionals. It targets college-educated businessmen with incomes of $30,000 to $60,000. Of the 256 pages in a sample issue, 141 contained consumer-oriented messages in advertisements for the following: 8 vehicles (Saturn, Toyota, Lexus, Lincoln, Ford, Cadillac, Dodge, Buick), 5 liquors (Absolut Brooklyn vodka, cognac, Miller, Coors, Busch), 3 cosmetics (Avon, Estyle, Dark and Lovely), 2 airlines (Delta, United Airlines) and others (Allstate, HBO, McDonald's, Hertz, Bell South, Federal Express, IBM, MCI, Xerox, Pepsi, coffee, Kodak, cigarettes, Sears, DisneyWorld, Seven-Eleven, Marriott/Hyatt, American Express). There were no ads that stressed home ownership, debt management, long-term investment options or financial programs for economic stability.

In his work *New Essays on the Psychology of Art,* Arnheim Rudolf has a chapter entitled "A Plea for Visual Thinking." His clean, terse argument is worthy of consideration in this consumer-oriented society:

> Perceiving and thinking require each other. They complement each other. The task of perception is supposed to be limited to collecting raw materials for cognition. Once the material has been gathered thinking enters the scene, at a supposedly high cognitive level, and does the processing. Perception would be useless without thinking; thinking without perception would have nothing to think about.[6]

Targeted consumer-oriented advertising has replaced the slave master, and with calculated slick wording the utilization of heroes and irresistible ocular appeal are poisoning perception and trivializing thinking. Consumerism specializes in capturing the eye, which becomes the determining factor in what little is thought and what much is bought. Thoughtlessness of this kind takes place in the realm of the visual, not perceptual; it is not about intellectual reasoning or logical reductionism, but about sentimental gratification. Consequently, thinking becomes visual thinking, whereas when careless thinking is practiced even the Bible and being a Christian steward have quaint influence on the Christian consumer. The visual appeal is clearly demonstrated in the following ad from *Omega:*

> She carried you; she raised you; she fixed lasagna just the way you like it; now you are breaking her heart. How could you forget your mother's e-mail address?
>
> Everyone and their mother is on the Internet these days. So how can your business thrive in this strange new world?

Accompanying this advertisement is a beautiful African-American woman with no makeup, nail polish or jewelry, and with meticulously structured wrinkles cascading under the vigilance of warm enlightened eyes—a beautiful personification of parenthood. "She fixed lasagna just the way you liked it." What is wrong with this? How many African-Americans over thirty-five, especially if they were reared in the South, had mothers who prepared lasagna? They prepared sweet potato custard, pinto beans, even macaroni and cheese—but lasagna? What is the correlation of a thriving business and Mom being on e-mail? If she is like most mothers who enjoy talking to their sons, this becomes a corporate expense, and if you own a business you ought to be able to call your mother from home.

Economic Resources and Racial Disparities

A Jamaican proverb says, "Save money and money will save you." However, everywhere we look the message is spend-charge, spend-charge, spend-charge. A 1994 survey by the National Foundation for Consumer Credit found that nearly 18 million U.S. households need some form of help in dealing with debt. *The State of Black America 1995* reports that "economic disparity between urban America and urban Black America is becoming more pronounced whether in central cities, suburbs or edge cities," as figure 9.1 shows.

	Black	White
Median net worth per person	$ 4,169	$43,279
Median net worth per household	$10,278	$79,169

Figure 9.1. Black and white households by net worth, 1988[7]

Poverty rates are high for older black women, in spite of their presence in the labor market, because of lower earnings in their prime age years and insufficient pension coverage in the jobs they have held. Since black men have also received low incomes and often die younger than white men, black women had fewer opportunities than white women to combine their earnings with those of a male partner with greater earning potential. Thus savings, social security benefits and the accumulation of assets were much lower.[8] Figure 9.2 illustrates the disparities in poverty rates by race.

	Black	White	Hispanic
Females			
65 and over	49.6	20.9	38.2
65 to 74	45.3	15.8	35.0
75 and over	55.8	27.8	44.5
Males			
65 and under	38.5	10.2	27.0
65 to 74	34.7	8.5	26.0
75 and over	46.4	13.2	29.2

Figure 9.2. Percent of elderly who are poor or near poor, 1990[9]

This disparity is evident in all sorts of families, whether headed by a male or a female, as shown in figure 9.3.

Household income (in dollars)	Black	White
Less than 5,000	11.9	3.0
Less than 10,000	27.3	8.5
10,000 to 34,999	46.7	43.2
More than 35,000	25.9	48.2
More than 50,000	12.6	27.4

Figure 9.3. Percentage of families receiving income in selected ranges, 1988

The limited resources available to African-Americans dictate the level of consumption of some items. At best we take trips through the pages of *National Geographic* or seek other ways to deaden the pain of this ethos. The lack of opportunity to accumulate long-term savings spawns the desire for short-term purchases that can be paid for in six to thirty-six, maybe as much as sixty, months. This reality is compounded by the fact that in the past banks would not grant African-Americans loans. As author James Noel said, "you couldn't get a loan during the '50s and '60s for a business, land or house. You could borrow money for nonsense, cars, clothes and furniture." Has anything changed? An article by Elizabeth Gleick entitled "The Impossible Dream" in the February 19, 1996, issue of *Time* substantiates what Noel said forty years ago. Despite all the grand talk about rebuilding Los Angeles, business owner Terrence Payne cannot get the credit to start over.

Payne's business had been in the family since 1944. If anyone had told him on April 29, 1992, as he watched a wall of flames destroy his grocery store, laundry and rental apartments, that four years later his lot would still be empty, he would have refused to believe it. He thought he would be able to rebuild his family-owned business within a year of the L.A. riots. "I never thought it would take this long; I never imagined it could be so painful." "He's not atypical," says Linda Griego, a former deputy mayor who is now president of a redevelopment organization. "There were others like him who every time they took two steps forward went back ten."

Two years before the riots, Payne's insurance policy had been canceled because he was in a "geographically undesirable location." Payne spent his life's savings of $100,000 plus an additional borrowed $85,000 on building permits, blueprints and the like but could not get a city-sponsored loan for his $1.2 million project. When Payne threatened to file a complaint with the Federal Reserve Bank, accusing the city of redlining, he was offered $585,000 on the condition that he put up his lot and $100,000 of his mother's property as collateral. Even after this he still needed $350,000 to begin construction. Left vacant, the land was declining in value. "This puts me on a 'slippery slope.' I have no income, I have no building and I have a debt of more than $1,000 a month." According to Linda Griego, "Even now, black applicants are rejected more than twice as often as whites with similar income and credit histories."

Getting Back to "Making Do"

We have seen but a glimpse of the economic conditioning realities faced by African-Americans. They are encouraged through marketing efforts to spend-charge, spend-charge, spend-charge, yet are being controlled by a society that has not practiced social, economic or racial parity. Credit cards gave African-Americans the opportunities to meet short-term gratification needs. Around 1965 we became mainline consumers in a limited, controlled market. However, this credit was not for major items, business ventures, acquisition of land for development, investments or houses in certain neighborhoods, and insurance was higher in the Negro neighborhoods. The lines of credit were limited; African-Americans had to have more for down payments and collateral. Terms were for twelve to seventy-two months with a range of $1,800 to $10,000 at the highest interest rates.

Yet as a people, we found ways to survive our economic oppression. Stewardship was praxis before the principle was articulated: we shared hand-me-downs, used everything, shopped in bargain basements, specialized in leftovers and scrapings (a "mess of this" and a "mess of that"), and as Grandpa sang every Sunday morning, "Somehow we made it, through it all God brought me through." We were thrifty with the money we had. As Ida B. Wells taught, "We do need to have money in our bank accounts. It allows us to live without desperation, and thereby frees us from a subservient position. Let us use money wisely, refrain from spending it as if there is no tomorrow and learn how to make our money work for us."[10]

Our consumer-oriented society intentionally creates the desire for unlimited wants through short-term, thoughtless purchasing. Christian African-Americans seem to be practicing limited restraint in this consumer-oriented society. A restricted economic position controls the appetite of African-Americans but has not diminished the taste. Historically, there was more discipline relative to the Christian faith, wedded with limited resources in a structured segregated society. These parameters—"just gettin' by," "making do," "barely making ends meet"—all made us prudent consumers. "Saving for a rainy day" was preached at home and reaffirmed in church every Sunday. Much of what society deprived us of, the church took on the responsibility to provide. As Gregory J. Reed points out,

Wholistic is a word mentioned frequently today whenever the ministry and mission of the black church is discussed. What it means is that the black church has begun to *re-focus* its attention on the critical needs of the whole individual and the whole community rather than on just spiritual or religious needs. I say *"re-focus"* because in the early days of the church, a wholistic ministry was taken for granted; there were no alternatives for African-American Christians because religious needs always included survival, or common needs as well as spiritual needs.[11]

According to C. Eric Lincoln and Lawrence H. Mamiya, the following statements summarize the varied economic roles of the black church:

1. The Black church helped to create the black self-help tradition and an ethos of economic rationality for free and enslaved blacks.

2. Through its priestly function, the Black church provided comfort, nurture and care among an outcast people, "a refuge in a hostile white world." They also took part in the liberation tradition by becoming economically independent institutions.

3. Black churches, along with quasi-religious mutual aid societies and fraternal orders, created important economic institutions during the late nineteenth and early twentieth centuries.

4. Black churches are themselves significant economic institutions in black communities. Recent studies indicate that the churches and the area of religion receive the highest percentage of charitable donations (75.4 percent) and volunteer time (35.3 percent).

5. Spurred by their participation in the activism of the Civil Rights period and the "war on poverty" programs, a growing number of pastors in large black churches (also a number of small and rural churches) are becoming involved again in economic initiatives and projects in their own communities.[12]

Unofficially, the African-American church receives about $2 billion a year through dues, donations, tithes and other charitable gifts. With in-kind gifts and volunteerism the figures could be doubled. The African-American church is the most successful and adequately funded institution in our communities. We have met the challenges of providing resources for economic development and services. This strong commitment to the stewardship of giving, however, must be complemented by the stewardship of restraint so that the Christian consumer is not controlled by unlimited wants. As the twenty-first century approaches, we African-American Christians can practice some responsibility over what we purchase and move from short-term gratification to medium-term planning relative to our finances. African-American Christian leadership must build and broaden consumer awareness while escalating biblical teachings about effective stewardship. This era calls the African-American church to empowerment through economic education grounded in the belief that Jesus Christ is Lord. It is essential that African-Americans become proactive for economic stability and freedom rather than reactive to economic disaster.

The African-American church and other African-American religious organizations have always risen to the challenges posed by slavery, the lynching era, civil rights, human rights, urban displacement, integration and racism, and the twenty-first century still finds us in a valley of unlimited wants between slick advertising and years of neglect. Climb we will and must toward economic empowerment. Our base must encompass community groups and social groups and must be interdenominational as we plan and market strategies to educate the African-American as consumer.

Wholism has always been a practice in the African-American church. This belief is rooted tenaciously in the biblical teachings of Jesus and not the practices of the Protestant churches. The Holy Bible teaches that Jesus the Christ was about good; the kingdom of God was for all persons to have equal access to goods and services and to practice parity (distributing more to some, according to need) over equity (distributing equally to all) as long as necessary. The sick with AIDS/HIV and Alzheimer's disease are our responsibility; economic security is possible by seeking the kingdom first. Unfortunately, African-American Christians are practicing neither perception thinking nor the teachings of Jesus in this consumer-oriented society, and the Christian church must sound a clear, unapologetic message about stewardship empowerment through consumer education. African-Americans must become more responsible, using whatever resources available, regardless how marginal.

Churches may wish to consider a three-phase ministry toward interdependence as African-American Christian stewards:

Phase 1

a. Provide consumer counseling services for families, single adults and youth with volunteers from the church.

b. Develop strategies to break the psychological dependency for short-term gratification of unlimited wants.

c. Revisit the practice of "making do" (living within one's means).

d. Teach and preach the biblical perspective on money management, consumerism, saving, investing and community responsibility.

Phase 2

a. Teach youth the value of money management in the context of depreciation (i.e., nonsense purchasing).

b. Develop church/community investment groups, with the emphasis on ownership and education for our children and our neighbor's children.

c. Look into the church's purchasing property and sponsoring ethnic community businesses (e.g., grocery stores, franchises, apparel and appliance stores).

d. Develop a fund for providing business loans to congregants who have demonstrated faith, commitment, community responsibility and a structural work ethic.

e. Challenge congregants to exercise their responsibility as stewards to volunteer their time and gifts in the community.

Phase 3

a. Form coalitions with tenants to make landlords accountable; purchase rental property.

b. Promote health through eating less fast food and through cooking nutritious meals daily.

c. Create partnerships between older persons and younger families for consumer mentoring.

d. Have seminars and workshops using newspapers, magazines and other materials with advertisements so that Christian stewards can become wise consumers.

Conclusion

Numerous variables adversely affect Christian African-Americans in the consumer-oriented society. African-Americans do not experience parity in the workplace, redlining is practiced relative to loans, there are fewer dollars available for investments, and short-term gratification purchases are made in attempts to experience some of the good life. The tactics used to create an appetite to consume, purchase, charge, have, use and enjoy are infinite. Being deprived of these opportunities for so long created a fragile and vulnerable consumer. Precisely at this juncture is where the Christian church must offer a clear, crisp word: "But strive first for the kingdom of God and his righteousness, and all these things will be given to you as well" (Mt 6:33). This text does not call for a vow of providentially ordained poverty but to place everything in and about one's life in perspective to the kingdom of God. Being gratified in the short term requires an assembly line of new and different things and adventures that perpetuate debt for "nonsense items." The Christian church of the last five decades has become silent and sterile and has allowed materialism and greed to become the litany in worship. Consequently, faith has been limited from having any bearing on the Christian as consumer.

Historians and anthropologists have been baffled as to how Negro slaves, who became colored tenants and who are now African-Americans, could seemingly be so happy and exemplify the epitome of joy. How could these people, possessed with so little of this world's goods, robbed and maligned, mistreated and called derogatory insensitive names, seem secure and live with such hope? The answer has been in our undaunted faith in a just and merciful God, experienced in Jesus the Christ whose name is above every name; who promised to make a way out of no way; who promised to provide for our children and grandchildren. Our hope was in a God who can be trusted. Until the African-American Christian of the twenty-first century embraces this same faith and hope, unlimited wants and instant gratification will be the order of the day.

Part 3

●●●●●●●●●●●●●●●●●●●●●●●●●●●●●●●●●●●

Consumption &
the Future of Faith

10
The Theology of Consumption & the Consumption of Theology

Toward a Christian Response to Consumerism
Rodney Clapp

Every person under the sun must eat to live. In that sense we are all blameless and—as at a feast lovingly prepared by a grandmother—glorious consumers. There is nothing wrong, and much that is right, about consuming to live. Hence I have heard a rabbi speak winningly from his tradition of "consecrated consumption." What worries some people about consumption (and I confess at the outset to be one of these ambivalent creatures, fat but troubled in paradise) is that the affluent, technologically advanced West seems more and more focused not on consuming to live but on living to consume. The problem with consumption, and the consumer capitalism that has pushed it to feverish historical extremes, is that it has become so all-consuming.

Even Americans—we citizens of what Harvard historian of marketing Richard Tedlow cites as the premier "nation of consumers"—recognize problems with the extremes to which we have taken consumption as a way of life.[1] The trash buckets for recycled garbage, nonexistent ten years ago but now standing sentry outside every suburban home in my neighborhood, bear testimony to one of the most obvious problems. We are sensitized to the ecological damage fostered by the centralized, technology-intensive, intentionally wasteful ("planned obsolescence") society fostered by consumer capitalism. Perhaps the environmentalists sometimes go too far, but however overstated their warnings may be, there is no denying the murky brown clouds of smog hanging over Los Angeles or the swimming beaches shut down on Lake Michigan as tides of sewage roll ashore.

A hardly less obvious, or problematic, feature of consumer capitalism is the inescapable barrage of advertising, coaching and coaxing multitudinous desires innocent and not-so-innocent. One observer estimates that the average American is exposed to 16,000 commercial messages, symbols and reminders every single day.[2] So inundated, we are hardly aware how pervasive and even invasive these images and messages are.

Their force struck me in 1996 while, in the course of researching the subject of consumption, I spent three days at a Christian community bereft of televisions and radios and removed from billboard-besieged highways. When I arrived back at Chicago's O'Hare Airport, the Abercrombie & Fitch and Calvin Klein posters in the terminal were the same ads I passed three days before with hardly a second thought, except to notice a pretty face here or a shapely figure there. Half a week out and the ads seemed decidedly hollow, ridiculously mannered, artificial, even unnatural. And driving away from the airport down I-294, I was greeted—no, *assaulted,* as it seemed to senses gentled by a brief respite—by a gauntlet of towering billboards. One of the first on the route was a garish yellow and red pitch for a nightclub called Bare Assets, teasing, "Do you like to watch?" I muttered under my breath, "This is not the way things are supposed to be."

But consumer capitalism is much more pervasive, and much less obvious, than smog or billboards. Look harder, and you can see it at work all around: shaping attitudes, bending behaviors, grinding and refracting an endless series of lenses through which to see and experience the world in a particular way.

Tracking the sly beast, I flew to New Hampshire to visit Lendol Calder, a Christian and historian concerned enough with consumerism that he devoted his dissertation study to the subject.[3] When, I asked him, did you first begin to notice the depth and width of consumerism in our culture? He recalled a Christian camp in college, composed of persons from several nations. A get-acquainted exercise involved dividing campers up by their nationalities and assigning them to come up with a song representing their culture that all could agree on and sing to the rest of the assembly. Most groups had agreed on a song (nearly all were indigenous folk songs), practiced it, and were ready in ten to twenty minutes. But not the Americans. They debated over twenty minutes, then an hour. Some wanted a rock song but could achieve no consensus. Others suggested a series of country songs, only to have them roundly rejected. At last they settled—on Coca-Cola's "I'd Like to Teach the World to Sing." The jingle ringing in his ears, Lendol realized that commercial culture was what finally and ultimately bound these Americans—these American *Christians*—together.

This is what I am after. Not just consumerism in its most undisguised, hackneyed manifestations, but as an ethos, a character-cultivating way of life that seduces and insinuates and acclimates. This, too often, is consumption that militates against all sorts of Christian virtues, such as patience and contentedness and self-denial, but almost always with a velvet glove rather than an iron fist. It speaks in tones sweet and sexy rather than dictatorial, and it conquers by promises rather than by threats.

Consumerism envelops us, as surely as the air we breathe—but not as naturally as the air. Consumerism (and the capitalism that created and sustained it) is not a force of nature. It has a history. Of course it cannot, and should not, be replaced overnight. It did not appear overnight, but over the course of centuries. Yet the fact that it cannot be changed wholesale and immediately is no excuse—at least not for Christians—for failing to engage it critically, understanding it as best we can for what it is, and resisting its ill effects in nooks and crannies, bits and pieces, as vigorously as we can. That unplanned obsolescent, Karl Marx, was right about this much: people can make history, change the course of cultures, even if not within circumstances of their own choosing. Consumer capitalism, both for good and for ill, is a pervasive and foundational reality of our day, yet people can respond to it in significant ways and potentially change its course.

Christianity Before Capitalism
With the fall of Soviet communism and the political successes of

Thatcherism and Reaganism in the 1980s, capitalism appears to need no justification. To argue for or against it today, from almost anywhere in the world, seems to make about as much sense as arguing for or against the force of gravity or the wind in your face. Capitalism is natural, a kind of cosmic given. It seems as inevitable and ineradicable a feature of the social landscape as the Rockies are of the geographical landscape.

But unlike the Rockies, which have stood beyond justification for millions of years, capitalism has been naturalized only over the last three or four centuries. In fact, several essential characteristics of capitalism, especially of the advanced or consumption-oriented variety we now know, were either unimaginable or positively condemned throughout most of Christian history. We do not question the legitimacy of making money with money. But the church through the Middle Ages, Martin Luther included, proscribed the charging of interest and would have regarded speculation of the sort we now routinely engage in with our stocks and bonds as nothing more than profligate gambling. We suffer no crisis of conscience, nor even a second thought, about consuming goods or experiences solely for relaxation and amusement. Yet Puritans and Christians of many other stripes understood consumption principally for pleasure as outright sinful indulgence.

We presume the obvious rightness, so long as it is done legally, of making a profit, indeed of maximizing that profit. It did not so easily make sense to the church fathers. At the end of the first century, the author of the *Didache* exhorted, "Never turn away the needy; share all your possessions with your brother, and do not claim that anything is your own. If you and he are joint participators in things immortal, how much more so in things that are mortal?" In the second century the *Shepherd of Hermas* counseled directly against investment and the accumulation of profit, observing that Christians are aliens to this world and have no call to amass worldly wealth. "Instead of fields, then, buy souls that are in trouble. . . . Look after widows and orphans and do not neglect them. Spend your riches and all your establishments you have received from God on this kind of field and houses!"[4] Much later, in Boston in 1635, a Puritan merchant was charged by the elders of his church with defaming God's name. He was hauled before the general court of the commonwealth and convicted of greed because he had sold his wares at a 6 percent profit, 2 percent above the maximum allowed.[5]

One more example should suffice to drive home the point that capitalism and consumerism have a history and at one time needed justification. Max Weber reminds us that modern capitalist employers depend on increased "piece-rates," or more pay for more production, and that such a thing was not at all second nature to a traditional or precapitalistic way of life. Again and again, he says, incipiently capitalistic employers found that raising piece-rates did not automatically raise production.

A man, for instance, who at the rate of 1 mark per acre mowed $2\frac{1}{2}$ acres [of hay] per day and earned $2\frac{1}{2}$ marks, when the rate was raised to 1.25 marks per acre mowed, not 3 acres, as he might easily have done, thus earning 3.75 marks, but only 2 acres, so that he could still earn the $2\frac{1}{2}$ marks to which he was accustomed. The opportunity of earning more was less attractive than that of working less.[6]

Weber continues that it was not just that working less was more attractive than earning more. There simply was no conception of an economy that might rise limitlessly, of progress and career tracks and salary increases. The traditional man or woman saw no sense in making more than necessary to meet his or her customary needs. As Weber puts it, "A man does not 'by nature' wish to earn more and more money, but simply to live as he is accustomed to live and to earn as much as is necessary for that purpose. Wherever modern capitalism has begun its work of increasing the productivity of human labour by increasing its intensity, it has encountered the immensely stubborn resistance of this leading trait of pre-capitalistic labour."[7]

Given the inescapably Christian history of the West and the West's prodigy, including consumer capitalism, it is a matter of concern (and not just to Christians) to rehearse how it is that capitalism came to be justified and finally, as it is now, go beyond justification. That is to say that there once had to be a working theology of consumption. Pervasively Christian polities and people did not, in fact could not, suddenly one day simply assume the rightness and goodness of profit-making, of taking interest on loans, of consumption for pleasure, of the accumulation of resources exceeding immediate needs. Through centuries they honestly and reverently grappled to interpret and shape their material lives in the light of God. They theologized, and only so did they legitimize, what we now call capitalism and consumerism.

Of course the fact that capitalism no longer needs justification is an indication that it no longer needs theology. Economists rarely consult theologians; quite a number of them actually consider the market outside theological and moral inquiry. So do the rest of us most of the time. As Ronald Reagan remarked when he defended the mania of the 1980s for getting and growing personal wealth, "That is not materialism. That is Americanism."[8] In Oedipal fashion, consumption has consumed theology. Thus, if there is any worry about where we stand and where we are going, Christians at least must understand both the theology of consumption and the consumption of theology.

The Beatification of the Merchant

As we begin to consider what I am calling a theology of consumption, it is only fair to observe that at no point did any theologian set out to consciously construct such a theology, let alone to justify such abuses of consumptive economies as price gouging, addictive shopping or ecological damage. Most of their theologizing, if not all, was done without economic matters directly in mind, so that in sketching a "theology of consumption" we are talking about indirect and often even undesired effects. That said, the place to begin is the Reformation, and as you might expect, the leading guide is the venerable Max Weber and his *The Protestant Ethic and the Spirit of Capitalism.*

As Weber and many others note, the mercantile way of life was not held in high esteem prior to the Reformation. If America's business is business and the businessperson is our saint, we stand as a historical anomaly. For good and for ill, it is Luther and Calvin who laid the groundwork for the respectability and later the beatification of the merchant. In the church before Luther, the exemplars of faith were found in the monastic system. The laity lived by a comparatively relaxed ethic. The religious answered to the higher and more demanding ethic of the evangelical counsels, which included vows of poverty and celibacy. Luther, himself formerly an Augustinian monk, challenged this system head-on. He asserted that God called the individual to a particular way of life within and among the world, and so that calling had to be fulfilled within and among the world. He could paint the monastic life as selfish and indulgent compared to the lives of believers who, by working out their calling in the world, served their neighbors.[9]

To understand how this concept and practice of calling took on a deeper and more urgent significance, however, we must turn to Calvin and his followers. As Weber demonstrates for purposes of understanding its economic effects, Calvinism made the doctrine of individual predestination key. Calvinists emphasized the absolute transcendence and sovereignty of God. This God's ways are incomprehensible, mysterious and incontrovertible. And this is the God who, at the dawn of time, predestined every individual who would exist to everlasting blessedness or everlasting damnation. So, in Weber's words, the meaning of our individual destiny is "hidden in dark mystery which it would be both impossible to pierce and presumptuous to question." Weber believes this doctrine, in its terrible and "magnificent consistency," must have had enormous psychological consequences for those who were enthralled by it. "That was a feeling of the unprecedented inner loneliness of the single individual. In what was for the man of the age of the Reformation the most important thing in his life, his eternal salvation, he was forced to follow his path alone to meet a destiny which had been decreed for him from eternity. No one could help him."[10] No church, no priest, no sacraments, no ritual of confession. The Calvinist relied on unmediated grace; consequently the "Calvinist's intercourse with God was carried on in deep spiritual isolation." Weber offers the example of John Bunyan's pilgrim setting off in his quest for his own salvation. The pilgrim's wife and children cling to him, but he stops his ears to their cries and trudges off alone.[11]

There must have been a great deal of psychological and spiritual pressure here. The afterlife is paramount, and yet God's electing ways are profoundly obscure. In addition, the individual cannot rely for reassurance on the church or any other social system. So how do I know if I am elect? How can I be sure I am in a state of grace? This is excruciating, like waiting on medical tests for cancer and knowing that even once the results come back the physician cannot effectively mediate them for me, and they will be almost impossible to decipher.

Later Protestants would deal pastorally with this pressure in a variety of ways, including, as we will see, direction to a powerful inner feeling and sense of union with the Holy Spirit. But not the earlier Calvinists. With their utterly sovereign and transcendent God, these pastors would not imagine the human vessel in any way containing or supplementing or commingling with the divine energy. But they could and did imagine the divine energy acting on, directing and controlling the alien human vessel. You could not enter into union with the Holy Spirit, but you might be a "tool" of the Holy Spirit. So individual Calvinists were urged to be conscious of their worldly conduct, the living of their Protestant calling, trusting that their conduct worked for the glory of God because the power of God worked on and guided them from the outside. These Calvinists certainly did not create their salvation, but by fulfilling their callings they attained conviction of their salvation.[12]

It is important to note that the Calvinists fulfilled their calling in the entirety of their lives, not just in any one part or specifically "religious" sphere of life. Before the Reformation a believer, if I can put it this way, was most holy or drew nearest to God through demanding, ascetic prayer or contemplation. With their doctrine of calling and their abolition of monastic orders, Protestants universalized or declericalized asceticism. For the Catholic laity, ascetic acts had been separated from each other or from life generally. In repentance, you might undertake the occasional fast, and you would make confession to a priest monthly or on some other occasional basis. Your asceticism or religious devotion happened at particular times and in particular places, such as the confessional booth. For Protestant laity, on the other hand, asceticism or religious devotion was undertaken in one's calling, and one's calling was nothing less (if a bit more) than one's daily work—everything one did from sunup to sundown. Asceticism had been carefully planned, rationalized and accounted for prior to Protestantism, but only for life in the monastery. Protestantism, and early Calvinism preeminently, wove asceticism into a systematic, carefully calculated program for organizing and shaping the whole lives of an entire people. From this flow the rationalization of time and admiration of industriousness so necessary for capitalism to thrive.[13]

Thus did the Protestant Ethic enable the spirit of capitalism. Strictly speaking, it is perhaps more correct to call this a theology of production than a theology of consumption. For as Weber is at pains to remind us, the Protestant Ethic was not originally consumer-oriented, let alone hedonistic. In fact it featured a "strict avoidance of all spontaneous enjoyment of life."[14] Yet I think it fair to say that the early Protestant Ethic at least laid the groundwork for a theology of consumption by rationalizing and submitting all of life to the criterion of efficiency, by rendering the making of money honorable, by isolating or individualizing the believer, and by so doing turning the believer's attention inward, toward introspection. I make no global judgment on the Protestant Ethic, and in fact certainly appreciate aspects of it. But as historian Jackson Lears comments, "The consequences were ironic and unintended. The Protestant Ethic provided the psychological justification for the organizational spirit of rational capitalism; a drive toward systematic control of the inner self eventuated in a drive toward systematic mastery of the outer world."[15] This "systematic mastery" is the overly zealous exploitation of the earth now routinely lamented for its ecological effects.

The ecological was not the only ironic consequence. As John Wesley worried, the Protestant Ethic must "necessarily produce both industry and frugality, and these cannot but produce riches. But as riches increase, so will pride, anger, and love of the world in all of its branches." On the one hand, he said, "we must exhort all Christians to gain all they can, and to save all they can; that is, in effect, to grow rich." Yet on the other hand, "wherever riches have increased, the essence of religion has decreased in the same proportion."[16] We have here a hint that the line between a theology of production and a theology of consumption quickly and easily blurs. Determining where the theology of production ends and the theology of consumption begins is probably as difficult as determining where the snake's tail begins. I am satisfied to argue that we step into the region of the tail as soon as the Protestant Ethic moves out of strict Calvinism and into other, later forms of Protestantism. Pietism would lay more emphasis on enjoyment of salvation in this life than on the ascetic struggle for certainty about the afterlife. With Puritanism, it would introduce the idea that success in one's labors was a reassuring sign of God's election. Methodism would put more emphasis than Calvinism on emotion and teach that certainty of salvation rested on an intense feeling at a conversion that could be pinpointed to an exact moment. Baptists would play up the role of individual conscience and so further tendencies to introspection.[17] With these developments the snake's head is in the tent. And the tail, it seems, is sure to follow.

The Theology of Consumption

To track the progress of head to tail, we need to switch sociological guides. In 1987 the British sociologist Colin Campbell published in a Weberian vein his *The Romantic Ethic and the Spirit of Modern Consumption.* To show how Christian theology and ways of life laid the groundwork for the later Romantic preoccupation with self and the self's pleasures, Campbell focuses on those extremely influential later Calvinists, the Puritans. Earlier Calvinist churches and movements were territorial and Constantinian, closely allied with regional or national authorities and self-admittedly consisting of merely nominal as well as true believers, of the tares mixed with the wheat. The Puritans, of course, wanted to establish a pure church, composed only of genuine believers. To demonstrate one's authentic belief, a confession of faith was necessary but not sufficient. Nor were good works guaranteed to filter out hypocrites. Thus, Campbell writes,

> the Puritans were necessarily drawn to place an ever-greater importance upon signs of saving grace as the crucial ingredient in any test of suitability for membership in the church of Christ. . . . What this meant in practice was that the test adopted was one in which the confession of faith included the declaration of the experience of the work of grace, that is, of how the individual became convinced that he had experienced such an event.[18]

So it is that "an intensely personal, subjective experience" is used to gauge the authenticity of faith. "It is not the individual's knowledge or conduct which is under scrutiny so much as the nature and quality of his inner state of being. The queries raised were typically about such issues as the depth and genuineness of his 'humiliation' or conviction of sin, the authenticity of his grief for his sinfulness, the pervasiveness of doubt, and the continuing bouts of despair."[19] As the historian William Haller put it, Puritans "were taught to follow by intense introspection the working of the law of predestination within their own souls." The "theatre" of the most intense drama imaginable was inside "the human breast."[20] Consequently it comes to pass that a melancholy bearing, self-debasement and fascination with one's own death were considered outward signs of inward godliness. True faith was associated with a certain "profound emotional sensibility." And "a link was forged between displays of feeling and assumptions about the fundamental spiritual state of an individual which was to long outlive the decline of Calvinism and to influence profoundly the eighteenth-century movements of sensibility."[21]

In short, Campbell argues that Romanticism is in part Puritanism secularized. The eighteenth century saw increases in technology and affluence that lengthened life expectancy and prompted more optimistic attitudes about life and the world. The Enlightenment took hold, and religion was forced to let go, or at least relax its grip. But with secularization, the religiously created emotional sensibility of godly melancholy did not pass away; it was instead transformed. Even as old beliefs in sin, hell and eternal damnation paled, "there was a reluctance to abandon the subjective states with which they had been associated," since these "religiously generated emotions had became a source of pleasure in themselves." As Campbell observes, "Once convictions become conventions . . . the possibility of emotional self-indulgence is a real one."[22] In describing intense emotion as enjoyable, Campbell is talking about something like our relishing the frights of a horror movie so long as we know there really is no lunatic with a butcher knife behind us, or delighting in an amusement park ride so long as we know that the roller coaster is not going to fly off the track. We pay money to savor the tears we weep, on cushioned theater seats, at a Shakespearean tragedy. So have our feelings become "a source of pleasure in themselves" and, as we will see, the primary consumer "object" of late modernity.

Campbell persuasively argues that the gradual move from conviction to convention, from intense faith to secularization, accounts for the transformation of Calvinist sensibilities into sentimentalist sensibilities. Both sensibilities value similar emotions, but the sentimentalist artificially stimulates emotion for the pleasure it gives. The seventeenth-century terror of death gives way to "a typical eighteenth-century liking for pensive sadness. . . . Death, having lost some of its power to sting, becomes romanticized." As Campbell acutely observes, "One way of looking at this change is to regard the Puritans as having developed a 'taste' for the strong meat of powerful religious emotion, and when their convictions waned, seeking alternative fare with which to satisfy their appetite." Those who inherited the Puritans' mentality "had become addicted to the stimulation of powerful emotions, and were now seeking substitutes for the original."[23]

So it was that gradually and subtly, between 1660 and 1760, the middle classes reinterpreted Protestantism sentimentally rather than Calvinistically. As literary critic Hoxie Neale Fairchild remarks, the influences of the Enlightenment decay the Calvinist's beliefs and leave the Calvinist's descendants with, "in a blurred and softened form, the emotions which his creed had both reflected and fostered. The God above him becomes more shadowy than the God within him, until at last he is left with the basic attitude of sentimentalism—a sense of inward virtue and freedom which must find corroboration in the nature of the universe."[24] This is what Campbell calls the "Other Protestant Ethic." Weber's Protestant Ethic stresses "rationality, instrumentality, industry and achievement."[25] The Other Protestant Ethic stresses fervent feeling, sentimentality, luxurious introspection and an abiding emphasis on self-fulfillment.

As historian Jackson Lears comments, for those shaped by the Other Protestant Ethic, "a state of constant, feverish, spiritual yearning was the sine qua non of salvation." People were exquisitely attuned to intense emotion and so primed to stimulate it and repeatedly play infinite variations on it. "This was the dynamic of deprivation at the heart of expanding consumption: purchase brought momentary satisfaction, followed by dissatisfaction and renewed longing."[26]

This Other Protestant Ethic had a great influence on both evangelical and liberal Protestantism, as well as secular cultures. We do well to remember that Western civilization did not go to bed one night full of faith and wake up the next morning absolutely secular. Even today, of course, faith is not finally vanquished; neither is it unmarked by secularization. In the actual, messy world, Christians—quite apart from their ancestors' sobriety and wariness of hedonism—still had a thing a two to teach the world about consumption. Consider the example of revivalism.

Revivalism and Christian Architects of Consumerism
By underscoring the importance of making a decision for Christ, Charles Finney and other revivalists helped along the sanctification of

choice. Revivalism encouraged rapturous feelings and a liquid self, open time and time again to the changes of and the choice for conversion and reconversion. This became translated into a propensity toward "conversion" to new products, a variety of brands and fresh experiences. As Jackson Lears writes, "By popularizing a pattern of self-transformation that would prove easily adaptable to advertisers' rhetorical strategies, evangelical revivalists . . . played a powerful if unwitting part in creating a congenial cultural climate for the rise of national advertising."[27]

In fact, peddlers were fixtures on the fringes of revival meetings, where they hawked counsel and medicines promising transformation of the buyers' lives. Modern advertising grew directly out of the patent medicine trade. Advertising testimonials drew directly on the before-and-after pattern of evangelical testimonies. The difference, as Lears notes, was that "in the patent medicine literature, soul-sickness took bodily form and required physical intervention. Suffering was caused not by sin but by constipation, catarrh, bilious liver, seminal losses, or the ubiquitous 'tired feeling.'" Not unlike a witness at a revival meeting, a Mr. Karl Barton in 1875 confessed that his life before his first bottle of Dr. Chase's nerve pills was a mess. "It was a pretty hard matter for me to call attention to anything in particular. It was a general, debilitated, languid, played-out feeling, and while not painful, depressing."[28] In the ads the nerve pills were, of course, his salvation and road to a new, born-again life.

Other examples might be added to that of revivalism. In fact, Christians were in a remarkable number of cases architects of twentieth-century consumer culture. Many influential advertising managers and copywriters, for instance, were the offspring of ministers. But some famous individuals stand out, such as Coca-Cola magnate Asa G. Candler and department-store impresario John Wanamaker.[29]

Candler bought the formula for Coke from its pharmacist-inventor in 1891. Brother to a Methodist bishop and a devout Methodist himself (Emory University's Candler School of Theology bears the family name), Asa, according to his son, made his faith "the central purpose" of his life.

Candler believed Coca-Cola cured his chronic headaches and promoted it with something like evangelistic zeal. "If people knew the good qualities of Coca-Cola as I know them," he said, "it would be necessary for us to lock the doors of our factories and have a guard with a shotgun" to control demand. In such spirit, he liked to conclude sales meetings with a group singing of "Onward Christian Soldiers."

Coca-Cola was one of the earliest commodities to be massively advertised. In 1912, the Advertising Club of America declared it the best-advertised product in the United States. Economic historian Richard Tedlow believes that Candler's breadth of marketing vision grew out of his involvement in national and international missions.

John Wanamaker, founder of Wanamaker department stores, was a lifelong, intensely faithful Presbyterian. He was an inveterate Bible reader and a close friend and supporter of Dwight L. Moody. He was also heavily involved in the Sunday-school movement and refused the sale of wine and liquor in his stores "on principle."

At the same time, Wanamaker, more than any other merchant of his time, brought French fashion and merchandising to America. He had the country's biggest furniture showrooms and was pleased that he could translate "luxuries into commodities or into necessities" more rapidly than any other merchant.

From the 1910s until his death in 1922, Wanamaker was also a main player in the commodification of the Christian holy days of Christmas and Easter. At Christmas time, Wanamaker turned the grand court of his Philadelphia store into a veritable cathedral, replete with stained glass, stars and angelic statuary. The effect was so churchlike that gentlemen, upon entering, instinctively doffed their hats. The store was also sacredly decked out at Easter, when Wanamaker displayed giant paintings of *Christ Before Pilate* and *Christ on Calvary*.

This brief look at revivalism and such men as Candler and Wanamaker shows that, following historian R. Laurence Moore, Protestantism in clear if sometimes strange ways "was excellent preparation for the pleasures of . . . modern consumer hedonism." It sanctified choice. It brought Christianity lock, stock, barrel and Bible into the marketplace and redefined faith in terms of the marketplace. It refined close observation and exquisite stimulation of feelings, and "since the Protestant imagination was free to venture forth on its own without the intervention and control of priests, it luxuriated in novelty."[30]

Making Consumers

Such examples indicate that Christians, acting out of particular Christian understandings and motivations, played an important role in the creation and growth of consumerism. If our Christian predecessors, using Christian means, helped create it, then likewise we might use Christian means to correct, modify and offset its ill effects. That said, it would of course be a gross distortion to act as if Protestantism alone invented and sustained consumer capitalism. It is crucial to note other historical factors essential to the birth and growth of consumerism.

In terms of the push and pull of the everyday economy, historians are agreed that production-oriented capitalism moved on to become consumption-oriented capitalism because it was so successful. We need to recall that until the twentieth century most American homes were sites not only of consumption but also of production. Even as late as 1850, six of ten people worked on farms. They made most of their own tools, built their homes and barns, constructed their furniture, wove and sewed their clothes, grew crops and raised animals, chopped wood and made candles to provide heat and light. One nineteenth-century Massachusetts farmer, for instance, produced so much of what he needed at home that he never spent more than ten dollars a year.[31]

The Industrial Revolution changed all that, very quickly. As the factory system and mass production became dominant over the space of decades, it displaced home production by drawing and forcing millions into wage labor, by driving out cottage industry, and by cheaply producing a host of commodities formerly made at home. From 1859 to 1899 the value of manufactured goods in the United States shot from $1.9 billion to $13 billion annually. Factories grew from 140,000 to 512,000.[32]

Suddenly this economic system could produce many, many more goods than the existing population, with its set habits and means, could afford and consume. For instance, when James Buchanan Duke procured just two Bonsack cigarette machines, he could immediately produce 240,000 cigarettes a day—more than the entire U.S. market smoked. When Henry P. Crowell of Quaker Oats built an automated mill in 1882, most Americans ate meat and potatoes, not cereal, for breakfast. Such overproduction was the rule, not the exception, throughout the economy. From flour manufacturers to stovemakers, there was a widespread and acute recognition that the amount of goods available had far surpassed the number of buyers for those goods. There was, in short, a huge gap between production and consumption. How to close it? Industrial production's momentum was on the rise, so cutting production was not feasible. Manufacturers decided instead to pump up consumption, to in effect invert neoclassical economics and increase demand to meet supply.[33]

However, manufacturers realized consumption was a way of life that had to be taught and learned. People had to move away from habits of strict thriftiness toward habits of ready spending. To be adequate consumers, they had to depart from a dependence on traditional skills, on production by family and artisans, on local merchants. In turn they had to convert to a trust and reliance on a multitude of products and services manufactured and promoted from far away, by complete strangers.

By trial and error, manufacturers arrived at methods for just such training and rehabituation. They instituted money-back guarantees and credit buying. They introduced brand names and mascots to give their mass-produced goods an appealing "personality." They introduced mail order and, as in the case of Sears, coached and reassured semiliterate customers to order by post ("Tell us what you want in your own way, written in any language, no matter whether good or poor writing, and the goods will promptly be sent to you").[34] And, of course, they advertised.

Advertising and the Cultivation of Consumers

As we have seen, many other factors were important in the rise of consumerism, but since advertising is the most insistent and undisguised face of advanced consumption, it merits special attention.

Until the late nineteenth century, advertising had been mainly informational. Ad pages in eighteenth-century newspapers looked like the classifieds in today's papers. There were no pictures, and rather like news items, the ads simply did such things as announce when a shipment of rice would arrive from the Carolinas. But faced with a mass market and the crisis of overproduction, manufacturers by the late nineteenth century initiated an advertising revolution. New advertising departed the realm of information, incorporating images and a host of persuasive tactics. It was, and remains, a primary tool in teaching people how to be consumers.

Colgate, for instance, used advertising to teach people who had never heard of toothpaste that they should brush their teeth daily. King Gillette, the inventor of the disposable razor, coaxed men to shave daily and to do it themselves instead of seeing a barber. His ads included shaving lessons ("Note the angle stroke"). Eastman Kodak used ads to tutor the masses in making the portable camera their "family historian." Food manufacturers such as Shredded Wheat published cookbooks training housewives to cook with exact measures of (branded) products. Newly empowered by preservatives and far-flung distribution networks, Domino Gold Syrup sought in 1919 to explicitly "educate" people that syrup was not only for wintertime pancakes. Said the sales manager, "Our belief is that the entire year is syrup season and the people must be educated to believe this is a fact."[35]

The effectiveness of advertising in selling any specific product remains debatable. What cannot be doubted is that early advertising successfully introduced an expansive array of products and services, playing a key role in the replacement of traditional home production by storebought commodities. Furthermore, advertising and related media have served and still serve as important shapers of an ethos in which the good life is attained through the constant acquisition and consumption of new products and new experiences.

Indeed, advertisers soon recognized that they must not simply cater to preexisting needs but create new needs. As Crowell of Quaker Oats noted, "[My aim in advertising] was to do educational and constructive work so as to awaken an interest in and create a demand for cereals where none existed." And as *The Thompson Red Book on Advertising* put it more generally in 1901, "Advertising aims to teach people that they have wants, which they did not recognize before, and where such wants can be best supplied." The nonadvertisers at whom ads were targeted intuitively realized what advertising was about early on. Said one newspaper reader in 1897, not so long ago people "skipped [ads] unless some want compelled us to read, while now we read to find out what we really want."[36]

Advertisers did not act alone in the training of consumers. Government began in the early twentieth century to solidify and boost the newly emerged strength of business corporations, capping this alliance with Herbert Hoover's expansion of the Department of Commerce in the 1920s.[37] Schools quite self-consciously cooperated with corporations in molding young consumers. One 1952 Whirlpool short subject, for instance, featured three teenage girls around a kitchen table, at work on a report about the emancipation of women. Did emancipation mean winning the vote or assuming property and other legal rights? No, the girls decide, as the host rises from the table to attend a shiny washing machine. Real emancipation came with release from the drudgery of chores, from washing machines and dryers that liberated women from clotheslines and "dark basements." *Business Screen* magazine gave clear instruction for the film's use in its review: "Some good clean selling takes place during this half-hour. . . . The film will have special appeal to women's groups of all kinds and to home economics classes from teenage on up."[38]

In short, consumers were made, not born.

What Consumption Is

Into the nineteenth century, then, advertising and consumption were oriented to raw information and basic needs. It was only in the late nineteenth century, with the maturation of consumer capitalism, that a shift was made toward the cultivation of unbounded desire. We must appreciate this to realize that late modern consumption, or consumption as we now know it, is not fundamentally about materialism or the consumption of physical goods. Affluence and consumer-oriented capitalism have moved us well beyond the undeniable efficiencies and benefits of refrigerators and indoor plumbing. Instead, in a funhouse world of ever-proliferating wants and exquisitely unsatisfied desire, consumption has become, most profoundly, the consumption of novelty. As Colin Campbell puts it, individuals consume for the "pleasure which they derive from the self-illusory experiences that they construct out of the images or associations attached to products."[39]

Sex appeal, for instance, sells everything from candy bars to toothpaste. (Recently a cancer detection ad on the back of a Christian magazine headlined, "Before you read this, take your clothes off," then in fine print counseled how to do bodily self-examinations.) Cigarette and alcohol ads do not even depict their product being consumed, but instead prime us to associate them with robust cowboys and spectacular mountain vistas. By 1989 the American Association of Advertising Agencies explicitly stated that consumer perceptions "are a fundamental part of manufacturing the product—as much as size, shape, color, flavor, design, or raw materials."[40]

As early as 1909 an advertising manager for Winton Motor Cars complained, "When a man buys an automobile he purchases a specific entity, made of so much iron, steel, brass, copper, leather, wood, and horsehair, put together in a specific form and manner. . . . Why attract his attention to the entity by something that is foreign thereto? Has the car itself not sufficient merit to attain that attention? Why suggest 'atmosphere,' which is something he cannot buy?"[41]

By 1925 "atmosphere" no longer seemed beyond the reach of the market. In that year advertising copywriter John Starr Hewitt wrote, "No one has ever in his life bought a mere piece of merchandise—per se. What he buys is the satisfaction of a physical need or the gratification of some dream about his life."[42] In the same year Earnest Elmo Calkins, the cofounder of the Calkins and Holden ad agency, observed, "I have spent much of my life trying to teach the business man that beauty has a dollars and cents value, because I feel that only thus will it be produced in any quantity in a commercial age." Calkins recognized that "modernism offered the opportunity of expressing the inexpressible, of suggesting not so much the motor car as speed, not so much a gown as style, not so much a compact as beauty."[43] All, of course, with a dollars and cents value attached.

Thus, for modern consumers, speed, style, beauty, sex, love, spirituality have all become categories of ideals to be evoked and sampled at will by selecting from a vast array of products, services and commodified experiences. Colin Campbell considers contemporary tourism a prime example. Tourism as an industry and a commodity depends for its survival on an insatiable yearning for "ever-new objects to gaze at." The same can be said for shopping, spectator sports, concert-going, movie-viewing and other quintessential "consumer" activities. "Modern consumers will desire a novel rather than a familiar product because this enables them to believe that its acquistion and use will supply experiences they have not encountered to date in reality."[44]

Moreover, as the many now blissfully lost in cyberspace will attest, reality can be more inconvenient and less purely pleasurable than virtual reality. Virtual camping is camping without mosquitoes and smoky clothes and two days of caked-on perspiration. Virtual war is war with some glory and thrill of conquest, but no stench of rotting corpses and no real risk of one's getting killed.

In 1627 Francis Bacon's *New Atlantis* dreamed of a utopia in which technology could adjust growing seasons and create synthetic fruit tastier and better looking than natural fruit.[45] In our culture the New Atlantis has, after a fashion, come into being, and its plenty includes cosmeticized fruit, artificial sweeteners, nonalcoholic beer and fat-free junk food.

Such matters remind us, as Campbell writes, that "actual consumption . . . is . . . likely to be a literally disillusioning experience, since real products cannot possibly supply the same quality of perfected pleasure as that which attends imaginatively enjoyed experiences."[46] So we modern consumers are perpetually dissatisfied. Fulfillment and lasting satisfaction are forever just out of reach. And if we cannot escape completely to cyberspace, we reach for and grab again and again the product or commodified experience that provides temporary pleasure. We are profoundly schooled and thousands of times daily reinforced— remember, the average American is exposed to more than 16,000 sales messages daily—into an insatiability that is, as the theologian Miroslav Volf remarks, "unique to modernity."[47] Insatiability itself is as old as humanity, or at least the fall of humanity. Unique to modern capitalism and consumerism are the idealization and constant encouragement of insatiability—the deification of dissatisfaction.

So it is that consumption has devoured classical Christian theology, and with it much of classical Christian practice. From the theology of production we moved to a theology of consumption. But consumption all too easily becomes an end in itself. Economics and the consumerism it serves are, as the economist Robert Nelson candidly admits, "our modern theology." Modernity is that age that has believed in the future against the past, in limitless progress that would eliminate not just the practical but the moral and spiritual problems of humanity. Many of the major concerns and practices of classical Christianity were accordingly redefined along economic lines. Material scarcity and the resulting conflict over precious resources were seen as the sources of human sinfulness. So economic progress and the building of consumer societies have "represented the route of salvation to a new heaven on earth." Economic efficiency has replaced the providence of God. Christian missionaries traveled to spread the gospel; economic theology has missionaries such as the Peace Corps and international development agencies, delivering the good news of "economic progress, rational knowledge, and human redemption." Christianity understood history's supreme revelatory moment to be the coming of Christ. Economic theology considers it to be the discoveries of modern science and technology. Twentieth-century religious wars are no longer fought between Roman Catholics and various Protestants but "among men often inspired by Marxist, fascist, capitalist, and still other messages of economic salvation."[48]

The Importance of Character

"Whoever has the power to project a vision of the good life and make it prevail," writes historian William Leach, "has the most decisive power of all. In its sheer quest to produce and sell goods cheaply in constantly growing volume and at higher profit levels, American business, after 1890, acquired such power and has kept it ever since."[49] Since consumer capitalism—today not just in America but around the world—so effectively promotes its version of the good life, and since consumers are made rather than born, a Christian response demands a consideration of character.

That is, every culture or way of life requires a certain kind of person—a "character" with fitting attitudes, skills and motivations—to sustain and advance the good life as that culture knows it. Thus Sparta was concerned to shape its citizens in the character of the warrior, Aristotle hoped for a polity that would make aristocrats, and twentieth-century America charged its public schools with the task of instilling the American way of life in their students.

In the postwar boom days of 1955, retailing analyst Victor Lebow echoed his advertising predecessors, declaring,

> Our enormously productive economy . . . demands that we make consumption our way of life, that we convert the buying and use of goods into rituals, that we seek our spiritual satisfaction, our ego satisfaction, in consumption. . . . We need things consumed, burned up, worn out, replaced, and discarded at an ever increasing rate.[50]

Can there be any doubt that we now live in the world Lebow prophesied and desired? That shopping has become one of our signal rituals is facetiously but tellingly betrayed in such slogans as "I shop, therefore I am," and "They came, they saw, they did a little shopping," scrawled on the Berlin Wall shortly after East Germans were allowed to pass freely into West Germany. Planned obsolescence, installment buying and credit cards—all creations of this century—were key means to making consumption a way of life. Now we can see on the evening news the president of the United States dutifully buying a pair of socks to inaugurate the Christmas season, as George Bush did several years ago.

Our language is one significant indication that consumption is a way of life. We are encouraged to see and interpret more and more of our activities in terms of consumption. People who go to movies are no longer "audiences" but "consumers"; people who go to school are no longer "students" but "educational consumers." Those who visit the physician are no longer "patients," those who go to church are no longer "worshipers," those who go to libraries and bookstores are no longer "readers," those who go to restaurants are no longer "diners." All are as frequently, and in many respects more fundamentally, designated "consumers." Social scientist Daniel Miller comments,

> As is often the case in such shifts in the language of legitimation, this represents a movement in ideology with specific political implications. Increasingly in market-driven politics, all action is being termed consumption choice. No account is made of the relative access to resources that make choices illusory or real. . . . There need be no concern with the imperatives behind consumption, the moralities, the experiential aspects of consumption or its responsibilities, since all these are discounted by the economists' notion of individual rationalities that simply secure self-interested needs through choice.[51]

The church must examine and challenge consumerism at exactly this point. What sort of people would consumer capitalism have us be? What are the key character traits of the consumer par excellence? And how do these stack up against the standards and aims of Christian character?

The Character of the Consumer
As we have observed, the consumer is schooled in insatiability. He or

she is never to be satisfied, at least not for long. The consumer is taught that persons consist basically of unmet needs that can be requited by commodified goods and experiences. Accordingly, the consumer should think first and foremost of himself or herself and meeting his or her felt needs. The consumer is taught to value above all else freedom, defined as a vast array of choices.

One of the most striking ways we are trained and reinforced in the consumptive way of life is exactly through a flood of ever-proliferating choices. In 1976 the average American supermarket carried nine thousand products; today it stocks thirty thousand. The typical produce section in 1975 had 65 items; today it stocks 285. The median household with cable now picks up more than thirty TV stations. During the 1980s a new periodical appeared for every day of every year.[52]

Is this all bad? Certainly not. As a movie lover, I can tell you that the typical video store stocking five thousand videos is more likely than another stocking one thousand to carry first-rate foreign films. Most of us can affirm much about the undergirding philosophy of freedom as noncoercive choice, and surely the diversity of commodities and commodified experiences can (although not necessarily) foster increasing openness to people and cultures different from our own. Yet we are so trained and reinforced in understanding freedom as choice that we fail to question if many of our choices are actually significant. Is quality of life really improved by having four rather than two brands of catsup to choose from? Is rock troubador Bruce Springsteen too far from the mark when he complains of TV that there are "fifty-seven channels and nothing on"?

No less important, we have become obtuse in noticing a whole array of significant possibilities that are eliminated when consumer choice rules all. As Alan Ehrenhalt relates in marvelous detail in his book *The Lost City,* the worship of choice and the spread of the market mentality have without doubt weakened communities. These developments have dissolved locally owned banks, newspapers, grocery stores and restaurants. As late as the 1950s, "the very act of shopping was embedded in the web of long-term relationships between customer and merchant, relationships that were more important than the price of a particular item at a particular time. The sense of permanence that bound politicians to organizations, or corporations to communities, reached down to the most mundane transactions of neighborhood commercial life."[53]

This is a way of life that we can longer choose, even should we want, for it has been practically obliterated. Instead, as Ehrenhalt eloquently concludes:

> Too many of the things we do in our lives, large and small, have come to resemble channel surfing, marked by a numbing and seemingly endless progression from one option to the next, all without the benefit of a chart, logistical or moral, because there are simply too many choices and no one to help sort them out. We have nothing to insulate ourselves against the perpetual temptation to try one more choice, rather than to live with what is on the screen in front of us.[54]

The Character of the Christian

Classical Christianity, as we have earlier observed, was wary of insatiability. There was, in fact, only one acceptable sort of insatiability: the unquenchable desire for relationship with the God of Israel and Jesus Christ. In the psalmist's words, "As a deer longs for flowing streams, so my soul longs for you, O God" (Ps 42:1). Augustine would surely consider our consumer compulsions a symptom of disordered desire, of the sort of desire that should be directed only to God instead of to God's creatures. This is theologically a serious matter indeed, since such disordered desire can verge on, if not become outright, idolatry.

Additionally, though Christianity offers a tremendously fulfilling way of life for the individual, it does not teach or promise fulfillment construed in individualistic terms. The church ultimately hopes and yearns for the fulfillment of all creation through the rightful worship of God and fulfillment of God's kingdom. Thus the initial petition of the Lord's Prayer implores (in the first-person plural), "Our Father, who art in heaven, hallowed be thy name; thy kingdom come, thy will be done, on earth as it is in heaven." Likewise Paul sees the church as a formative community whose members are variously gifted by the Holy Spirit "for the common good" (1 Cor 12:7). The Christian hope to overcome evil and death is not, according to the New Testament, for the escape of the individual soul to heaven (or of individual pleasure fulfilled in a consumeristic heaven on earth) but for the creation of a new heaven and earth and, at that occasion, the corporate resurrection of all the blessed.

Finally, it bears mentioning that the consumer way of life fosters a number of virtues at loggerheads with many Christian virtues. Can we simultaneously seek and to some degree realize both instant gratification and patience? What about instant gratification and self-control? Is gentleness cultivated in an ethos that must become ever more coarse and gross to excite overloaded, jaded consumers, or joy cultivated by an economic system that deifies dissatisfaction? Since these virtues are at the heart of Christian character, they deserve more extensive consideration. We can explore these matters in more detail by turning to a related, cardinal Christian virtue that the other virtues are all rooted in: fidelity.

Fidelity and the Consumer Way of Life

Among other things, the Christian practice of marriage is an exercise in the virtue of fidelity. Christians aspire to be enduringly faithful to one particular God, not to a succession or collection of gods, and in this manner a Christian marries and commits himself or herself exclusively to a particular mate—"till death do us part." Yet the consumer marries because marriage will serve his or her interests as he or she understands them at the moment. Commitment in the Christian way of life is an ideal and a goal; commitment in the consumer way of life is an instrumental and typically temporary good. Like any careful contract, marriage in the consumer ethos should continually be open to reevaluation. If at any point it fails to promote the self-actualization of one spouse or the other, the option of ending the partnership must be available. In the Christian way of life, lifetime monogamy makes sense. In the consumer way of life, serial polygamy (a succession of mates over a lifetime) is a much more sensible practice. A high increase in divorce rates signals many things, but one of them surely is that consumption is our way of life.

Another sign of our commitment to consumption is the profound societal confusion and ambivalence about children. On the one hand, we idealize children as innocents and perhaps sentimentalize them more than any other society in history. On the other hand, as the sociologist David Popenoe bluntly says, "American communities are strikingly unfit for children." Children want and need social stability, yet our communities are "transient, anonymous, diverse and increas-

ingly unfriendly to children."[55] Children need communities in which
they are physically secure, yet even those of us in comparatively safe
suburbs can hardly allow our younger children to walk to school by
themselves. Children need communities that are accessible to them,
yet there are few self-contained neighborhoods, so that most activities
require automobile, and thus adult, transportation.

The fact is that under the sway of the consumer ethos we have
shifted from child-centered to adult-centered families, fostering
higher divorce rates and constructing communities that often subordinate the needs of the young to the needs (and felt needs) of
grownups. Frankly, consumption as a way of life renders it difficult
to justify having children, since children represent the commitment
of a lifetime. In the wonderfully apt phrase of novelist Michael
Dorris, children "hold us hostage to the future." They limit a parent's mobility, dictate through their needs the spending of much
parental money and create "agendas" a parent otherwise would
never have imagined, let alone chosen. Attempting to stay true to
consumption as a way of life, we soberly build daycare centers that
label children Precious Commodities, fixate on the monetary costs
of rearing a child from diapers through college and seriously wonder whether or not we should "force" our faith and morality on our
children.

Beginning the Resistance

I hope it is abundantly clear by now that consumerism is an ethos or
way of life that envelops and in many ways defines our world. There are
aspects of consumer capitalism that Christians can certainly appreciate
and defend, but it is so dominant and unquestioned in our setting that
I have emphasized characteristics and tendencies that bring it into
tension with the faith. Consumer capitalism grew over centuries; it will
not change overnight. People of faith living amid overweening consumerism have a responsibility to resist where they can, to cultivate the
good life as it is understood in the Christian tradition. So we are
impelled both theologically and strategically to devote attention to the
peculiarly and explicitly Christian formation of character, to building
a Christian way of life or, if you will, culture.

To get a sense of how Christians can undertake such a resistance, I visited believers who represent three socioeconomic classes: the afflu-ent (Malcolm Street), the middle class (Lendol and Kathy Knight Calder) and the voluntary poverty of intentional Christian communi-ties (the Bruderhof). The financial means and lifestyles of some of these folk are closer to my own than others, but I found that I could learn something from each about vital Christian responses to the challenge of consumerism.

Intentionally Vulnerable

Malcolm Street grew up in the wealth of a Texas oil family. At least in financial terms, he has always been well off. Yet he is anything but a comfortable or complacent man. During our three days together, he repeatedly prodded me to ask him the hard questions, to push the line of faithful logic past the point of his own comfort. Congruently, his reading is engaged and critical. Browsing through Christian magazines in his apartment, I found margins laden with scribbled comments ("Enlightened social policy won't get it. Only Lordship will.") and grades ("B+," "A+," "A++") assigned to articles in the table of contents. With such glimpses of Street, I was not surprised to learn that his vigorous confrontation of consumerism and the temptations of wealth grew out of determined questioning and examination.

During the fifties, while studying finance in college, he had a summer job at a bank in Fort Worth. Upon graduation he was given a full-time position, and by the time he was in his late twenties Malcolm was an upper-level officer. It was then that he had a conversion that brought to life the Methodism in which he had been reared.

He noticed that several of the older, economically successful men and women he counseled financially were deflated, sometimes despair-ing, wondering (in the words of the old Peggy Lee song), "Is that all there is?" Street says, "All their lives they had focused on climbing the ladder, only to find when they got to the top that it was leaning against the wrong building."

The young banker then began a process of reexamination. Intense and willingly self-critical as I have noted, Malcolm reacted to the prologue of 1 Corinthians 13 by deciding he had a "calloused heart." He realized, among other things, that it was too easy for the affluent to be disconnected from the pains and needs of "ordinary" folk. "If the public school goes downhill, we send our kids to a private one. If the neighborhood gets violent, we move behind the walls of a peaceful one. If we don't get satisfactory medical care, we switch doctors."

Now fifty-three, Malcolm Street has in the intervening decades repeatedly exposed himself to the neediest of the needy, with mission trips to such places as Haiti, Liberia and Honduras. He devotes 30 percent of his time to service on the boards of Christian organizations. He believes that money has a purpose—"to make friends for God"— which in practice means that business is about "maximizing human benefit, not profit." Profits, he says, "are essential if services are to be proportional to human needs, but they are not the ultimate 'bottom line.'" In keeping with that perspective, he has over the last thirteen years built and operated "assisted living" apartments for the frail elderly. Determined to make himself vulnerable to the needs of those who are not as insulated as he, Malcolm lives on the premises of a Fort Worth complex called the Courtyards, where he leads a weekly Bible study for residents and meets monthly with male residents for breakfast.

Street's way of life demonstrates that a kind of intentional vulnerability can help revivify sensibilities and empathies dulled by satiating overconsumption. A degree of affluence not only insulates us from a keen awareness of our limits and mortality but, through indulgence, can coarsen the senses of sight, sound, taste, smell and touch so that we require increasingly gross stimuli to experience pleasure. To help others and to reawaken our truest senses, we can regularly draw close to those suffering from want, sickness or loneliness. Malcolm has also learned from spiritual director Henri Nouwen the importance of periodic spiritual retreats. To withdraw for a weekend of vulnerability to silence, away from television, radio and bookshelves, is to force a reconnection with things deeper than the inundating ephemera of mass consumer culture.

Finally, Street emphasizes that generosity is a crucial, life-enriching habit for wealthy Christians. "Giving proportionately to your ability is a way to force yourself out of the insulation of affluence, beyond your comfort zone. For the upper-income Christian, a 10 percent tithe is just the threshhold of your capacity to give 'to the least of these.'"

Hearing the Water Speak

Until their summer move to a college in Illinois, Lendol and Kathy Knight Calder lived near New London, New Hampshire, where Lendol taught history at Colby-Sawyer College. I visited them at their New Hampshire home, nestled in the White Mountains and a five-minute walk from a breathtakingly beautiful mountain lake.

Kathy and Lendol, who met in a college InterVarsity chapter, have had their sensitivity to consumerism heightened by Lendol's doctoral dissertation on that subject. Their modest New Hampshire home, also occupied by their two small children, was filled with wall-hung quilts and furniture passed down from family members.

They worry that consumer culture tends to mediate all "reality." People in a mass consumer society watch television and movies created, promoted and distributed by other people, they listen to prerecorded music rather than make their own, and they buy birthday cards instead of writing a poem. Consumer reality, then, is secondhand and often sanitized—you can, for instance, "play" basketball by watching Michael Jordan without ever straining a muscle or touching a ball. Lendol is struck that most of his CSC students could look out their dorm windows at mountains that they might hike, ski and climb, but instead spent their time watching television and listening to CDs. Likewise, on a splendid spring day in New Hampshire, "in the safest place in the world," he says, residents of his town exercised on a treadmill inside a gymnasium.

In contrast, the Calders try to take full advantage of their natural surroundings. Lendol runs, bikes and, when in New Hampshire, climbs mountains. He and Kathy take frequent walks with their children. They encourage the kids to appreciate and participate in the wonder of creation. (One afternoon we walked to the lake, still and serene as a mirror, and three-year-old daughter Abigail proclaimed that the lake was not talking or laughing today. Lendol explained that they have discussed how different parts of creation "speak" to God.)

Kathy and Lendol agree that consumer culture reigns partly because it so thoroughly defines time for most people. In response, they try to pay more attention to natural and liturgical rhythms. As Episcopalians, they prize the church year on this count, believing it provides a significant alternative to consumer holidays and the values they promote. In Kathy's words, the weeks leading up to Christmas are in the church year a time for penitence, not "stuffing your face." During Advent the Calders eat more simply, so that they might truly feast at Christmas.

Such appreciative celebration is reinforced by the cultivation of gratitude. Consumer culture would have us feel constantly unsatisfied. In response, Kathy practices gratitude as a kind of spiritual discipline. In difficult times, such as when she is tempted to feel dissatisfied, she sometimes lists simple, basic things she has enjoyed that day but easily taken for granted. "Thank you for the roof over my head," she prays. "Thank you for the good, warm bed I slept in last night. Thank you for the cup of tea I had at breakfast. Thank you for my husband." As the list lengthens, she finds herself less desperately in need of a new dress or book.

Like Malcolm Street, the Calders emphasize the importance of generosity. While the consumer mentality focuses on the immediate and ceaseless gratification of our own desires, Lendol and Kathy have found gift-giving an excellent and enjoyable way to resist that constant inward pull. They present gifts not just on birthdays, but to friends on special occasions or to those who welcome them into their homes overnight.

In all this I was perhaps most impressed that the Calders' down-to-earth attempts to resist and reshape consumer culture were undergirded by a profound sense that they (and other like-minded Christians) are in this struggle for the long haul. Lendol suggests one of the best analogues to resistance of consumer culture is the challenge of Eastern European Christians and intellectuals to communism. They did not, in the apparently "small" and mundane actions of their lives, set out to overthrow communism. In fact, many have since said they expected to live the rest of their days under the sway of communism and recognized that they were a part of a system they considered the Big Lie. Yet they stood against it when and where they could, and one thing eventually led to another.

Likewise, we Western Christians cannot escape consumer culture. We are part of it and in many ways (again, not all for ill) molded by it. The Christians of the East remind us that even small exercises in resistance are significant. They open our imaginations, and who knows where that will take us, or our children, or our children's children?

VCRs and Song

The Bruderhof is a collection of eight communities in the Eastern United States and in England, most made up of three hundred to four hundred men, women and children, and descended from the Anabaptist tradition of the Hutterian Brethren. Members hand over all personal wealth (including automobiles and inheritances) upon entering and make major life decisions, such as where to live, with the assistance of the "hof." I visited the Woodcrest and Pleasant View communities in upstate New York.

What most forcefully struck this outsider is that the Bruderhof is a kind of family monasticism. Marriage is vigorously encouraged, and since members do not practice birth control, most families have six to eight children. Children are prized as children but also as exemplars of true Christian spirituality—Bruderhofers take very seriously Matthew 18:3, "Unless you change and become like children, you will never enter the kingdom of heaven."

The Bruderhof is certainly a radical response to consumer capitalism; this only underlines how profoundly pervasive and penetrating that system is. The Bruderhofers in no way think it can be completely avoided, nor that all aspects of it should be. They operate thriving businesses, providing furniture and play equipment for preschools. On visiting their operations at Woodcrest, I found twenty-some men and women seated at computers, the women wearing telephone headsets over their characteristic Bruderhof headscarves, all taking orders from around the country. I overheard two computer specialists discussing how they might find an out-of-print book via the Internet and talked with the Bruderhof equivalent of a business manager (they do not go for titles) about what he called a looming "paradigm shift" in preschool furniture.

Still, the Bruderhof's communitarian way of life enables members to be much more judicious in their appropriation of consumeristic technologies and lifestyle than is the typical North American Christian. When I asked elder Christoph Arnold for an example of a consumer technology that the Bruderhof tried and then quit, he thought only briefly before he replied, "VCRs. We had VCRs for a while, but then we noticed the children weren't singing. They weren't playing and running and making up songs. They wanted to put in a tape and sit in front of the TV. So we locked up the VCRs. Now the children are singing again."

In such ways the Bruderhof exemplifies the importance of a culture that encourages and supports practices alternative to a pervasive and powerful consumerism. Although most Christians may not be prepared to relinquish the degree of autonomy necessary to be a Bruderhofer (I confess I am not), we can take steps toward openness and accountability that may loosen the uncontested stranglehold of consumeristic attitudes.

After all, focusing on consumption only or primarily as an issue for individuals plays right into the consumption ethos (which, as we have seen, was partly created by an overly individualized and introspective Christianity). For instance, one of the most popular and enduring responses to Christian worries over materialism has been the counsel that the Christian may hold any amount of possessions so long as he or she has the right attitude—an inner detachment—toward those possessions. There is surely much value in this approach, but we have at the same time left the assessment of *genuine* inner detachment up to the isolated, individual Christian. (Ask yourself how much you actually know, in some detail, about any other believer's salary or tithing.) Thus any authority the faith has in regard to our economic behavior is entirely privatized.

As Robert Wuthnow indicates (and Bruderhofers would surely agree), in practice this amounts to complete capitulation to consumerism. Attitude and behavior are of course not so easily separable. Nor are we wise to think that we can accurately assess our attitudes in solitude, apart from the counsel and discernment of others. With such powerful social forces as the market and the media constantly exhorting us to excesses of consumption, it is ludicrous to think the most viable and faithful response is to face these forces as an isolated individual or family.

Yet the taboo on discussing what we do with our money is so strong that according to Wuthnow's data, churchgoers are less likely than the general population to discuss their finances with someone else—and less likely yet to discuss finances with a fellow Christian![56] Consumerism will continue to exercise undue influence over Christians until we desecrate this unholy taboo and stop regarding our economic lives as an entirely private matter, finding ways to open our wallets and checkbooks in front of trusted Christians. In this and in so many other ways, we need what Wuthnow calls a "critical and *collective* resistance."[57]

The Bruderhof, by its radical embodiment of faith, hopes to call other Christians to just such a critical and collective resistance—however different it may look from their own.

Whither Stewardship?

Malcolm Street, the Calders and the Bruderhof are all fine examples of Christian stewardship, of spending time, money and the resources of the earth for the service of God. Yet though *stewardship* has been used since the 1970s to encapsulate the dominant Christian response to issues of materialism and environmental crises, I have not mentioned the term until now.

There is a reason for this. In the last two decades the concept has come in for considerable (and often effective) criticism from many angles. A number of Christian environmentalists, among others, have urged the church to dispense with the term altogether. I agree that in our current setting, without careful attention, *stewardship* can be too easily coopted and subverted by the consumer ethos. But stewardship has a genuine and dignified Christian pedigree. I do not think it can be dismissed without loss, but it would be better complemented and corrected with another venerable biblical concept—that of priesthood.

Priestly Stewardship

Priesthood is a biblical notion of such centrality that it might be said biblical narrative operates by a kind of priestly logic. That is to say that priesthood most fundamentally has to do with Israel being chosen by God to declare and exemplify the will of God to creation, and in turn to represent the needs and praise of all creation to God. This is expressed most concisely in Exodus 19:6, when Yahweh tells Moses that he is Creator and owner of the whole earth, but Israel "shall be for me a priestly kingdom and a holy nation."

This priestly logic is such that Israel's status as "a light unto the nations" is necessary for Yahweh to be revealed to the nations. Without Israel's engagement with God, and the telling of the story of that engagement, this God simply will not be known by the nations. Priestly

logic also entails that Israel's witness cannot be interpreted individual-
istically. Jewish political scientist Gordon Lathrop observes:

> The institutions of solidarity that mark off Jews' commitments to one
> another from their more minimal obligations to outsiders are not
> designed to be applied as universal law governing relations among all
> people, but rather to be reiterated within each particular nation. This,
> then, is the universalist mission of Judaism: not to be "a light unto all
> individuals," not to establish an international system of justice, but
> rather to teach specific nations how to live *as* a nation.[58]

The church is expected to live by this same priestly logic, so that in
1 Peter 2:9 it is designated "a chosen race, a royal priesthood, a holy
nation." Just as Israel must tell and embody its story to make known its
God, so must the church tell and embody Israel's story and the story
of Jesus Christ. Thus theologian George Lindbeck asserts that the
church is called to an ecclesiology "more Jewish than anything else."
And against individualistic conceptions of this representative and
mediatorial priesthood, Lindbeck writes, "It is above all by the character of its communal life that [the church] witnesses, that it proclaims
the gospel and serves the world."[59]

Complementing stewardship with priesthood is helpful in confronting consumerism because it helps Christians retain the classical and
uniquely God-centered basis of our stewardship.[60] *Stewardship* today can
have a decidedly managerial tone to it and in fact is often employed in
purely secular fashion. Yet Christians are stewards not simply or primarily for a corporation or for humanity, but for God. And though Christian
stewardship has its individual component, it is most fundamentally a
corporate or communal stewardship.[61] Luther's priesthood of all believers, understood as he intended it, means that we mediate God's care to
other Christians and to all humanity. Priestly stewardship can remind us
that the fundamental Christian witness is not that of the isolated individual
but that of the church.

Priesthood can protect stewardship from another destructive vulnerability. Since the 1980s, stewardship has met with increasing opposition from environmentalists.[62] Some fear that stewardship promotes
anthropocentrism and the assumption that the world and its resources
are at our human disposal, to use or abuse as we like. The concept, they
suggest, can reinforce human detachment from the world and so

strengthen the sense that "nature" is nonrational and even "dead" matter, fit merely for human manipulation.[63]

Here priesthood provides a marvelous complement. Priesthood indicates that all of creation, human and nonhuman alike, exists ultimately for and to the praise of God. A host of Old Testament texts demonstrate that the nonhuman creation does not exist solely for human benefit. Significantly, God in Genesis 1 pronounces the rest of creation "good" *before* humanity is created.[64] The psalmist as well as the prophets Isaiah, Jeremiah and Ezekiel speak of mountains, trees, sun and moon praising God.[65] Unlike an office complex or gymnasium, which have no value if people do not inhabit them, creation can glorify and bring God delight apart from human presence. Flora and fauna exist first and foremost not for human use or enjoyment but for God's pleasure.

A priestly stewardship is quick to admit and encourage as much, since it emphasizes that the right end and ordering of all creation is doxological. Human and nonhuman creation alike exist ultimately for the praise of God. Priestly stewardship interprets all creation as the sign and means of God's love, wisdom and power. Yet it does understand humanity to have a special role within God's creation, and that is the role of priest. In the Jewish and Christian conception, Orthodox theologian Alexander Schmemann observed, woman and man are called to stand "in the center of the world and [unify] it in the act of blessing God, of both receiving the world from God and offering it to God" in thanksgiving.[66] Something of this conception seems to be at work in Paul's writing of Romans 8. Here the nonhuman creation is seen to groan, as in childbirth, both in pain and anticipation, for the redemption of the world. C. E. B. Cranfield comments that

> the non-human creation is frustrated because it has not been able properly to fulfill the purpose of its existence, God having appointed that without man it should not be made perfect. We may think of the whole magnificent theatre of the universe together with all its splendid properties and all the chorus of sub-human life, created to glorify God but unable to do so fully, so long as man the chief actor in the drama of God's praise fails to contribute his rational part.[67]

So faithful humanity articulates the praise of all creation; it pronounces the resounding and thankful "yes" grateful creatures would utter to their Maker, Sustainer and Redeemer.

Exactly on the point of redemption, priesthood offers another, and final, complement to stewardship. Stewardship language can obscure and neglect the great hope of redemption. It can imply that "nature," or the nonhuman creation as we know it, is basically in fine shape. All humans need do is tend it as it is and otherwise stay out of the way of its "natural" tendencies. But "nature" is not synonymous with unfallen creation. All of creation, even innocent "nature," is awry and in need of redemption.[68] Moreover, creation suffered its fall before it reached maturity and fullness. Christians hope for a redemption that is much more than a return to the Garden of Eden. Fulfilled, consummated creation will be grander and richer by far than the unsullied but also unripened creation of Eden. The venerable Irenaeus poetically anticipated grapevines that would grow each vine with ten thousand twigs, each shoot with ten thousand branches, each cluster with ten thousand grapes, and each grape yielding 225 gallons of wine! Demonstrating that the tradition of what I am calling priestly stewardship goes back to the early days of the church, he wrote, "And when any of the saints shall take hold of one of the clusters, another cluster shall call out, 'I am a better cluster; take me, and bless the Lord through me.'"[69]

Thus, acting as priestly stewards to preserve and enhance the other parts of creation given into our care, we look not only back to Genesis but also ahead to the coming kingdom of God in Christ. Then lion will lie with lamb, and no child will want for food, and every act of consumption will be an act of praise.

GOD
HUMAN ITY
WORLD
CREATOR
CREATURE
CREATION

HUMAN
NATURE

Notes

Introduction: Consumption & the Modern Ethos/Clapp

[1] On the public and political understanding of the church in Christendom, see Oliver O'Donovan, *The Desire of the Nations* (Cambridge, U.K.: Cambridge University Press, 1996) and John Milbank, *Theology and Social Theory* (Oxford, U.K.: Basil Blackwell, 1990).

[2] To take a more profound example, the term *nature* is not coextensive with the Christian term *creation*. Nature, used to designate a nonhuman world radically contrasted to the human, is a modern term that obliterates the embarrassing religious connotations of *creation*. Moreover, *nature* in the modern use is employed to indicate what is "natural" or as it should be, thus obscuring the Christian understanding that nature as we now know it is not natural, but fallen and broken. Finally, the term also sets the human off against the nonhuman, emphasizing otherness and so rationalizing the manipulability and exploitation of the nonhuman. In contrast, *creation* encompasses plants, animals and humanity as part of a gracious, interrelated whole. We get a sense of how different our conversation about and responses to consumption might be when attending to Wendell Berry's criticisms of a related word, *environment:* "This word came into use because of the pretentiousness of learned experts who were embarrassed by the religious associations of 'Creation' and who thought 'world' too mundane. But 'environment' means that which surrounds or encircles us; it means a world separate from ourselves, outside us. The real state of things, of course, is far more complex and intimate and interesting than that. The world that environs us, that is around us, is also within us. We are made of it; we eat, drink, and breathe it; it is bone of our bone and flesh of our flesh. It is also a Creation, a holy mystery. . . . This world, this Creation, belongs in a limited sense to us, for we rightfully require certain things of it—the things necessary to keep us fully alive as the kind of creature we are—but we also belong to it, and it makes certain rightful claims on us: that we care properly for it, that we leave it undiminished not just to our children but to all the creatures who will live in it after us. None of this intimacy and responsibility is conveyed by the word *environment*." (From Berry, *Sex, Economy, Freedom and Community* [New York: Pantheon Books, 1993], p. 34.)

[3] R. Laurence Moore, *Selling God* (New York: Oxford University Press, 1994), p. 14.

[4] Ibid., p. 16.

[5] Ibid., p. 17.

[6] Ibid., p. 34.

[7] Ibid., p. 20.

[8] Ibid., p. 21.

[9] Ibid., p. 35.

[10] Ibid.

[11] Quoted in William Leach, *Land of Desire* (New York: Vintage Books, 1993), p. 348.

[12] Quoted in ibid., p. 192.

[13]Quoted in ibid., p. 193.

[14]"The Cross of Gold," as reprinted in Donald K. Springer, *William Jennings Bryan: Orator of Small-Town America* (New York: Greenwood, 1991), p. 134.

[15]John Paul II, *Centesimus Annus* (Washington, D.C.: United States Catholic Conference, 1991), para. 34, p. 66.

[16]Ibid., para. 25, pp. 48-49. At another place in the encyclical, the pope notes that the state and the market both threaten the real good of contemporary societies: "The individual today is often suffocated between two poles represented by the State and the marketplace. At times it seems as though he exists only as a producer and consumer of goods, or as an object of State administration. People lose sight of the fact that life in society has neither the market nor the State as its final purpose, since life itself has a unique value which the State and the market must serve" (para. 49, p. 97).

My sense is that westerners, and Americans in particular, are now well sensitized to the dangers of the overbearing state but are only beginning to recognize that the unlimited market has dangers as well. Among intellectuals, however, many have worried about both poles, from both conservative and liberal political perspectives. See, for instance, Robert Nisbet, *The Present Age* (New York: Perennial Library, 1988), and Alan Wolfe, *Whose Keeper? Social Science and Moral Obligation* (Berkeley: University of California Press, 1989). On the covert morality and teleology of the marketing techniques so fundamental to consumer capitalism, see Philip D. Kenneson and James Street, *Selling Out the Church* (Nashville: Abingdon, 1997).

[17]John Paul II, *Centesimus Annus*, para. 19, p. 39.

[18]Ibid., para. 35, pp. 66-69.

[19]Ibid., para. 17, p. 35.

[20]Ibid., para. 41, p. 80.

[21]Ibid., para. 36, p. 71. Reformed philosopher Nicholas Wolterstorff reads Weber's *Protestant Ethic* in a similar cultural-formational light, noting that the book "invites us to consider . . . that materialism and acquisitiveness may be promoted by the character formation produced by, and required for, participation in our capitalistic economy." (From Nicholas Wolterstorff, "Has the Cloak Become a Cage? Charity, Justice and Economic Activity," in *Rethinking Materialism*, ed. Robert Wuthnow [Grand Rapids, Mich.: Eerdmans, 1995], p. 163.)

[22]Although it appeared well after these essays were written, a recent book by a Catholic political scientist quite skillfully examines and contrasts the consumption ethos and the Christian ethos. See Michael Budde, *The (Magic) Kingdom of God: Christianity and the Global Culture Industries* (Boulder, Colo.: Westview, 1997).

[23]Rodney Clapp, "Why the Devil Takes Visa," *Christianity Today*, October 7, 1996, pp. 18-33. Readers seeking an overview of the sociological study of consumption may consult Robert Bocock, *Consumption* (New York: Routledge, 1993).

Chapter 1: Sensualists Without Heart/Gay

[1]Christopher Dawson, *Progress and Religion: An Historical Inquiry* (1931; reprint, Peru, Ill.: Sherwood Sugden, 1991), p. 228.

[2]Thorstein Veblen, "The Theory of the Leisure Class," in *The Portable Veblen*, ed. Max Lerner (New York: Penguin, 1976), p. 77.

[3]Alexis de Tocqueville, *Democracy in America*, trans. George Lawrence (Garden City, N.Y.: Doubleday/Anchor, 1969), pp. 691-92.

[4]Ibid., p. 462.

[5]Ibid., p. 430.

[6]Ibid., pp. 614-15.

[7]Ibid., p. 645.

[8]José Ortega y Gasset, *The Revolt of the Masses* (New York: Mentor, 1932), p. 32.

[9]Mike Featherstone, "Perspectives on Consumer Culture," *Sociology* 24 (February 1990): 7.

[10]Georg Simmel, "The Metropolis and Mental Life," in *The Sociology of Georg Simmel*, ed. and trans. Kurt H. Wolff (Glencoe, Ill.: Free Press, 1950), pp. 409-24.

[11]Ibid., p. 414.

[12]Ibid.

[13]Søren Kierkegaard, *The Present Age* and *Of the Difference Between a Genius and an Apostle*, trans. Alexander Dru (New York: Harper & Row, 1962), pp. 40-41.

[14]Thomas Luckmann, "The Invisible Religion," in *Secularization and the Protestant Prospect*, ed. James F. Childress and David B. Harned (Philadelphia: Westminster, 1970), pp. 74-75.

[15]Max Weber, *The Protestant Ethic and The Spirit of Capitalism*, trans. Talcott Parsons (Los Angeles: Roxbury, 1996), pp. 181-82.

[16]Colin Campbell, "Romanticism and the Consumer Ethic: Intimations of a Weber-Style Thesis," *Sociological Analysis* 44 (Winter 1983): 279-96.

[17]Ibid., p. 282.

[18]Ibid., p. 286.

[19]Colin Campbell, *The Romantic Ethic and the Spirit of Modern Consumerism* (Oxford: Basil Blackwell, 1987), p. 134.

[20]Ibid., pp. 136-37.

[21]C. S. Lewis, *The Abolition of Man* (1943; reprint, Glasgow: Collins, 1978), p. 20. See also William Barrett, *Death of the Soul: From Descartes to the Computer* (New York: Anchor, 1986).

[22]Leszek Kolakowski, "The Illusion of Demythologization," in *Modernity on Endless Trial* (Chicago: University of Chicago Press, 1990), p. 99.

[23]Leo Strauss, "The Three Waves of Modernity," in *Introduction to Political Philosophy: Ten Essays*, ed. Hilail Gildin (Detroit: Wayne State University Press, 1989), p. 81.

[24]Ibid., p. 87.

[25]Karl Marx, "A Contribution to the Critique of Hegel's Philosophy of Law: Introduction," in *Karl Marx: Early Writings*, trans. Rodney Livingstone and Gregor Benton (Harmondsworth, U.K.: Penguin, 1975), p. 342.

[26]Sigmund Freud, *The Future of an Illusion*, trans. James Strachey (New York: W. W. Norton, 1961), pp. 49-50.

[27]Friedrich Nietzsche, *Thus Spoke Zarathustra: A Book for All and None*, trans. Walter Kaufmann (New York: Viking Penguin, 1966), pp. 17-18.

[28]Philip Rieff, *The Triumph of the Therapeutic: Uses of Faith after Freud* (London: Chatto & Windus, 1966), pp. 24-25.

[29]Wendell Berry, "Preface: The Joy of Sales Resistance," in *Sex, Economy, Freedom and Community: Eight Essays* (New York: Pantheon Books, 1993), p. xii.

[30]St. Neilos the Ascetic, as cited in St. Nikodimos of the Holy Mountain and St. Makarios of Corinth, comp., *The Philokalia: The Complete Text*, trans. and ed. G. E. H. Palmer, Philip Sherrard, and Kallistos Ware (Boston: Faber & Faber, 1979), p. 246.

[31]Søren Kierkegaard, *The Sickness unto Death: A Christian Psychological Exposition for Upbuilding and Awakening*, trans. Howard V. and Edna H. Hong (Princeton, N.J.: Princeton University Press, 1980), p. 41.

[32]Berry, "Preface," p. xi.

[33]Kierkegaard, *Sickness Unto Death*, pp. 38-39.

Chapter 3: Money & Misery/Myers

[1]Reported in *Public Opinion*, August/September 1984, p. 25.

[2]Angus Campbell, *The Sense of Well-Being in America* (New York: McGraw-Hill, 1981), p. 41. A seemingly less scientific national survey, published in James Patterson and Peter Kim, *The Day America Told the Truth: What People Really Believe About Everything That Matters* (New York: Prentice-Hall, 1991), asked Americans, "If you could change one thing about your life, what would it be?" The number one answer was wealth, mentioned by 64 percent.

[3]George Gallup Jr. and F. Newport, "Americans Widely Disagree on What Constitutes 'Rich,' " *Gallup Poll Monthly*, July 1990, pp. 28-36.

[4]Reported by W. Randall Jones in *Worth*, December/January 1996, p. 14.

[5]Alexander W. Astin, Kenneth C. Green and William S. Korn, *The American Freshman: Twenty Year Trends* (Los Angeles: Higher Education Research Institute, Graduate School of Education, UCLA, 1987). This is a report of the Cooperative Institutional Research Program sponsored by the American Council on Education. Post-1985 data are recorded in annual *American Freshman* reports by Astin and others, and in *The Chronicle of Higher Education*, January 12, 1996, pp. A34-35.

[6]Thomas H. Naylor, "Redefining Corporate Motivation, Swedish Style," *The Christian Century* 107 (1990): 566-70.

[7]Robert H. Frank, Thomas Gilovich and Dennis T. Regan, "Does Studying Economics Inhibit Cooperation?" *Journal of Economic Perspectives* 7 (1993): 159-71.

[8]Ronald Inglehart, *Culture Shift in Advanced Industrial Society* (Princeton, N.J.: Princeton University Press, 1990).

[9]Michael Argyle summarizes data on India and on the diminishing returns of increasing wealth, in "Causes and Correlates of Happiness," in D. Kahneman, E. Diener and N. Schwartz, *Understanding Well-Being: Scientific Perspectives on Enjoyment and Suffering* (New York: Russell Sage Foundation, in press).

[10]Inglehart, *Culture Shift*, p. 242.

[11]Ed Diener, with J. Horwitz and Robert A. Emmons, "Happiness of the Very Wealthy," *Social Indicators* 16 (1985): 263-74.

[12]Kathleen Chwalisz, Ed Diener and Dennis Gallagher, "Autonomic Arousal Feedback and Emotional Experience: Evidence from the Spinal Cord Injured," *Journal of Personality and Social Psychology* 54 (1988): 820-28. See also A. L. Allman and Ed Diener, "Measurement Issues and the Subjective Well-being of People with Disabilities," unpublished paper, Department of Psychology, University of Illinois, 1990; R. M. Bostick, "Quality of Life Survey Among a Severely Handicapped Population," Ph.D. diss., University of Houston, 1977; and Susan D. Decker and Richard Schulz, "Correlates of Life Satisfaction and Depression in Middle-Aged and Elderly Spinal Cord-Injured Persons," *American Journal of Occupational Therapy* 39 (1985): 740-45.

[13]A. L. Allman, "Subjective Well-Being of Students with and Without Disabilities," paper presented at the Midwestern Psychological Association Convention, Chicago, May 1989.

[14]Richard Kammann, "Objective Circumstances, Life Satisfactions and Sense of Well-Being: Consistencies Across Time and Place," *New Zealand Journal of Psychology* 12 (1983): 14-22.

[15]This example was suggested by Cornell University economist Robert Frank at a conference on "Understanding Quality of Life: Scientific Perspectives on Enjoyment and Suffering," Princeton University, November 1-3, 1996.

[16]Quoted by wire services in *Grand Rapids Press*, December 14, 1990, p. A3.

[17]Quoted by *Life,* January 1991, p. 23.

[18]Philip Brickman, Dan Coates and Ronnie J. Janoff-Bulman, "Lottery Winners and Accident Victims: Is Happiness Relative?" *Journal of Personality and Social Psychology* 36 (1978): 917-27; and Michael Argyle, *The Psychology of Happiness* (London: Methuen, 1986).

[19]Inglehart, *Culture Shift,* p. 212.

[20]Robert H. Frank, "The Empty Wealth of Nations," unpublished manuscript, Johnson Graduate School of Management, Cornell University, 1996.

[21]From a Census Bureau report, "Tracking the American Dream," summarized by Associated Press in *Grand Rapids Press,* September 13, 1994, p. A4.

[22]Data from 1963 and 1995 editions of *Statistical Abstract of the United States.* In 1992, Americans spent \$200.2 billion in eating and drinking places, 12.43 times the \$16.1 billion spent in 1960. Dividing 12.43 by the 3.37-fold consumer price increase and 1.4-fold population increase over this time period yields increased per person spending of 2.4 times (or, I estimate, about 2.5 times as of 1995).

[23]*Statistical Abstract of the United States 1978* (table 1383) and *1995* (table 1233). Technical note: Table 1383 reports 15 percent "room" air conditioners in 1960, which apparently accounted for virtually all air conditioning. Tables 1073 and 1074 of the 1963 *Statistical Abstract of the United States* report that 6,584 of 58,326 housing units, or 11 percent, had air conditioning. The 15 percent estimate may therefore be high.

[24]*Statistical Abstract of the United States 1995,* table 1214. This table reports that 21 percent of new homes had more than 2,000 square feet in 1970. Tracking that figure back as far as possible in earlier editions, the earliest data available are from 1966.

[25]Baird cited the statistics in this paragraph in a presentation to the Third Annual White House Conference on Character Education, June 1996.

[26]National Opinion Research Center surveys reported by Richard Gene Niemi, John Mueller and Tom W. Smith, *Trends in Public Opinion: A Compendium of Survey Data* (New York: Greenwood, 1989).

[27]Martin E. P. Seligman, "Explanatory Style: Predicting Depression, Achievement and Health," in *Brief Therapy Approaches to Treating Anxiety and Depression,* ed. Michael D. Yapko (New York: Brunner/Mazel, 1989).

[28]Gerald L. Klerman and Myrna M. Weissman, "Increasing Rates of Depression," *Journal of the American Medical Association* 261 (1989): 2229-35. See also Cross-National Collaborative Group, "The Changing Rate of Major Depression," *Journal of the American Medical Association* 268 (1992): 3098-105.

[29]Garrison Keillor, quoted by Martin Marty in *Context,* May 15, 1989.

[30]William Bennett, "Redeeming Our Time," *Imprimis,* November 1995, pp. 1-8.

[31]Richard Easterlin, "Will Raising the Incomes of All Increase the Happiness of All?" *Journal of Economic Behavior and Organization* 27 (1995): 35ff.

[32]Data on household material goods and incomes available in the *Annual Abstract of Statistics,* published annually by the Central Statistical Office. From 1984 to 1994, for example, the percentage of households with cars increased from 61 to 69 percent. Those with telephones increased from 78 to 91 percent. And those with central heating increased from 66 to 84 percent. (Data from table 15.4 of 1996 edition.)

[33]Robert Wuthnow, *God and Mammon im America* (New York: Free Press, 1994).

[34]Evolutionary psychologists would say there *was* a point. Men compete for mates by acquiring resources that females seek for themselves and their offspring. Psychologist David Buss explains: "Women who selected men who were able to invest resources in them and their offspring would have been at a considerable advantage in survival and

reproductive currencies compared to women who were indifferent to the investment capabilities of the man with whom they chose to mate" (from David Buss, "Sexual Conflict," in *Sex, Power, Conflict,* ed. D. M. Buss and N. M. Malamuth [New York: Oxford University Press, 1996], p. 302). Because (according to this view) we guys come from a long line of men who successfully attracted mates, we carry genes that predispose us to want to accumulate more and more resources. In this theory one hears an echo of Freud: It all comes down to sex.

Mind you, little of this is conscious. Donald Trump is not asking, "How can I, by accumulating wealth and trophy wives, maximize the number of genes I leave to posterity?" Rather, say evolutionary psychologists, our natural yearnings are our genes' way of making more genes.

[35]Private hourly earnings, in 1982 dollars, declined from an average $7.78 per hour in 1980 to $7.40 in 1994 (*Statistical Abstract of the United States 1995,* table 673). In 1993 dollars, the average hourly wage rate peaked at about $12.75 in 1973 and had declined to nearly $11.00 by 1993, reports Reynolds Farley in *The New American Reality* (New York: Russell Sage Foundation, 1996), p. 79.

[36]"The Census Bureau reports that the distribution of income tends to become more unequal during expansions. Gini coefficients for household income [an index of income inequality] have risen in every year since 1968, except three: 1974, 1980 and 1990, all of them years of recession," reports John C. Weicher in "Changes in the Distribution of Wealth: Increasing Inequality?" *Review* (a publication of the Federal Reserve Bank of St. Louis), January/February 1995, pp. 5-23.

[37]From a study of subjective well-being in fifty-five nations by Ed Diener, Marissa Diener and Carol Diener, "Factors Predicting the Subjective Well-Being of Nations," *Journal of Personality and Social Psychology* 69 (1995): 851-64.

[38]"The Billionaires," *Forbes,* July 17, 1995, pp. 137-36.

[39]Report of the U.S. Census Bureau, June 17, 1996, available on the World Wide Web at http://www.census.gov/pub/hhes/income/incineq/p60tb1.html

[40]George J. Church, "Are We Better Off?" *Time,* January 29, 1996, pp. 37-40.

[41]Jill Smolowe, "Reap As Ye Shall Sow," *Time,* February 5, 1996, p. 45. This represents a substantial increase from the 143 to 1 ratio discovered in a 1993 survey as reported in Holly Sklar, "Losing Ground on Jobs, Wages: Profits Are Rising, but the Benefits Haven't Trickled Down," *Asbury Park Press,* September 3, 1995, p. C3.

[42]*Time,* September 4, 1995, p. 21.

[43]*Wall Street Journal,* April 11, 1996, p. R1.

[44]M. I. Roemer, *National Health Systems of the World,* vol. 1, *The Countries* (New York: Oxford University Press, 1991); R. Fein, "Health Care Reform," *Scientific American* (November 1992): 46-53; *Information Please Almanac.*

[45]*Forbes,* December 18, 1995, p. 212.

[46]Holly Sklar, *Chaos or Community: Seeking Solutions, Not Scapegoats for Bad Economics* (Boston: South End, 1995), p. 9.

[47]Data from Edward N. Wolff, as reported in Sklar, *Chaos or Community,* p. 6. The United Nations' *Human Development Report 1996* indicates that the world's 358 wealthiest people have assets equal to the combined income of 2.3 billion of the world's people, nearly half the global population (New York: Oxford University Press, 1996).

[48]In a 1996 interview, Ted Turner recalls feeling ambivalent two years earlier before giving away $200 million "because I knew I was taking myself out of the running for the richest man in America.... I talked to both Bill Gates and Warren Buffett, the two

richest men in the country, and they would be inclined to give more if there was a list of who did the giving rather than the having" (*New York Times Magazine*, October 12, 1996, pp. 34ff).

[49]Kevin Phillips, *The Politics of Rich and Poor: Wealth and the American Electorate in the Reagan Aftermath* (New York: Random House, 1990), p. 10.

[50]Newt Gingrich, "I Am Not in a Teaching Job," *Time*, December 25, 1995—January 1, 1996, pp. 84-85.

[51]*Statistical Abstract of the United States 1995*, table 733.

[52]Gertrude Himmelfarb, "The National Prospect," *Commentary*, November 1995, pp. 65-66.

[53]Alan Ehrenhalt, *The Lost City: Discovering the Forgotten Virtues of Community in the Chicago of the 1950s* (New York: BasicBooks, 1995).

[54]National Research Council, Panel on High-Risk Youth, Commission on Behavioral and Social Sciences and Education, *Losing Generations: Adolescents in High-Risk Settings* (Washington, D.C.: National Academy Press, 1993), p. 236.

[55]Arloc Sherman, *Wasting America's Future: The Children's Defense Fund Report on the Costs of Child Poverty* (Boston: Beacon, 1994).

[56]Aletha C. Huston, Vonnie C. McLoyd and Cynthia Garcia Coll, "Children and Poverty: Issues in Contemporary Research," *Child Development* 65 (1994): 272-82.

[57]Greg J. Duncan, with Jeanne Brooks-Gunn and Pamela Kato Klebanov, "Economic Deprivation and Early Childhood Development," *Child Development* 65 (1994): 296-318. There is, admittedly, another possible reason for the poverty-pathology correlation: genetic influences that put people at risk for pathology may also put them at risk for poverty. Genetics cannot, however, explain the post-1960 social megatrends.

[58]David Buss, *The Evolution of Desire: Strategies of Human Mating* (New York: BasicBooks, 1994).

[59]M. Belinda Tucker and Claudia Mitchell-Kernan, eds., *The Decline in Marriage Among African Americans: Causes, Consequences and Policy Implications* (New York: Sage, 1995).

[60]Lillian B. Rubin, "'People Don't Know Right from Wrong Anymore,'" *Tikkun* 9 (1995): 13-18, 83-87.

[61]Census Bureau data and Parnell quote from Mitchell Landsberg, "Benton Harbor Leads Single Parent Parade," Associated Press in *Grand Rapids Press*, September 19, 1994, p. A3.

[62]U.S. Department of Health and Human Services, *Trends in the Well-Being of America's Children and Youth: 1996*, p. 290.

[63]Council on Families in America, *Marriage in America: A Report to the Nation* (New York: Institute for American Values, March 1995). The council attributes these figures to William J. Bennett, *The Index of Leading Cultural Indicators* (New York: Touchstone, 1994).

[64]National Conference of Catholic Bishops, "Putting Children and Families First: A Challenge for Our Church, Nation and World," pastoral letter, November 1991.

[65]Robert H. Frank, "The Empty Wealth of Nations," unpublished manuscript, Johnson Graduate School of Management, Cornell University, 1996. Frank does not include charity in his draft consumption formula, but he tells me he agrees it needs to be there.

[66]Jack Kemp, "A Cultural Renaissance," *Imprimis*, August 1994, pp. 1-5.

[67]Dan Quayle, "At Last We Agree: Fix the Family," *USA Today*, April 14, 1994, p. 11A.

[68]C. Eugene Steurle, remarks at the Communitarian Teach-In on the Future of the Family, Rayburn Office Building, Capitol Hill, November 3, 1993.

[69]Reported by Richard Morin, "Unconventional Wisdom," *Washington Post*, March 10,

1996, p. C5.

[70]Council on Families in America, *Marriage in America.*

[71]Quoted by David S. Broder, "GOP Makes Sure Rich Keep Getting Richer," Washington Post Writers Group in *Grand Rapids Press,* September 24, 1995, p. E2.

[72]Robert Rector, "Requiem for the War on Poverty," *Policy Review,* Summer 1992, p. 40.

[73]Dan Coats, *The Project for American Renewal* (Washington, D.C.: U.S. Senate, 1995).

[74]Quayle, "At Last We Agree," p. 11A.

[75]Quoted by Molly Ivins, "How About the Welfare Fathers?" Creator's Syndicate in *Grand Rapids Press,* January 25, 1995, p. A10.

[76]Support for this idea comes from sources from the Clinton welfare reform proposal (*Time,* June 20, 1994, p. 30) to Senator Bill Bradley ("Civil Society and the Rebirth of Our National Community," *The Responsive Community,* Spring 1995, pp. 4-10).

[77]Irwin Garfinkel, "Child Support Assurance," Communitarian Teach-In on the Future of the Family, Rayburn Office Building, Capitol Hill, November 3, 1993.

[78]Jay Belsky, "Effects of Infant Day Care: 1986-1994," invited address to the British Psychological Society Section on Developmental Psychology, Portsmouth, England, September 4, 1994.

[79]Amitai Etzioni, remarks to the 1995 White House Conference on Character Education for a Civil, Democratic Society, May 19, 1995.

[80]Jeremy Rifkin, presentation to the Federal Highway Administration, April 2, 1996. See also his book *The End of Work: The Decline of the Global Labor Force and the Dawn of the Post-market Era* (New York: Putnam's Sons, 1995).

[81]S. Grover and K. J. Crooker, "Who Appreciates Family-Responsive Human Resource Policies: The Impact of Family-Friendly Policies on the Organizational Attachment of Parents and Non-parents," *Personnel Psychology* 48 (1995): 271-88.

[82]"1995 Executive Compensation Committee Report" (in notice of Annual Meeting of Shareholders of Herman Miller, Inc.). See also C. Davenport, "America's Most Admired Corporations," *Fortune,* January 30, 1989, pp. 68-94, and Max De Pree, *Leadership Is an Art* (New York: Doubleday, 1989).

[83]Martin Luther King Jr., "Where Do We Go from Here: Chaos or Community?" in *A Testament of Hope: The Essential Writings of Martin Luther King Jr.,* ed. J. M.Washington (New York: Harper & Row, 1986).

[84]Andrew Billingsley, *Climbing Jacob's Ladder* (New York: Simon & Schuster, 1992), p. 36.

[85]Recent Asian-American immigrants are a case in point. See N. Caplan, M. H. Choy and J. K. Whitmore, "Indochinese Refugee Families and Academic Achievement," *Scientific American,* February 1992, pp. 36-42.

[86]Jonathan Alter, "The Name of the Game Is Shame," *Newsweek,* December 12, 1994, p. 41.

[87]Marian Wright Edelman, "Introduction: Cease Fire! Stopping the Gun War Against Children in the United States," in *The State of America's Children Yearbook 1994* (Washington, D.C.: Children's Defense Fund, 1994).

Chapter 4: Catholic & Protestant Ethics/Tropman

[1]Max Weber, *The Protestant Ethic and the Spirit of Capitalism,* trans. Talcott Parsons (New York: Allen & Unwin, 1956).

[2]For example, Larry Kersten wrote a book called *The Lutheran Ethic* (Detroit: Wayne State University Press, 1970).

[3]Michael Novak, *The Catholic Ethic and the Spirit of Capitalism* (New York: Free Press, 1993), and John E. Tropman, *The Catholic Ethic in American Society* (San Francisco: Jossey Bass,

1996).

[4]Lester Thurow, *Head to Head* (New York: Morrow, 1992).

[5]For a detailed discussion, see Tropman, *Catholic Ethic.*

[6]Weber, *Protestant Ethic,* p. 117 (emphasis added).

[7]Charles Curran, "Ethical Principles of Catholic Social Teaching Behind the United States Bishops' Letter on the Economy," *Journal of Business Ethics* 7, no. 6 (1988): 413-17.

[8]Katherine Newman, *Falling from Grace: The Experience of Downward Mobility in the American Middle Class* (New York: Free Press, 1986).

[9]Paul Misner, *Social Catholicism in Europe from the Onset of Industrialization to the First World War* (New York: Crossroads, 1991), p. 2.

[10]Ibid., p. 3.

[11]R. E. Pumphrey and M. W. Pumphrey, eds., *The Heritage of American Social Work* (New York: Columbia University Press, 1961), p. 132.

[12]Walter Rauschenbusch, *Christianity and the Social Crisis* (New York: Macmillan, 1907), p. 238.

[13]Arthur Schlessinger, *The Crisis of the Old Order* (New York: Houghton Mifflin, 1957), p. 179.

[14]John Montgomery, "Programs and Poverty: Federal Aid in the Domestic and International Systems," *Public Policy* 18, no. 4 (Summer 1970): 517-37.

[15]Kate DeSmet, "City Merchants' Anti-panhandling Campaign Raises an Issue of Morality," *Detroit News,* July 10, 1992, p. 12A.

[16]Thurow, *Head to Head,* pp. 36-37.

[17]Ibid., p. 32.

[18]Geert Hofstede, *Culture's Consequences* (Newbury Park, Calif.: Sage, 1980), p. 222, fig. 5.1.

Chapter 5: After Eden/Blanchard

[1]Consider the rabbinic commentary on the Hebrew *la'asot* (to do) in Genesis 2:3.

[2]My translation and editing follow the interpretation of Rashi.

[3]The rabbinic perspective was limited in important ways by the essentially agricultural society in which they lived. Today we must be willing to consider craft and industrial products, perhaps even "information," as points at which heaven and earth may meet.

[4]Perhaps blessings *(b'rakhot)* are a resacralization of the food which, after sacred eating was centralized in the Temple, had come to be viewed as mundane and not part of the Temple system and its special holiness. By attaching the symbolic ritual activities of the Temple to these otherwise mundane objects, the meaning of daily acts of consumption was transformed. In the end, rabbinic Judaism not only introduces holiness *(kedusha)* into the act of consumption itself but also transfers the locus of this holiness from the objects of the somewhat elite and isolated precincts of the Temple cults into the objects of the ordinary world.

[5]For an extended discussion of these questions see Peter Freund and George Martin, *The Ecology of the Automobile* (New York: Black Rose Books, 1993).

[6]This example is taken from the ongoing work of the National Jewish Center for Learning and Leadership (CLAL).

[7]This reflects my agreement with those theorists who insist on the important ways in which consumers actively shape products.

[8]Of course, the practical demands of the market will fix some price, but that price cannot be treated as if it were a true price, hence the legal prohibition of *ona'ah* does not apply.

The same seems to be true about regulations that must fix the value of a human life (e.g., how much do I owe if I pledge my "value" to the Temple?).

[9]How bizarre and ironic that the way of marking the infinite value of a Torah scroll is by denying one who has been overcharged for a Torah scroll the right to a refund of the difference between what he paid and the typical regional price. Such is the convoluted way of all cultural systems.

[10]This view, and its connection to other concepts I have introduced, derives in large measure from Rabbi Irving Greenberg's unpublished analysis of the attributes of being in the image of G-d *(tselem elohim)*. In our case, the relevant attributes are power, consciousness, freedom and relationship.

[11]Greenberg tries to avoid this problem by introducing the concepts of (a) the life-enhancing attribute of G-d and (b) the covenant, with its attendant ethical dimension, as a method for realizing a world moving in the direction of increasing the expression of the divine image.

[12]Freund and Martin, *Ecology of the Automobile.*

[13]Cf. Paul Hawken, *The Ecology of Commerce* (New York: HarperBusiness, 1993).

[14]A similar ritual reminder is the deliberate act of leaving a part of a new house unpainted to symbolize the Jewish situation of exile *(galut)*.

[15]Even where we differ with the specific ideals of this rabbinic text, it may still be instructive to see the process by which such "messianic envisioning" aids us in sketching out directions in which we may want to go.

[16]In one sense, it does not matter. Concluding that this particular product of the utopian imagination does not work would only require that we repeat the process for ourselves. This kind of revisioning has certainly been at the heart of many medieval and modern social movements. As we might expect, religious and reconstructed religious symbols and concepts have played an important role.

Chapter 6: Stewardship, Sabbath & Time/Mason

[1]*The New Palgrave: A Dictionary of Economics* (New York: Stockton, 1987) contains no entry for *steward* or *stewardship,* a fact true of all leading texts. Given the continued embrace of the distinction between positive and normative inquiry within the mainstream majority and the presumption that economists (as economists) do positive analysis (i.e., objective, factual inquiry), inattention to the notion of stewardship, with its implied normative (i.e., explicitly value-based inquiry) content, is less surprising. Despite this, most of these same economists concede at least one dominant norm—efficiency. Hence we conclude that the prevailing, though generally unstated, conception of stewardship for most economists is an *efficient* ordering of the personal or social household, an important and too often neglected value, to be sure.

[2]That the biblical witness is to inform all nations, see Genesis 18:18; 2 Kings 19:15; Job 12:23; Psalm 22:27-28; Isaiah 2:2-5; 42:4ff.; Daniel 7:27; Micah 4:1ff.; Zechariah 8:20ff.; Matthew 25:32; Galatians 3:8; Revelation 2:26, 21:24, 22:2, among many other similar citations. See also D. Van Winkle, "The Relationship of the Nations to Yahweh and to Israel in Isaiah XL-LV," *Vetus Testamentum* 35, no. 4 (October 1985): 446-58; C. Scobie, "Israel and the Nations: An Essay in Biblical Theology," *Tyndale Bulletin* 43, no. 2 (1992): 283-305. Commentators through the ages have debated precisely how to use the biblical (and especially pentateuchal) materials. Some within the Christian tradition argue that little ethical guidance is found in the Pentateuch, arguing we should be guided more by prophetic concerns for justice and New Testament emphases on love as the fullest

expression of the Mosaic Law. Others claim contemporary ethical guidance for all of the Bible but practically confine much of the pentateuchal materials to relevance primarily to the Christian community today and not to the broader society. The interpretation argued here is that God encoded, within the numerous legal and extralegal provisions designed to govern ancient Israel, ethical emphases that form a normative foundation that the remainder of the Bible then develops. These ethical urgings—along with the fuller understanding and greater refinement provided by the totality of the Bible and aided by subsequent commentary upon it—are to be held up before the households and nations today as a measuring rod for discerning what are just and righteous institutions and dealings. Christopher Wright has called the position taken here paradigmatic: "What God did with Israel in their land functions for us as a model or paradigm from which we draw principles and objectives for our socio-ethical endeavor in secular society." See C. J. H. Wright, *God's People in God's Land: Family, Land and Property in the Old Testament* (Grand Rapids, Mich.: Eerdmans, 1990) pp. 175-76.

[3]These provisions are detailed in the three standard law codes of the Pentateuch and refined by commentary spread throughout the Bible. See Exodus 21:2ff.; 23:10-12; Leviticus 25; and Deuteronomy 15:1-18. The concern here could be extended to embrace other provisions with similar intent, such as those dealing with gleanings and corners of fields (Lev 19:9-10, 23:22; Deut 24:19-21), the use of the third-year tithe (Deut 14:28-29, 26:12) and the general admonition to care for the poor and needy, such as by sharing feast days (Deut 16:11-14).

[4]See John D. Mason, "Biblical Teaching and Assisting the Poor," *Transformation* 4 (April/June 1987): 1-14, and "Biblical Teaching and the Objectives of Welfare Policy in the U.S.," in *Welfare in America: Christian Perspectives on a Policy in Crisis*, ed. S. Carlson-Thies and J. Skillen (Grand Rapids, Mich.: Eerdmans, 1996), pp. 145-85.

[5]The Sabbath, as Christ instructs us, was made for people and not people for the Sabbath. As God rested on the seventh day, so we (along with our servants!) can use rest. In his interchange with his critics, Christ tells us that healing and doing good can mark the Sabbath. In other words, Sabbath is offered for our good, that we be freed from the cares of this life to rest and be refreshed and enjoy the God who made us and who delivers us from bondage. In his *Anchor Bible Dictionary* essay on "Sabbatical Year" Christopher Wright observes the close relationship between the weekly Sabbath and the sabbatical year, both expressing primarily humanitarian concerns.

[6]A. J. Heschel, *The Sabbath: Its Meaning for Modern Man* (New York: Farrar, Straus & Giroux, 1951).

[7]The structure of the pentateuchal social provisions assumes the extended family unit, the *bet ab* or house of the father. The loan at issue in the Sabbath year forgiveness, for example, most likely came from a closely related *bet ab*. Ruth gleaned in the fields of a relative. Paul instructed Timothy that widows should become charges to the church community only if they do not have grandchildren to help them (1 Tim 5).

[8]I think here of the structure of the social security system, which financially assists the aged through direct state provision when an alternative could be achieved indirectly through the creation of tax inducements for extended family members to provide this assistance. Similarly with welfare programs, which replace nuclear as well as extended family assistance with state provision when it would be possible to create incentives (positive and negative) for extended family assistance. I understand that Japan does not face the pending problems with funding social security that the U.S. does because it relies far more on privately funded extended family responsibility.

[9]See particularly the work of Sara McLanahan and Gary Sandefur, *Growing Up with a Single Parent: What Hurts, What Helps* (Cambridge, Mass.: Harvard University Press, 1994). See also D. Popenoe, "American Family Decline, 1960-1990: A Review and Appraisal," *Journal of Marriage and Family* 55 (August 1993): 527-55. The *New York Times* recently (February 29, 1996) cited a study done in the Atlanta area by Child Trends, noting that children raised in welfare homes by single mothers were doing more poorly in cognitive development than other children.

[10]See Marvin Olasky's *The Tragedy of American Compassion* (Wheaton, Ill.: Crossway Books, 1992). Similarly: "The point is that most of the existing programs should not be maintained, that they are actually hurting the poor by putting and keeping them in a posture of dependency and perpetual political supplication." This quotation is from "Welfare: Moynihan's Counsel of Despair," *First Things*, no. 61 (March 1996): 8-10.

[11]Too many of the accounts of this nation's early history turn on the lives and commitments of the prominent figures, as important as these are for grasping the unique shape of the American experiment. To understand the foundations of this nation's moral sympathies more completely, I submit we need to rehearse how the majority of households lived in those early years. The observations of a Tocqueville become crucial in this regard, as are a growing number of works such as Barry Shain, *The Myth of American Individualism* (Princeton, N.J.: Princeton University Press, 1994) and Stephen Innis, *Creating the Commonwealth: The Economic Culture of Puritan New England* (New York: W. W. Norton, 1995), which find most households morally constrained by community obligations largely derived from the Judeo-Christian ethical tradition.

[12]J. Dilulio Jr., "The Coming of the Super-Predators," *The Weekly Standard*, November 27, 1996, pp. 23-28.

[13]W. J. Wilson, *The Truly Disadvantaged: The Inner City, the Underclass and Public Policy* (Chicago: University of Chicago Press, 1987). See also his more recent *When Work Disappears: The World of the New Urban Poor* (New York: Alfred A. Knopf, 1996). Elijah Anderson notes how the blocks and neighborhoods no longer are informally policed by "old heads" (older men or women) but increasingly are subject to dangerous gang and drug "policing"; see his *Streetwise: Race, Class and Change in an Urban Community* (Chicago: University of Chicago Press, 1990).

[14]David Cutler and Edward Glaeser, "Are Ghettos Good or Bad?" *Quarterly Journal of Economics* 112 (August 1997): 864-65.

[15]There is at least one exception to this general assessment: housing policy. From the 1930s to the 1960s the nonpoor (and generally nonblack) were offered loan assistance to purchase housing located in dispersed fashion in acceptable areas (an early form of redlining) while subsidies to the poor typically were concentrated into central city areas in high-rise rental housing often called "the projects." To be fair, when the high-rise rental housing was constructed, the expectation was that most residents would be intact nuclear families and that these settings would not become the difficult situations too often found today.

[16]We are reminded, in this regard, of Luke 16:19-31, wherein the rich man went to hell because he failed to attend to the running sores of Lazarus. There is no mention in this text of the rich man causing Lazarus's condition; to the contrary, having the Law and the Prophets before him, he should have acted when he did not. I have been struck repeatedly in recent decades with how meager our response to the deteriorating conditions of the inner cities has been. This nation was mobilized through volunteer efforts and government action when waters rose dangerously along the Mississippi, a

condition that threatened little loss of life but a great deal of property. On the other hand, we seem to become immobilized, even escapist, in the face of considerable loss of human life in our inner cities. What does this tell us about social stewardship?

[17]These suggestions grow out of my ongoing attempt to bring biblical teaching to the contemporary problems of poverty and our inner cities. See in this regard several earlier publications: "The Debate over the Ghetto Underclass: A Question of Obligation," background paper prepared for the Center for Public Justice and abbreviated for publication in *Public Justice Report* 12 (November 1988): 1; "The Biblical Jubilee and 'Human Capital' Provision," background paper prepared for the Center for Public Justice and abbreviated for publication in *Public Justice Report* 13 (January 1990): 4; "Centralization and Decentralization in Social Arrangements: Explorations into Biblical Social Ethics," *Journal of the Association of Christian Economists* (U.K.) 13 (Fall 1992): 3-47.

[18]See T. Williams and W. Kornblum, *Growing Up Poor* (Lexington, Mass.: D. C. Heath, 1985), which reports on a study funded by the U.S. Department of Labor that seeks to discern why certain youths from difficult, impoverished backgrounds were able to break the grip of their circumstances. A crucial factor in most of the success stories was the presence of a significant adult mentor exercising a form of tough love, showing they cared deeply and holding the youths accountable to high standards. In a similar attempt, Richard Freeman studied young Boston-area black males to observe what factors explained educational and labor market success. Among expected conditions, such as residence in a two-parent home, a seemingly unexpected one—contact with a church (acting independently of other explanatory variables)—contributed to favorable outcomes. See Freeman, "Who Escapes? The Relation of Church-Going and Other Background Factors to the Socio-economic Performance of Black Male Youths from Inner-City Poverty Tracts," in *The Black Youth Employment Crisis*, ed. R. Freeman and H. Holzer (Chicago: University of Chicago Press, 1986), pp. 353-76.

[19]See in this regard several of the chapters in G. Loury, *One by One from the Inside Out: Essays and Reviews on Race and Responsibility in America* (New York: Free Press, 1995).

[20]The best analytical framework for examining these realities is offered by economist Gary Becker in his "A Theory of the Allocation of Time," *Economic Journal* 75 (September 1965): 493. See also S. Burenstam-Linder, *The Harried Leisure Class* (New York: Columbia University Press, 1970).

[21]I have attempted to demonstrate the failure of leading systems of moral obligation today to offer us motivational reasons for living up to the prescriptions of those systems in a working paper entitled "Liberalism, Religious Belief and the New Communitarianism: Searching for a Workable System of Moral Obligation" (November 1995).

[22]Heschel describes the proper use of Sabbath time as a foretaste of eternity. The fact (and time) of eternity with God contains very practical implications for our worldly endeavors; we realize that this life hardly encompasses our being and only dimly provides what wonders await us, and therefore we should be willing to sacrifice for others. It is interesting in this regard that when in John's Gospel Jesus reveals himself as God incarnate, he repeatedly stresses the hope of eternal life (Jn 6:27, 40, 47, 54, 58).

[23]A colleague reacted to this claim by wondering whether cognitive realization of what God has done for us is sufficient, and whether more is needed to move us to sacrifice in the ways I am calling for. This colleague wondered if disciplined steps were needed to form one's character so that one acts in sacrificial ways and has opportunities for,

and models of, sacrificial service provided by the church.

[24]I thank those who have reacted to the conceptions of this essay when expressed in more cryptic form and who thereby provoked me to clarify and refine. I recall in particular Sharon Mason, Christiana and Matthew Ostrowski, David Richardson and especially Bruce Webb. I beg their forgiveness if I have not heard clearly or used their reactions wisely.

Chapter 7: ΘΕΩΣΙΣ in Freedom & Love/Wesche

[1]The incarnational content of *oikonomia* receives concrete illustration in ecclesiastical discipline. Salvation in the church is set forth as union with the divine, made possible by the divine's union with humanity in the Incarnation. Bringing about this communion is the church's chief goal as the "steward" of this divine mystery of the Incarnation. Suspending canonical norms, when this is the best way to unite a repentant individual estranged from the communion of the church, is called *oikonomia*.

Governed by the term's christological context, an *ecumenical* council or the *ecumenical* patriarch would refer to more than a council or patriarch whose significance is "worldwide" or "universal." It refers to the character that conditions all the capacities in which the church functions as the steward of God's *oikonomia:* it is charged with managing the work of Christ, which is to unite those who are sundered. It is commissioned to make all to know the manifold wisdom of God which has been revealed in the Son, Jesus Christ, who is the love of God (cf. Eph 3:10).

[2]Summarizing the line of reasoning in Eunomius's *Liber Apologeticus* §7, in *Eunomius: The Extant Works*, text and trans. Richard Paul Vaggione (Oxford: Clarendon, 1987), p. 41.

[3]Athanasius, *Select Treatises of St. Athanasius*, vol. 1 of *Works of Cardinal Newman* (Westminster, Md.: Christian Classics, 1911), p. 30.

[4]Cf. Gregory of Nyssa *Quod Non Sint Tres Dii* (that there are not three Gods), in *PG* 45, col. 121 AB.

[5]Gregory the Theologian *Oration* 31.14, in *Sources Chretiennes* 250 (Paris: Cerf, 1978), p. 304.

[6]Gregory the Theologian *Epistle 101 Ad Cledonium*, in *PG* 37, col. 180.

[7]Gregory the Theologian *Oration* 30.6, in *Sources Chretiennes* 250, p. 236.

[8]Gregory the Theologian *Oration* 38.13, in *PG* 36, col. 325.

Chapter 8: On New Things/Schneider

[1]This is the main underlying thesis of J. Gonzalez, *Faith and Wealth* (San Francisco: Harper & Row, 1990).

[2]On approaches to economic life in mainstream Reformation thought, John R. Schneider, *Godly Materialism: Rethinking Wealth and Possessions* (Downers Grove, Ill.: InterVarsity Press, 1994), pp. 33-36 and references, may be useful.

[3]H. Richard Niebuhr, *Christ and Culture* (New York: Harper & Row/Harper Torch Books, 1951).

[4]See both Gonzalez, *Faith and Wealth*, and Barry Gordon, *The Economic Problem in Biblical and Patristic Thought* (New York: E. J. Brill, 1989). Gordon is better than Gonzalez at conveying areas of disagreement and differences of approach among ancient theologians.

[5]See Schneider, *Godly Materialism*, pp. 19-41 with references, for a helpful historical review.

[6]This section is largely dependent for its claims on Gonzalez, *Faith and Wealth*, and Gordon, *Economic Problem*.

[7]Much has been written on the history of Gnosticism. For a popular treatment, more valuable for its readable survey of the ideas than for its philosophical thesis, see Elaine Pagels, *The Gnostic Gospels* (New York: Random House, 1980).

[8]Both Tertullian (160-c.220) and Clement of Alexandria (150-215), who disagreed intensely on matters of cultural vocation, agreed completely that the material creation and material things were religiously good. See Gordon, *Economic Problem*, pp. 84-88.

[9]This judgment became urgently important especially after Constantine declared Christianity legal in the Roman Empire and new economic freedom opened for Christians. See Gordon, *Economic Problem*, pp. 89-100.

[10]On various types of this approach, see Niebuhr, *Christ and Culture.*

[11]This seems to have been the majority and dominant opinion, reflected in the majesterial work of St. Augustine of Hippo (354-430) and St. Thomas Aquinas (1224-1274), as well as Protestant Reformers Martin Luther (1483-1546) and John Calvin (1509-1564). See Schneider, *Godly Materialism*, pp. 25-36 and references. Another critique of enjoyment, of the ascetic variety, came to powerful expression in the writings of Augustine, among others. It was part of his larger judgment that physical pleasure is evil. I presume, however, that most will agree that this line of thinking is more profoundly that of later Platonism than it is of biblical origin. See Gonzalez, *Faith and Wealth*, pp. 214-21, for a summation of Augustine's teachings on material wealth.

[12]A useful review of patterns of wealth distribution in premodern societies is in Michael J. Novak, *The Spirit of Democratic Capitalism* (Lanham, Md.: University Press of America/Madison Books, 1991).

[13]The most complete study I am aware of is given in S. Safrai, M. Stern, D. Flusser and W. C. van Unnink, eds., *The Jewish People in the First Century: Historical Geography, Political History, Social, Cultural and Religious Life and Institutions*, vol. 2 (Philadelphia: Fortress Press, 1987).

[14]A helpful presentation of this phenomenon appears in a little booklet written by a lay commission headed by William Simon and Michael Novak, entitled *Toward the Future: Catholic Social Thought and the U.S. Economy—A Lay Letter by the Lay Commission on Catholic Social Thinking*, American Catholic Committee, 1984.

[15]Ibid., p. 23.

[16]Quoted in ibid.

[17]See C. Gay, *With Liberty and Justice for Whom?* (Grand Rapids, Mich.: Eerdmans, 1991), pp. 20, 204-6. Gay cites Ron Sider as exemplary of a trend on the part of many "progressives" to adopt free market strategies of liberation.

[18]Ibid.

[19]Ibid., pp. 64-115.

[20]Leo XIII, *Rerum novarum* (Vatican City: Democrazia Cristiana, Direzione Nazionale, Dipartmento Formazione, 1991).

[21]John Paul II, *Centesimus Annus* (Washington, D.C.: United States Catholic Conference, 1991), pp. 8-24.

[22]For a helpful survey of these approaches as the debate was then unfolding, see R. North, *The Sociology of the Biblical Jubilee* (Rome: Pontifical Biblical Institute, 1954).

[23]John Paul II, *Centesimus Annus.*

[24]Quoted in Gay, *With Liberty*, p. 20.

[25]See ibid., pp. 205-6.

[26]*Toward the Future*, pp. 25-26, and John Paul II, *Centesimus Annus*, pp. 23-24.

[27]For an extended argument, see *Toward the Future*, pp. 26-52.

[28]Ibid., p. 25.

[29]Ibid., pp. 32-34.

[30]On Wesley's ethics, see P. Couture, *Blessed Are the Poor?* (Nashville: Abingdon, 1991), pp. 119-34.

[31]See Ronald J. Sider, *Rich Christians in an Age of Hunger,* 2nd ed. (Downers Grove, Ill.: InterVarsity Press, 1984). In the context of his own largely utilitarian argument, Sider cites with approval John Wesley's statement that anyone who keeps more for himself than "the plain necessaries of life" lives in "an open and habitual denial of the Lord" and has gained at once both "riches and hell-fire" (p. 164).

Ron Sider resists being classified as a utilitarian, but it is difficult not to understand the principles that emerge from his writings that way, given his support of Wesley on this subject. Merely stating that enjoyment of abundance can be good, as Sider does whenever pressed, is not the same as stating how it is good, or how it coheres with his more obvious principles of simpler living.

[32]For a useful discussion of the image of God in Old Testament terms, see J. Richard Middleton, "The Liberating Image? Interpreting the *Imago Dei* in Context," *Christian Scholar's Review* 24 (September 1994): 1.

[33]See G. Lilburne, *A Sense of Place: A Christian Theology of the Land* (Nashville: Abingdon, 1989), especially pp. 45-54.

[34]On the prophets, see J. Limburg, *The Prophets and the Powerless* (Atlanta: John Knox Press, 1977).

[35]See Schneider, *Godly Materialism,* pp. 83-99 and references.

[36]Sider, *Rich Christians,* p. 61.

[37]Gonzalez, *Faith and Wealth,* gives an good survey of this state of things, which reflects the well-known consensus of scholarship.

[38]Martin Hengel, *Property and Riches in the Early Church,* trans. John Bowden (Ann Arbor, Mich.: University Microfilms, Books on Demand, n.d.).

[39]Hengel, *Property and Riches,* p. 27.

[40]That certain evangelical scholars detect an unequivocal hostility to material wealth in New Testament ethics ought to concern every orthodox Christian. Such hostility makes sense only on something commensurate with a Gnostic view of the creation. For instance, see T. Schmidt, *Hostility to Wealth in the Synoptic Gospels* (Sheffield, U.K.: JSOT, 1987).

[41]For a fuller discussion and defense of this interpretation see Schneider, *Godly Materialism,* pp. 123-44.

[42]Richard Horsley, *Jesus and the Spiral of Violence* (San Francisco: Harper & Row, 1987), p. 78.

[43]Ibid.

[44]See Schneider, *Godly Materialism,* pp. 145-64, for a defense of this point.

Chapter 9: How a Christian African-American Reflects on Stewardship in a Consumer-Oriented Society/Jones

[1]Quoted in C. Eric Lincoln and Lawrence H. Mamiya, *The Black Church in the African-American Experience* (Durham, N.C.: Duke University Press, 1990), p. 244.

[2]Lincoln and Mamiya, *Black Church,* p. 245.

[3]Quoted in Eric V. Copage, *Black Pearls* (New York: Quill/W. Morrow, 1993), s.v. February 19.

[4]Lincoln and Mamiya, *Black Church,* p. 241.

[5]John S. Butler, *Entrepreneurship and Self-Help Among Black Americans* (Albany: State University Press of New York, 1991), p. 67.

[6]Rudolf Arnheim, *New Essays on the Psychology of Art* (Berkeley: University of California Press, 1986), p. 135.

[7]Paulette J. Robinson and Billy J. Tidwell, eds., *The State of Black America 1995* (New York: National Urban League, 1995), p. 108.

[8]Ibid., p. 157.

[9]This chart and the following chart are from ibid., p. 123.

[10]Quoted in Copage, *Black Pearls*, s.v. February 19.

[11]Gregory J. Reed, *Economic Empowerment Through the Church* (Grand Rapids, Mich.: Zondervan, 1993), p. 11.

[12]Lincoln and Mamiya, *Black Church*, p. 273.

Chapter 10: The Theology of Consumption & the Consumption of Theology/Clapp

[1]Richard Tedlow, *New and Improved* (Boston: Harvard Business School Press), p. 3.

[2]Leslie Savan, *The Sponsored Life* (Philadelphia: Temple University Press, 1994), p. 1.

[3]To be published by Princeton University Press as *Financing the American Dream: Debt, Credit and the Making of American Consumer Culture*.

[4]Quoted in William J. Walsh, S.J., and John P. Langan, "Patristic Social Consciousness— The Church and the Poor," in *The Faith That Does Justice*, ed. John C. Haughey (Nahwah, N.J.: Paulist, 1977), pp. 114-15.

[5]Robert Wuthnow, *God and Mammon in America* (New York: Free Press, 1994), p. 18.

[6]Max Weber, *The Protestant Ethic and the Spirit of Capitalism*, trans. Talcott Parsons (New York: Scribner's, 1958), pp. 59-60.

[7]Ibid., p. 60.

[8]Quoted in Robert Wuthnow, ed., *Rethinking Materialism* (Grand Rapids, Mich.: Eerdmans, 1995), p. 15.

[9]Weber, *Protestant Ethic*, pp. 80-81.

[10]Ibid., pp. 103-4.

[11]Ibid., pp. 106-7.

[12]See ibid., pp. 113-15.

[13]On this last point, see ibid., pp. 157-58. For much of the formulation of this paragraph I am indebted to correspondence from Tim Peebles, February 22, 1996.

[14]Weber, *Protestant Ethic*, p. 53.

[15]Jackson Lears, *Fables of Abundance* (New York: BasicBooks, 1994), p. 46.

[16]Quoted in Weber, *Protestant Ethic*, p. 175.

[17]Weber, *Protestant Ethic*, pp. 130, 133, 140, 151.

[18]Colin Campbell, *The Romantic Ethic and the Spirit of Modern Consumption* (Oxford: Basil Blackwell, 1987), p. 128.

[19]Ibid., pp. 129-30.

[20]Quoted in ibid., p. 130.

[21]Ibid., p. 131.

[22]Ibid., pp. 132-33.

[23]Ibid., p. 134.

[24]Hoxie Neale Fairchid, quoted in ibid., p. 136.

[25]Ibid., p. 137.

[26]Lears, *Fables of Abundance*, p. 47.

[27]Ibid., p. 57.

[28]Quoted in ibid., p. 143.

[29]On Candler, see Tedlow, *New and Improved*, pp. 22-111 and 349; on Wanamaker, see

Leach, *Land of Desire*, pp. 191-224, and Leigh Eric Schmidt, *Consumer Rites* (Princeton, N.J.: Princeton University Press, 1995), pp. 159-169.

[30]R. Laurence Moore, *Selling God* (New York: Oxford University Press, 1994), p. 38.

[31]See Richard Ohmann, *Selling Culture* (London: Verso, 1996), p. 9.

[32]Ibid., p. 49.

[33]Ibid., pp. 79, 86.

[34]Quoted in ibid., p. 78.

[35]See Susan Strasser, *Satisfaction Guaranteed* (New York: Pantheon, 1989), pp. 97-105, 133.

[36]For both citations, see Ohmann, *Selling Culture*, p. 109.

[37]See Leach, *Land of Desire*, p. 10.

[38]Cited in Rick Prelinger, *Ephemeral Films: 1931-1960* (New York: Voyager, 1994), CD-ROM. I am indebted to good friend and computer connoisseur Verne Becker for calling this fascinating resource—replete with actual film and television commercials—to my attention.

[39]Colin Campbell, "The Sociology of Consumption," in *Acknowledging Consumption*, ed. Daniel Miller (London: Routledge, 1995), p. 118.

[40]Cited in Earl Shorris, *A Nation of Salesmen* (New York: Avon Books, 1996), p. 105.

[41]Quoted in Lears, *Fables of Abundance*, p. 212.

[42]Quoted in ibid., p. 323.

[43]Quoted in ibid., pp. 311-12.

[44]Campbell, "Sociology of Consumption," p. 118.

[45]Quoted in Lears, *Fables of Abundance*, p. 32.

[46]Campbell, "Sociology of Consumption," p. 118.

[47]Miroslav Volf, "In the Cage of Vanities," in *Rethinking Materialism*, ed. Wuthnow, p. 172.

[48]Robert Nelson, *Reaching for Heaven on Earth* (Lanham, Md.: Rowan & Littlefield, 1991), pp. xx, xxi, xxii, 2, 8, 10, 17.

[49]Leach, *Land of Desire*, p. xiii.

[50]Victor Lebow, quoted in David A. Crocker, "Consumption and Well-Being," in *Philosophy & Public Policy* 15, no. 4 (Fall 1995): 13.

[51]Daniel Miller, "Consumption as the Vanguard of History," in *Acknowledging Consumption*, ed. Daniel Miller (London: Routledge, 1995), pp. 17-18.

[52]See Steven Waldman, "The Tyranny of Choice," *The New Republic*, January 27, 1992, pp. 22-25.

[53]Alan Ehrenhalt, *The Lost City: Discovering the Forgotten Virtues of Community in the Chicago of the 1950s* (New York: BasicBooks, 1995), p. 99.

[54]Ibid., p. 272.

[55]David Popenoe, "The Roots of Declining Social Virtue," in *Seeds of Virtue*, ed. Mary Ann Glendon and David Blankenhorn (Lanham, Md.: Madison Books, 1995), pp. 87-88.

[56]Wuthnow, *God and Mammon in American*, pp. 138-41.

[57]Ibid., p. 266; emphasis added.

[58]Gordon Lathrop, "Universalism and Particularism in Jewish Law: Making Sense of Political Loyalties," in *Jewish Identity*, ed. David Theo Goldberg and Michael Krausz (Philadelphia: Temple University Press, 1993), p. 196.

[59]George Lindbeck, "The Church," in *Keeping the Faith*, ed. Geoffrey Wainwright (Philadelphia: Fortress, 1988), p. 193.

[60]Along such lines theologian D. Stephen Long warns, "We must free ourselves from the rationality of the [omnivorous] market and recover a theological rationality grounded in the life and practice of the church. If we are not so converted, the church will simply

continue to be incorporated into the transnational corporation until the church can no longer give an account of itself in theological terms, or even feel the need to do so" (from D. Stephen Long, "A Global Market—A Catholic Church," *Theology Today* 52, no. 3 [October 1995]: 365).

[61]Ernest Best notes that "priest" in 1 Peter is corporate: "each is a priest . . . but never a priest in and by himself; it is only as a member of the corporate priesthood within one corporate existence of the church: the conception is not individualistic" (from Ernest Best, *1 Peter,* New Century Bible Commentary [Grand Rapids, Mich.: Eerdmans, 1971], p. 108). See also Peter H. Davids, *1 Peter,* New International Commentary on the New Testament (Grand Rapids, Mich.: Eerdmans, 1971), p. 91.

[62]See Robert Booth Fowler, *The Greening of Protestant Thought* (Chapel Hill: University of North Carolina Press, 1995), p. 80.

[63]See, for example, Wesley Granberg-Michaelson, *A Worldly Spirituality* (San Francisco: Harper & Row, 1984), pp. 62-63.

[64]See Christopher J. H. Wright, "The Theology and Ethics of the Land," in his *Walking in the Ways of the Lord* (Downers Grove, Ill.: InterVarsity Press, 1995), p. 184. The creation texts of Genesis 1 and 2 are, of course, much criticized in some discussions of consumption and environmentalism, particularly for the granting of human dominion over the rest of creation. For a helpful treatment of the texts that addresses such concerns, see Phyllis Trible, *God and the Rhetoric of Sexuality* (Philadelphia: Fortress, 1978), pp. 80-92.

[65]See, for example, Psalm 65:12-13; 98:8; 148:1-14; Isaiah 24:4, 7; 55:12; Jeremiah 4:28; 12:4; Ezekiel 31:15.

[66]Alexander Schmemann, *For the Life of the World* (Crestwood, N.Y.: St. Vladimir's Press, 1973), p. 14. I differ from Schmemann's wonderful portrayal of priesthood on two important points: he tends to see nonhuman creation existing solely for the sake of humanity and clearly excludes women from the ordained priesthood.

[67]C. E. B. Cranfield, *A Critical and Exegetical Commentary on the Epistle to the Romans* (Edinburgh: T & T Clark, 1975), 1:413-14. For an excellent and theologically responsible discussion on the praise that nonhuman creation may offer God, see Brian J. Walsh, Marianne B. Karsh and Nik Ansell, "Trees, Forestry and the Responsiveness of Creation," *Cross Currents,* Summer 1994, pp. 149-62.

[68]This important point on stewardship is made by Jonathan Wilson in his "Evangelicals and the Environment," a paper prepared for the Evangelical Ethics Interest Group, Society of Christian Ethics, 1996 annual meeting, pp. 7-8.

[69]Irenaeus *Adversus Haereses* 5.33.3-4, in *The Early Christian Fathers,* ed. and trans. Henry Bettenson (New York: Oxford University Press, 1956), p. 100

Contributors

Tsvi Blanchard is a senior teaching fellow at the National Jewish Center for Learning and Leadership, based in New York City. He has been a professor of philosophy, director of the Ida Crown Jewish Academy in Chicago, a Hillel director and a practicing psychologist. His most recent publication is *Joining Heaven and Earth: Maimonides on the Laws of Visiting the Sick* (published as a monograph by the Jewish Healing Center).

Rodney Clapp is senior editor for academic and general books at InterVarsity Press. He is the author of three books, including the award-winning *Families at the Crossroads* and *A Peculiar People* (both IVP). He has served on the editorial boards of *The Journal of Family Ministry* and *Marriage Partnership* and frequently contributes essays on theology, culture and ethics to a variety of periodicals.

Craig M. Gay is assistant professor of interdisciplinary studies at Regent College, Vancouver. He is the author of *With Liberty and Justice for Whom? The Recent Evangelical Debate over Capitalism* (Eerdmans) and has written on consumerism for various journals. He received the 1993-1994 Christian Scholar's Award from the *Christian Scholar's Review.*

Clifford A. Jones Sr. is senior minister at Friendship Missionary Baptist Church, Charlotte, North Carolina. He is also president of the Lott Carey Baptist Foreign Mission Convention and of the General Baptist State Convention of North Carolina. He has edited *From Proclamation to Practice: A Unique African-American Approach to Stewardship* (Judson).

Bill McKibben is a former staff writer for *The New Yorker* and a frequent contributor to *The New York Review of Books.* His books include *The End of Nature* (Random House), *The Age of Mission Information* (Random House), *The Comforting Whirlwind* (Eerdmans) and, most recently, *Hope, Human and Wild: True Stories of Living Lightly on the Earth* (Little, Brown).

John Mason is professor of economics and business at Gordon College. He is also chair of the division of social and behavioral sciences at Gordon. He is secretary-treasurer of the Association of Christian Economists and board president of the Emmanuel Gospel Center, Boston. From 1992 to 1995 he worked as a core team member of the Welfare Responsibility Project, overseen by the Center for Public Justice.

David Myers is professor of psychology at Hope College. He is best known for his widely adopted texts on introductory psychology and social psychology. He has published widely in professional journals and is the recipient of the Gordon Allport Prize for research studies of group influence. His latest book is *The Pursuit of Happiness: Who Is Happy and Why* (William Morrow).

John Schneider was formerly professor of systematic theology and chair of the department of religion and theology at Calvin College. He has published a number of articles with academic journals and popular periodicals. He is the author of *Godly Materialism: Rethinking Money and Possessions* (IVP).

John E. Tropman is professor of social policy and nonprofit management at the University of Michigan. He also directs the Catholic Ethic Project. He is the author of several books, the most recent of which is *The Catholic Ethic in American Society* (Jossey-Bass).

Kenneth Paul Wesche is pastor of St. Hermans Orthodox Church, Minneapolis. He is an associate edtor of *Pro Ecclesia* and president of the Minnesota Eastern Orthodox Clergy Association. He is the author of various journal articles and *Justinian on the Person of Christ* (St. Vladimir's).

RED/BLUE 205

READING 10

DESCARTES 22

CULTS 26

PROTESTANT SHIFT 30

CHANGED WORK 73

UPSTAIRS/DOWNSTAIRS 75

POST MODERN 104

SACRIFICE 116

HISTORY